JOHN LILBURNE AND THE LEVELLERS

John Lilburne (1615–1657), or 'Freeborn John' as he was called by the London crowd, was an important political agitator during the English Revolution. He was one of the leading figures in the Levellers, the short-lived but highly influential radical sect that called for law reform, religious tolerance, extended suffrage, the rights of freeborn Englishmen, and a new form of government that was answerable to the people and underpinned by a written constitution.

This edited book assesses the legacy of Lilburne and the Levellers 400 years after his birth, and features contributions by leading historians. They examine the life of Lilburne, who was often imprisoned and even tortured for his beliefs, and his role as an inspirational figure even in contemporary politics. They also assess his writings that fearlessly exposed the hypocrisy and self-serving corruption of those in power – whether King Charles I or Oliver Cromwell. They look at his contribution to political ideas, his role as a revolutionary leader, his personal and political relations with his wife Elizabeth, his exile in the Netherlands, his late decision to become a Quaker, and his reputation after his death.

This collection will be of enormous interest to academics, researchers, and readers with an interest in the English civil war, seventeenth-century history, and the contemporary legacy of radical political tradition.

John Rees is a visiting research fellow at Goldsmiths, University of London, UK. His doctoral research was on the Levellers and he was the organiser of the John Lilburne 400 conference in 2015. His previous publications include: *The Algebra of Revolution* (1998); *Imperialism and Resistance* (2006); *Timelines: A Political History of the Modern World* (2012); and *The People's History of London* (with Lindsey German) (2012). He is a member of the editorial board of Counterfire and a co-founder of the Stop the War Coalition.

ROUTLEDGE STUDIES IN RADICAL HISTORY AND POLITICS

https://www.routledge.com/Routledge-Studies-in-Radical-History-and-Politics/book-series/RSRHP

Series editors: Thomas Linehan, *Brunel University*, and John Roberts, *Brunel University*

The series *Routledge Studies in Radical History and Politics* has two areas of interest. Firstly, this series aims to publish books which focus on the history of movements of the radical left. 'Movement of the radical left' is here interpreted in its broadest sense as encompassing those past movements for radical change which operated in the mainstream political arena as with political parties, and past movements for change which operated more outside the mainstream as with millenarian movements, anarchist groups, utopian socialist communities, and trade unions. Secondly, this series aims to publish books which focus on more contemporary expressions of radical left-wing politics. Recent years have been witness to the emergence of a multitude of new radical movements adept at getting their voices in the public sphere. From those participating in the Arab Spring, the Occupy movement, community unionism, social media forums, independent media outlets, local voluntary organisations campaigning for progressive change, and so on, it seems to be the case that innovative networks of radicalism are being constructed in civil society that operate in different public forms.

The series very much welcomes titles with a British focus, but is not limited to any particular national context or region. The series will encourage scholars who contribute to this series to draw on perspectives and insights from other disciplines.

Titles include:

An East End Legacy
Essays in Memory of William J Fishman
Colin Holmes and Anne J Kershen

Sovereignty Revisited
The Basque Case
Edited by Åshild Kolås and Pedro Ibarra Güell

John Lilburne and the Levellers
Reappraising the roots of English radicalism 400 years on
Edited by John Rees

JOHN LILBURNE AND THE LEVELLERS

Reappraising the Roots of English Radicalism 400 Years On

Edited by John Rees

LONDON AND NEW YORK

First published 2018
by Routledge
2 Park Square, Milton Park, Abingdon, Oxon OX14 4RN

and by Routledge
711 Third Avenue, New York, NY 10017

Routledge is an imprint of the Taylor & Francis Group, an informa business

© 2018 selection and editorial matter, John Rees; individual chapters, the contributors

The right of John Rees to be identified as the author of the editorial material, and of the authors for their individual chapters, has been asserted in accordance with sections 77 and 78 of the Copyright, Designs and Patents Act 1988.

All rights reserved. No part of this book may be reprinted or reproduced or utilised in any form or by any electronic, mechanical, or other means, now known or hereafter invented, including photocopying and recording, or in any information storage or retrieval system, without permission in writing from the publishers.

Trademark notice: Product or corporate names may be trademarks or registered trademarks, and are used only for identification and explanation without intent to infringe.

British Library Cataloguing in Publication Data
A catalogue record for this book is available from the British Library

Library of Congress Cataloging in Publication Data
Names: Rees, John, 1957– author.
Title: John Lilburne and the Levellers : reappraising the roots of
English radicalism 400 years on / John Rees.
Other titles: Reappraising the roots of English radicalism 400 years on
Description: 1st edition. | Abingdon, Oxon, New York, NY: Routledge, [2018] |
Series: Routledge studies in radical history and politics | Includes index.
Identifiers: LCCN 2017020046 | ISBN 9781138926516 (hardback) |
ISBN 9781138060692 (pbk.) | ISBN 9781315680569 (ebook)
Subjects: LCSH: Lilburne, John, 1614?–1657. | Levellers–Biography. |
Great Britain–History–Civil War, 1642–1649–Biography. | Great Britain–
History–Puritan Revolution, 1642–1660–Biography. | Quakers–Great Britain–Biography. |
Radicalism–Great Britain–History. | Great Britain–Politics and government–1642–1660.
Classification: LCC DA407.L65 .R44 2018 | DDC 942.06/2092 [B]–dc23
LC record available at https://lccn.loc.gov/2017020046

ISBN: 978-1-138-92651-6 (hbk)
ISBN: 978-1-138-06069-2 (pbk)
ISBN: 978-1-315-68056-9 (ebk)

Typeset in Bembo
by Out of House Publishing

CONTENTS

Notes on contributors vii
Acknowledgements ix

   Introduction: John Lilburne, the Levellers, and the
   English Revolution 1
   John Rees

1 John Lilburne and the citizenship of 'free-born Englishmen' 6
   Rachel Foxley

2 Lilburne, toleration, and the civil state 32
   Norah Carlin

3 Women and the Levellers: Elizabeth and John Lilburne
   and their associates 49
   Ann Hughes

4 Lilburne and the law 61
   Geoffrey Robertson

5 John Lilburne as a revolutionary leader 69
   John Rees

6 Print and principals: John Lilburne, civil war radicalism,
   and the Low Countries 78
   Jason Peacey

7 The resurrection of John Lilburne, Quaker   95
   Ariel Hessayon

8 Reborn John? The eighteenth-century afterlife of John Lilburne   117
   Edward Vallance

Bibliography   *143*
Index   *152*

CONTRIBUTORS

Norah Carlin is the author of *The Causes of the English Civil War* (Blackwell/ Historical Association, 1999) and several articles on the Levellers and Ireland in the English Revolution. She taught history at Middlesex University and its predecessors 1965–2002 and now lives in Edinburgh.

Rachel Foxley is Associate Professor in Early Modern History at the University of Reading. She has published widely on political ideas and political discourse in the seventeenth century, particularly the thought of radicals and republicans. Her book *The Levellers: Radical Political Thought in the English Revolution* was published by Manchester University Press in 2013, and she is currently working on concepts of democracy in seventeenth-century republican thought.

Ariel Hessayon is a senior lecturer in the Department of History at Goldsmiths, University of London. He is the author of *'Gold Tried in the Fire'. The Prophet TheaurauJohn Tany and the English Revolution* (Ashgate, 2007) and co-editor/editor of several collections of essays: *Scripture and Scholarship in Early Modern England* (Ashgate, 2006); *Varieties of Seventeenth- and Early Eighteenth-Century English Radicalism in Context* (Ashgate, 2011); *An Introduction to Jacob Boehme: Four Centuries of Thought and Reception* (Routledge, 2013); *Gerrard Winstanley: Theology, Rhetoric, Politics* (special issue of *Prose Studies*, 2014); and *Jane Lead and her Transnational Legacy* (Palgrave Macmillan, 2016). He has also written extensively on a variety of early modern topics: antiscripturism, book burning, communism, environmentalism, esotericism, extra-canonical texts, heresy, crypto-Jews, Judaising, millenarianism, mysticism, prophecy, and religious radicalism. His recently completed edition of the *Complete Works of TheaurauJohn Tany* is forthcoming shortly with Breviary Stuff Publications.

Ann Hughes has written widely on the English revolution and her major works include *Gender and the English Revolution*, *Gangraena and the Struggle for the English Revolution*, and, as co-editor, *The Complete Works of Gerrard Winstanley*. She is Emeritus Professor of Early Modern History at Keele University.

Jason Peacey is Professor of Early Modern British History at UCL. He edited *The Regicides and the Execution of Charles I* (2001) and *The Print Culture of Parliament, 1600–1800* (2007), and co-edited *Parliament at Work* (2002), and is the author of *Politicians and Pamphleteers: Propaganda in the Civil Wars and Interregnum* (2004) and *Print and Public Politics in the English Revolution* (2013). Recent articles include 'Print, Publicity and Popularity: The Projecting of Sir Balthazar Gerbier, 1640–1662', *Journal of British Studies* (2012); and 'Sir Edward Dering, Popularity and the Public, 1640–1644', *Historical Journal* (2011). He is currently working on a project relating to overlapping and interlocking publics in seventeenth-century Europe.

John Rees is author of *The Leveller Revolution* (2016), based on his doctoral research at Goldsmiths, University of London, where he is a visiting research fellow. His other books incude *Timelines: A Political History of the Modern World* (2012), the co-authored *A People's History of London* (2012), *Imperialism and Resistance* (2008), and *The Algebra of Revolution* (1998). He edited and contributed to *Essays on Historical Materialism* (1998).

Geoffrey Robertson is the founder and head of Doughty Street Chambers. He is a leading human rights lawyer who was involved in the prosecutions of Pinochet and Hastings Banda and the defence of Salman Rushdie and Julian Assange. He served for many years as a Recorder (part-time judge) in London, and was the first president of the UN War Crimes Court in Sierra Leone and a 'distinguished jurist' member of the UN's Justice Council (2008–2012). His books include *The Case of the Pope* (Penguin), *Crimes Against Humanity – The Struggle for Global Justice* (Penguin), *The Justice Game* (Vintage), and *An Inconvenient Genocide – Who Now Remembers the Armenians?* (Biteback), which was awarded the 'Polemic of the Year' prize in 2015. His work on Lilburne and the Leveller movement is found in *The Tyrannicide Brief* (Random House) and *The Levellers: The Putney Debates* (Verso).

Edward Vallance is a professor of early modern British political culture at the University of Roehampton. He is the author of *A Radical History of Britain* (2009), *The Glorious Revolution* (2006), and *Revolutionary England and the National Covenant* (2005), and has written for *Albion*, *English Historical Review*, *The Historian*, *Historical Journal*, *Historical Research*, *History Workshop Journal*, *The Huntington Library Quarterly*, *Journal of British Studies*, *Renaissance Studies*, and *The Seventeenth Century*. Aside from academic journals, he has also written for the *Guardian*, the *New Statesman*, *Al Jazeera* (English), and *BBC History Magazine*, among others.

ACKNOWLEDGEMENTS

These essays mostly have their origin in the John Lilburne 400th anniversary conference held at the Bishopsgate Institute in London in March 2015. The conference marked Lilburne's birth with a wide range of contributions from novelists, artists, activists, and politicians, including Martine Brant and Peter Flannery, the writers of the TV series *The Devil's Whore*; singer and songwriter Rev Hammer; Jay Carver, the chief archaeologist of the Crossrail project; authors Katherine Clements, Michael Arnold, and Robert Wilton; activist Tariq Ali; and MP Jeremy Corbyn.

The essays collected here are based on the papers given by historians at the conference, with just two exceptions. At the last minute Geoffrey Robertson was unable to attend the conference but the paper reproduced here is the one that he intended to present. Ann Hughes's contribution is based on a paper given at the annual Levellers' Day seminar at the Communication Workers Union training centre at Alvescot Lodge in Oxfordshire in May 2016. I am grateful to the Amiel and Melburn Trust, Unite the Union, and the Goldsmiths Annual Fund for their financial support for the original conference and to the National Civil War Museum for promoting the conference.

Only two of the essays have been previously published: Rachel Foxley's 'John Lilburne and the citizenship of "free-born Englishman"' and Edward Vallance's 'Reborn John? The eighteenth-century afterlife of John Lilburne'. I'm grateful to the *Historical Journal* and the *History Workshop Journal* respectively for their permission to reprint this work and present it to a wider audience.

The essays here are presented in a roughly chronological order according the events of Lilburne's life. But this cannot be a complete biographical account of Lilburne's life, for which readers are encouraged to turn to Pauline Gregg's *Freeborn John* (Dent, 1961) and the forthcoming life of Lilburne by Mike Braddick, who also spoke at the Lilburne 400 conference.

The essays do, however, examine aspects of Lilburne's life and politics which have not previously been explored in this detail. In doing so, they reveal a complex and sophisticated revolutionary figure whose political thought and organisational capacities stood at the very epicentre of the epoch-making events of the English Revolution.

John Rees, London, January 2017

INTRODUCTION

John Lilburne, the Levellers, and the English Revolution

John Rees

Origins

The Levellers had their name bestowed upon them by their enemies in 1647 at the time of the Putney Debates. But they were recognisable to both friends and enemies as a distinct political grouping some time before this, known as the 'London agents', or more simply as John Lilburne's supporters. Lilburne had managed to assemble an organised group of supporters and considerable notoriety because he personally embodied experiences that were common to, or spoke to, much wider layers of society, at least on the parliamentary side of the great divide opening up across society in the late 1630s and 1640s.

Lilburne was the son of gentry in the northeast of England, but he was not first in line for succession and so could not expect to prosper in life merely by inheritance. In this he was representative of a social phenomenon well recognised by contemporaries. 'Second son' was a term that carried a social meaning rather like the phrase 'angry young men' did in the 1950s. It indicated a discontented and volatile group with a sense of social exclusion. Like many in this condition, including other future Levellers, Lilburne was apprenticed to trade in London. His master was cloth merchant Thomas Hewson in London Stone, now in Cannon Street.[1]

London apprentices were perhaps the largest group of young people in any kind of training before the expansion of higher education in the 1960s. Despite, or perhaps because, they lived in their master's home for the period of their apprenticeship, they were famously prone to disorder on public holidays. There was not necessarily any political meaning to these outbursts before the crisis of the late 1630s, but the apprentices did become markedly more politically engaged as that crisis broke apart Stuart government in the early 1640s. Lilburne was one of the apprentices and they were one of his first political audiences.[2]

But it was a narrower political affiliation that first created Lilburne as a political actor. He was a religious radical, a critic of the Church of England under Charles I's Archbishop Laud, and a direct disciple of the 'Puritan martyrs' William Prynne, John Bastwick and Henry Burton. These men had been imprisoned and mutilated by Laud's regime. And Lilburne, through his associations with gathered churches – those that stood at the most radical end of the spectrum of the Puritan critics of the established Church – became their close confidant.

Indeed, it was an attempt to smuggle copies of John Bastwick's *Letany* into England from a press in the Netherlands that led to Lilburne's first arrest. He was brought before the prerogative Court of Star Chamber. For his refusal to recognise the court, and specifically for his claim that no freeborn Englishman should be tried in such a way, he became famous to the London crowd as Freeborn John. His reputation was enhanced by his physical bravery. When he was punished by being tied to the back of a cart and dragged from the Fleet prison to Westminster Yard, beaten 500 times with a three-thonged, knotted leather whip on the way, he remained defiant, even when he was put in the stocks at the end of the ordeal. He was still throwing copies of Bastwick's pamphlet from his coat and making speeches until his gaolers gagged him.[3]

Lilburne's defiance and thus his reputation would not have travelled so far without his involvement with secret printing. From gaol he had already smuggled out and had distributed an appeal to the apprentices and soon his own story of his persecution, the *Christian Man's Trial*, was printed by William Larner, who would become a lifelong printer of Leveller material.[4]

So it was that by the time John Lilburne was freed from his imprisonment by the Long Parliament he already stood at the confluence of very powerful, and organised, currents of political opposition. He was part of the generation of 'second sons', a London apprentice, a religious radical, an ally of the Puritan martyrs, a survivor of arrest, torture and imprisonment himself, and closely related to the secret printing presses of the parliamentary opposition.

Lilburne emerged from prison to play a leading role in the street protests that resulted in Charles I's decision to flee his capital in 1642. But Lilburne was developing intellectually as well as as a practical agitator. The radicals of the English Revolution had little ideological heritage to guide them. They could not, as subsequent generations of radicals have done, look back to the experience of previous revolutions because they were in essence experiencing the first modern revolution. Neither did they have any specifically democratic or revolutionary theoretical frameworks on which they could rely. Lilburne rested on an egalitarian interpretation of the Bible, the history of Puritan persecution, in particular Foxe's *Book of Martyrs*, the tradition of English common law as interpreted by Edward Coke's *Institutes*, in part on the Magna Carta, and, as it developed, Parliament's own 'resistance theory', which justified its defiance of the king. As Rachel Foxley demonstrates, Lilburne materially added to this body of thought the notion of freeborn citizenship, an essentially modern departure from seeing individuals as subjects of the monarch. Geoffrey Robertson accounts for Lilburne's pioneering use of English common law throughout his political career.

The meaning of war

The onset of the cataclysmic civil war once again saw Lilburne at the leading edge of military and political developments. He fought with bravery and distinction at Edgehill and at Brentford, where he was captured by the royalists. Taken to the king's new capital at Oxford he was once again imprisoned and then put on trial for his life. He was not released until Parliament threatened to execute the royalist prisoners it held if Lilburne lost his life. This decision was only transmitted to Oxford in the nick of time by Lilburne's heavily pregnant wife, Elizabeth. She made the hazardous journey between London and Oxford passing through the outposts of friends and enemies to free her husband. Elizabeth Lilburne was a formidable activist in her own right and it was not the last time she would be consumed by the defence of her imprisoned husband. Ann Hughes charts the sometimes difficult relationship between John and Elizabeth Lilburne and the toll taken on them by political engagement.

Supporters of Parliament were continually grappling with the questions of what the war was meant to achieve and how it should be conducted. Was it merely a form of armed negotiation meant to bring the king back on terms more agreeable to Parliament? Or was it a war to defeat the king more completely? Along these lines, a peace party and a war party formed in Parliament, in the army, and in the wider society. And once the parliamentary leadership under John Pym successfully engaged the Scottish army on its side, this division was overlain and reinforced by a wider religious debate. The Scots had agreed to lend their military support to Parliament in return for a promise that their Presbyterian form of church government would be introduced in England. For a significant layer of Puritan opinion stretching from proponents of Independent churches (inside the national church but not controlled by a church hierarchy), like Oliver Cromwell, to supporters of gathered churches (outside the national church structure altogether), like Lilburne and other future Levellers, this was unacceptable.[5] They feared, as John Milton memorably put it, that 'New *presbyter* is but old *priest* writ large'.[6] Norah Carlin describes how the issue of religious toleration and political freedom developed Lilburne's political thought.

Lilburne and other future Levellers like William Walwyn and Richard Overton had, until the controversies of 1643–44, operated as the most radical wing of Independency, the rapidly rising star of which was Oliver Cromwell. But Lilburne and his allies were always less focused on elite politics than on popular mobilisation. As debates about the postwar settlement of the nation became central, Lilburne and his supporters emerged with their own political movement and with demands and methods of operation that were sometimes compatible with those of their old allies and sometimes not.[7] Lilburne was the best known Leveller but he was also acting as part of a powerful collective leadership which had a number of bases of popular support among apprentices, in the gathered churches, and in the army. In

'John Lilburne as a revolutionary leader' I examine a powerful image of Lilburne, one which sees him primarily as a malcontent and troublemaker, and argue that his considerable political achievements are obscured by this reputation.

Revolution and republic

The Levellers did not survive the revolution they helped to create. In the wake of the execution of the king in January 1649, two possible courses were presented to the English Republic. One was a democratic republic outlined in the Levellers' *Agreement of the People*, now adopted by the entirety of the revolutionary forces assembled in the Whitehall Debates, but quickly laid aside by the MPs of the purged Long Parliament.[8] The second course, the one now taken, was an essentially military republic under the army commanded by Cromwell. The Levellers revolted against this turn of events in word and deed. The title of Lilburne's pamphlet *England's New Chaines Discovered* was a four-word summary of their view. Their supporters in the army mutinied and were defeated by forces under Cromwell, at Bishopsgate in London, at Burford, and in the Oxford garrison. That broke the Levellers as an effective and coherent organisation.[9]

Leveller leaders were imprisoned and Lilburne was put on trial for his life. Lilburne escaped conviction, in part due to a remarkable deployment of popular rhetoric which convinced the jury that they had a better right to decide the law than the government or the judges.[10] But Lilburne did not escape being sent into exile. Jason Peacey recreates the politics of Lilburne's exile in the Low Countries, tracing the thread of radical politics in the era of defeat. Lilburne did return to England, but only to face a second treason trial in 1653. Again, the courtroom Houdini escaped conviction – but not imprisonment, this time on the island of Jersey. Here he remained until the final months of his life. Ariel Hessayon looks at John Lilburne's last battles and his late conversion to Quakerism, challenging those interpretations that have seen this as a final surrender to quietism.

The ways in which Lilburne's reputation and the history of the Levellers have come down to us is long, complex, and contested. There has never been a moment when it has not interacted with contemporary politics or been refracted through modern political debate.[11] In 'Reborn John?' Edward Valance charts the first of these great transitions, as radicals and others in the eighteenth century debated the lineage of the first modern revolutionary leader and the movement he represented. Lilburne had a premonition it might happen this way when he wrote, 'though we fail, our truths prosper'.[12]

Notes

1 P. Gregg, *Free-born John, a Biography of John Lilburne* (London: Dent, 1986), chs. 1 and 3; M.A. Gibb, *John Lilburne the Leveller, a Christian Democrat* (London: Lindsay Drummond, 1947), pp. 19–22; H.N. Brailsford (C. Hill, ed.), *The Levellers and the English Revolution* (Nottingham: Spokeman, 1961), ch. 6; G.E. Aylmer, 'Gentlemen Levellers?', *Past and Present*, No. 49 (November 1970).

2 N. Carlin, 'Liberty and Fraternities in the English Revolution: The Politics of the Artisans' Protests, 1635–1659', *International Review of Social History*, Vol. 39, Issue 2 (August 1994); P. Baker, '*Londons Liberty in Chains Discovered*: The Levellers, the Civic Past, and Popular Protest in Civil War London', *Huntington Library Quarterly*, Vol. 76, No. 4 (2013).
P. Earle, *The Making of the English Middle Class* (London: Methuen, 1989), ch. 3; J. Rees, *The Leveller Revolution* (London: Verso, 2016), pp. 23–27.
3 P. Gregg, *Free-born John, a Biography of John Lilburne* (London: Dent, 1986), chs. 4 and 5; M. Tolmie, *The Triumph of the Saints, the Separate Churches of London 1616–1649* (Cambridge: CUP, 1977), esp. ch. 7.
4 J. Lilburne, *The Christian Man's Triall* (London, 1641), E181[7].
5 J.H. Hexter, *The Reign of King Pym* (Cambridge, Mass.: Harvard University Press, 1941).
6 J. Milton, 'On the New Forcers of Conscience Under the Long Parliament' (1646). For Leveller objections to the Scottish alliance, see, for example, *An Unhappy Game at Scotch and English* (1646), E.364[3] attributed to Overton and Lilburne, and by Sarah Barber to Henry Marten, see S. Barber, *A Revolutionary Rogue, Henry Marten and the English Republic* (Stroud: Sutton, 2000), p. 170.
7 J. Peacey, 'John Lilburne and the Long Parliament', *The Historical Journal*, Vol. 43, No. 3 (September 2000); J. Rees, *The Leveller Revolution* (London: Verso, 2016), pp. 126–27.
8 B. Taft, 'The Council of Officers' Agreement of the People, 1648/9', *The Historical Journal*, Vol. 28, No. 1 (March 1985); C.H. Firth (ed.), *Clarke Papers*, Vol. I and II (London: Royal Historical Society, 1894); P. Baker and E. Vernon, *Foundations of Freedom: Agreements of People, Levellers and Constitutional Crisis of the English Revolution* (Basingstoke: Palgrave Macmillan, 2012); C. Polizzotto, 'What Really Happened at the Whitehall Debates? A New Source', *Historical Journal*, Vol. 57, No. 1 (2014).
9 J. Lilburne, *Englands New Chaines Discovered; or The Serious Apprehensions of a Part of the People, in Behalf of the Commonwealth* (London, 1649), E545.27; H.N. Brailsford (C. Hill, ed.), *The Levellers and the English Revolution* (Nottingham: Spokeman, 1961), ch. 26; C.H. Firth, 'The Mutiny of Col. Ingoldsby's Regiment at Oxford in September, 1649', *Proceedings of the Oxford Architectural and Historical Society*, New Series, No. XXX (1884).
10 T. Varax (Clement Walker), *The Triall of Lieu. Colonell John Lilburne* (London, 1649), E584[9].
11 For some discussion of this, see B. Worden, 'The Levellers in History and Memory, c.1660–1960', in M. Mendle (ed.), *The Putney Debates of 1647, the Army, the Levellers and the English State* (Cambridge: CUP, 2001); J. Rees, *Leveller Organization and the Dynamic of the English Revolution* (Goldsmiths, University of London, PhD, 2014) ch. 1.; J. Rees, 'Revolution Denied', in L. German and R. Hoveman (eds.), *A Socialist Review* (London: Bookmarks, 1998).
12 J. Lilburne, *Englands New Chaines Discovered* (London, 1649), E545.27.

1

JOHN LILBURNE AND THE CITIZENSHIP OF 'FREE-BORN ENGLISHMEN'[1]

Rachel Foxley

John Lilburne was a charismatic figure who could rally impressive popular support in London. As one of the leaders of the Leveller movement, which flourished from the mid-1640s in the period of uncertainty following the end of the first English civil war, he was in and out of prison repeatedly, and communicated his experiences and his political vision in his prolific pamphlet writing. Central to these was his self-depiction as a 'free-born Englishman'.

Lilburne's writings emerged out of the context of parliamentarian argument during and after the first civil war. There has been a tendency to classify political theories of the early to mid-seventeenth century in England by asking whether they resulted from historical or theoretical modes of thought.[2] This question has been particularly pressing with regard to the Levellers, who have been put at both ends of the spectrum (as historically-minded defenders of an ancient constitution still largely embodied in the common law, or as natural law consent theorists who broke away from a dependence on historical precedent), and in the middle (as theorists of the Norman Yoke, harking back to heavily idealised Anglo-Saxon liberties).[3] It is surely worth asking how the Levellers have managed to be read so differently by different historians. The answer lies partly in the lack of uniformity between Leveller leaders, as well as in the habitual combining of different modes of argument that was characteristic of many civil war writers, including Lilburne and the other Levellers. In this article I will situate Lilburne's political thought in relation to the language of the common law, while acknowledging that the centre of gravity of his colleagues' thinking was much closer to natural law. This further raises the question of how their collaboration could have been so fruitful: I hope to suggest answers here, too, showing how Lilburne's thinking, developed through common law language, offered a useful complement to the consent theory more consistently employed by his colleagues.[4]

The interpretation of the Levellers has turned on this question of the historical or theoretical basis of their thinking partly because it has been taken to be some measure of 'conservatism' or 'radicalism'.[5] The historical mode of thought, basing political prescription and analysis on the ancient constitution, has been linked to the use of the language of the common law, and has been taken to be inherently conservative for a number of reasons. Clearly, treating as ideal the past constitution, and the existing law which is said to preserve it, is unlikely to be a prescription for radical change; but also it is widely agreed that the common law was the almost unchallenged 'language' in which early Stuart politics was conducted: it would be those who wanted to change the basis of argument, presumably, who would see the need to move outside this consensual language.[6] These claims, however, need to be modified in significant ways. Using the common law as a means for preserving the ancient constitution could be, and was, seen as a very dynamic process involving constant struggle and reassertion of liberties through the exercise of the law itself, which both embodied and guaranteed those liberties. This means, too, that however predominant the language of the common law was in pre-civil war politics, it was not a univocal carrier of political consensus as revisionist historians have sometimes suggested. Recognising what Greenberg calls the 'radical face of the ancient constitution' allows us to see that our much-touted 'languages' of politics really do function as languages: they enable thought as much as they constrain it, and arguments can be carried on *within* as well as *between* them.[7]

In this chapter I suggest that Lilburne was using the language of the common law in innovatory ways, but ways which had their origin in the 'radical' common law tradition that had begun to develop before the civil wars. He made the phrase 'free-born Englishman' into a shorthand for an emerging concept of citizenship. He did this by restructuring, from within, the legal language out of which much of his thought grew: the legal vocabulary continues to be used, but the foundational assumptions underlying it have changed.

I

The collocation 'free-born Englishman' is not common before Lilburne. Its novelty may have been overlooked because historians have found its ingredients unremarkable, and perhaps one of the advantages of the phrase was that contemporaries would be familiar both with the appeal to 'free-born' status and with patriotic language, and would thus find the idiom unthreatening. Lilburne himself had been nicknamed 'free-born John' at the time of his earliest public defiance of the authorities in 1638, an earnest of the availability of the phrase 'free-born'.[8] The usual context for the expression was not 'free-born Englishman' but 'free-born subject'. The phrase 'free-born subject' is the correlate of the standard parliamentarian (and pre-civil war) call for the 'liberties of the subject' – the topic avowedly at issue, for example, in the debates leading up to the Petition of Right.[9] Indeed, Levellers and pamphleteers of similar political hue did not completely abandon this vocabulary themselves – which makes it notable how far Lilburne himself did abandon it, and how early. In Lilburne's early writing we do find references to 'subjects', and in January 1645, in a hint of things to come, he refers to 'freeborne English Subjects'.[10] By the summer of 1645, however, he seems to have found his own language which avoids the word 'subject' altogether, replacing it with the notion of the 'free-born Englishman'. Lilburne creates a consistent language in which 'subjects' become 'Englishmen'. The modern opposition between subjects and citizens might push us towards understanding Lilburne's linguistic shift as a move in the direction of a notion of citizenship; I will argue that the details of Lilburne's language support such a view. The transformation of 'subjects' into citizens is marked by the appearance of the term 'Englishman' as much as by the disappearance of the word 'subject'. Cognates of the word 'subject', when they do recur at a later period of Leveller discourse, are clearly pejorative: to be subjected is to be vassalised, enslaved; one can only be 'subjected' to an arbitrary power.[11] The logic of Lilburne's elimination of the word 'subject' in favour of 'Englishman' is borne out by this later development.

II

Who are Lilburne's 'free-born Englishmen'? In talking of the 'free-born' and of 'free-men', or 'free men', Lilburne might be thought to be distinguishing these men from others who fell outside this status. I think it is clear, however, that these terms are inclusive rather than exclusive in their force.

It has been well demonstrated by Thomas, Hampsher-Monk and Wende that the term 'free-born' was not used by Leveller writers to distinguish a select group of Englishmen from the remainder, as C.B. Macpherson had argued. All Englishmen were taken to be free-born. One opponent of the Levellers remarked that it was redundant to talk about free-born Englishmen, asking rhetorically, 'are there any Englishmen that are not Free-borne?'[12]

There is more scope for confusion with 'free-men', as the term has two different meanings. To be a freeman of a guild or company, and hence of a city, was certainly to be a member of an exclusive group. Such status was connected to a locality, however, and not to the nation as a whole. So when Lilburne talks about 'freemen of England' we can be fairly sure that he does not mean only those men who were freemen in the narrower sense. The broader sense of 'freeman' is exactly parallel with 'free-born'. One of Lilburne's favourite references was to chapter 29 of Magna Carta, which set out what could not be done to a 'free man'. Keith Thomas's discussion shows that the status contrasted with freedom in the seventeenth-century texts is either slavery or villeinage. Since villeinage had been ended, the 'free men' referred to in Magna Carta would now be all Englishmen. Coke's discussion of the 'liber homo' of Magna Carta chapter 29 included in it even villeins, 'saving against their lord', and made no other exclusions.[13]

Even in contexts where we might expect the narrow meaning of 'freeman' to be dominant, Lilburne and his associates often either use, or clearly invoke, the broader meaning. Lilburne reprints a petition, on behalf of 'all the freemen of England', that complains that charters of incorporation to specific merchants 'disfranchis[e] [...] all other the free-borne people of England'.[14] Playing consciously on both the narrower and broader meanings of 'free-man', Lilburne laments that 'the poor *Weavers*, though Free-men of *London*, are not only in miserable poverty, but in the miserablest slavery (in the City where they by name are Free-men)'.[15] In Leveller idiom, the status of Englishman could even be used to *override* the status distinctions of London politics. In *Londons Liberties in Chains*, Lilburne's co-author urges London freemen to demand the right to elect the Lord Mayor; he justifies his own interest in the topic by saying that, though he was not a citizen of London, 'yet [he was] no stranger, nor forreigner, but a free-man of England who hath freely hazarded all, for the recovery of the common Liberty, and my Countries freedom'.[16] In fact, as a non-citizen of London, the writer *was* technically a 'foreigner': this was the word used to describe English London residents who were not freemen of the city.[17] But his status as 'a free-man of England' outweighs, for him, the fact that he is not a freeman of London.

In his writings specifically on London – where he avoids spelling out exactly which 'free-men' he is talking about – Lilburne is again driving at inclusiveness, although he surely draws on his readers' familiarity with the assertion of the liberties of the city's privileged freemen. The whole thrust of his argument is against the exclusiveness of 'these Prerogative-Monopolizing Patentee-men of London'; 'the Prerogative-Monopolizing arbitrary-men of London'. Their offensive activities take place through their

> Patentee-Monopolizing Companies, Corporations and Fraternities. So that to speak properly, really, and truly, their Brotherhoods are so many conspiracies to destroy and overthrow the lawes and liberties of England, and to ingrosse, inhance, and destroy the trades and Franchises of most of the Freemen of London.[18]

These 'conspiracies' and 'monopolies' of private interest are diametrically opposed to the Leveller ideal of the common good as exemplified in the equal freedoms of individuals. Carlin points out that this makes the Levellers very different from the guild-members who agitated *within* their corporations in these years; Houston is, I think, right to assert that Lilburne does attack monopolies and the company system directly, as part of this campaign against private interests.[19] Lilburne himself pointed to his own writings as demonstrations of 'the unjustnesse of Corporations and Monopolies, which are both sons of one father'.[20]

The inclusive force of Lilburne's insistence on calling Englishmen 'free-born' and 'free-men' is clear. The assumption that Englishmen were free and not bond is not controversial. What is controversial is the assertion that the free status of Englishmen gave them, as individuals, political status. Sir Thomas Smith had written that the lowest class of free men 'have no voice or authoritie in our common wealth, and no account is made of them but onelie to be ruled, not to rule other'.[21] Ireton, at Putney, was quite prepared to put free Englishmen into that category.

The Levellers' innovation is not in saying that all Englishmen were free men, but in drawing extensive conclusions about political rights from that.

III

I have said that for Lilburne being a free-born Englishman brought with it political status. The content of that status, and indeed the argument that it did, in some sense, already exist, are fleshed out through Lilburne's richly textured usage of legal terminology. His treatment of the word denizen, in particular, works to justify his claim that Englishmen possess a set of political rights.

The phrase 'free denizen' is another alternative for 'free-born Englishman'; denizen in this context simply means 'inhabitant'. Thus Lilburne amplifies his claim to be a free-man with the phrase 'a free-borne Denizen of England',[22] where the added ingredient seems to be the reference to Englishness, backed up by the connotations of birth in England (free-born) and residency in England (denizen). Again, Lilburne refers to good laws made for the protection of 'all the free Denizens' of the country.[23]

Denizen, however, had a technical legal meaning as well; and as the *Oxford English Dictionary*'s examples show, this was familiar enough to be usable figuratively as well as literally. Coke, giving a false etymology, sums up the two meanings:

> he that is borne within the King's liegeance is called sometime a Denizen, quasi deins nee, born within ... But many times ... Denizen is taken for an Alien borne, that is infranchised or denizated by Letters Patents.[24]

Two things are notable in the latter case: firstly, that the denizen only gains rights similar to those of an English person by being formally granted them; secondly, that the denizen never gains *all* the rights of a native subject. Thus the definition of the phenomenon in *Les Termes de la Ley*: 'where an Alien born becommeth the Kings subject, & obtaineth the Kings letters patents for to enioy all priuiledges as an Englishman, but if one be made denizen, he shall pay customes & diuers other things as aliens'.[25] Cowell is even more explicit about the status of denizens: the word

> signifieth in our common law, an Alein [sic] that is infranchised here in England by the Princes Charter, and inabled, almost in all respects, to doe as the Kings native subjects doe, namely to purchase, and to possesse lands, to be capable of any office or dignitie.
>
> Yet it is said to be short of naturalisation, because a stranger naturalised, may inherit lands by descent, which a man made, onely a Denizen cannot.[26]

One useful connotation of this technical sense of 'denizen' is that it implies freedom. An alien becomes a denizen by being 'infranchised', which literally means being made free or given freedoms. This literal meaning was clear to at least some of Lilburne's contemporaries: Henry Cockeram's *Dictionary* defined 'Enfranchise' as

'To make free' and 'Disfranchise' as 'To make one lose his freedome'.[27] Cowell's *Interpreter* gives a suggestive definition of 'Enfranchisement':

> It signifieth in our common law, the incorporating of a man in any society, or body politicke. For example, hee that by Charter is made Denizen of England, is said to be enfranchised; and so is hee that is made a Citizen of London, or other City, or Burgesse of any Towne Corporate, because hee is made partaker of those liberties that appertaine to the Corporation, wherinto he is enfranchised. So a villaine is enfranchised, when hee is made free by his Lord, and made capable of the benefits belonging to Free-men.[28]

Thus being enfranchised means several things: being made part of a group; being granted liberties belonging to the members of a particular body; and being literally made free from a status regarded as a kind of servitude.[29] This set of associations is a powerful one for Lilburne to draw on, as he clearly does in his use of the term 'disfranchise', and the often linked term 'denizen'.

As well as using the noun 'denizen', apparently in its original sense of native inhabitant, Lilburne also uses various versions of the word 'undenize/undenizenize' to denote the removal of liberties. This is often linked with the notion of disfranchisement. The two ideas are linked, for example, when he talks of what might lead 'to the disfranchising me of being a Denizon and freeman of England'.[30] A supporter of Lilburne writes that through the imposition of the Covenant in the army, 'men of excellent publique principles' would be 'disfranchised, and undenized'.[31] In *Londons Liberty* Lilburne uses the term 'disfranchise' to refer to the denial of a vote both to Londoners who were not livery men in choosing their MPs, and of those elsewhere falling short of the 40s. income required to vote:

> and this undenezing of those Corporations, is an undenezing to all the towns and villages adjacent, in which live thousands of people, that by name are free-men of England, and divers of them men of great estates in money and stock; which also are disfranchised and undenezed, by the fore-mentioned unrighteous Statute; because they have not in land 40s. *per annum*.[32]

Thus references in an almost modern vein to disfranchisement as the deprivation of a vote are linked with references to 'undenezing'. By depriving someone of a vote, the authorities had made him less of a denizen. Someone who was 'undenezed' was pushed outside that group of people whose consent was considered essential to government.

Lilburne drew on the concept of granting a set of quasi-native rights to (foreign) denizens in order to reinforce his own conceptualisation of just such a coherent set of rights belonging to natives by birth. Given that there was no bill of rights comprehensively stating what was due to all native English subjects, the granting of denizen status was in a way a legal acknowledgement that there *was* a set of rights which accrued to native Englishmen precisely because of their status. The denizen could be seen as being granted exactly that package, minus a couple of important entitlements.

When Lilburne uses the word 'denizen' he blends its two meanings, combining the idea of a package of entitlements for Englishmen with the emotive appeal of being a native inhabitant of England, a denizen. The word in Lilburne's usage takes on some of the connotations of the modern term 'citizen'. Thus he laments the result of monopolies as 'but an indenosonizing of a few, to undenosonize a many', and juxtaposes this with the comment that England is supposed to be 'a Kingdom governed by one Law made by universall and common consent'.[33] Thus a legal grant (a corporation's patent) makes a few people into denizens, in the way that letters patent could 'indenosonize' an alien; the effect of this is to 'undenosonize' most people – not from rights that they had ever been *granted*, but from those rights due to them as denizens, native inhabitants who are supposed to be equal in the eyes of the law.

What are the uniform entitlements of Lilburne's free-born Englishmen? Wende has pointed out that the Leveller writers used a whole list of interchangeable terms, in both singular and plural forms, to denote what they were fighting for: rights, liberties, freedoms, free customs, privileges, property, safety, laws, immunities. He rightly sees this as significant. His explanation is that freedom is seen by the Levellers as a composite, resulting from all these things. It would perhaps be more accurate to say that the Englishman's freedom *consists* in his rightful claim to all of these things; this explains why it often seems to be identified with the liberty of every subject to enjoy the benefit of the law. Wende perceptively emphasises this logical shift from plural liberties to the single 'liberty' of the law.[34] Lilburne's language actively remodels individual legal freedoms into a more unified conception of a set of citizenship rights. Law is the mediating term in this transformation: freedoms under law retain their names but come to signify the single and universal freedom guaranteed by the law.

One unifying expression denoting the entitlements of an Englishman is 'birth-right'. Like the terms 'denizen' or 'freeman', which come to connote the role of citizen, 'birth-right' comes to connote all that is due to a citizen. On occasion Lilburne may use the term with quite specific entitlements: he opposes monopolies 'that so all the people may inioy their birth right, free trade'.[35] But generally, birth-right comprehends all that an Englishman is entitled to claim under English law, and sometimes under higher authorities, too: the 'inheritance of our Fathers, and the Birth-right of us and our children' is 'our Fundamentall Lawes and Liberties, Franchises and Priviledges, that God, Nature, and the just Customes of the Land in which wee live, hath given us'.[36] The term is an indicator of the crucial influence of the legal tradition, and specifically of Coke's interpretation of English law. In the speech he reports himself giving to the Committee of Examinations, Lilburne firstly declares: 'I am a free-man, yea, a free-borne Denizen of England'. He goes on to quote Magna Carta to justify his rights: 'Sir, the Priviledges contained herein is my Birth-right and Inheritance'.[37] This follows Coke's Ciceronian assertion that the law is 'the best birth-right the subject hath', which Lilburne quotes directly elsewhere.[38] Lilburne found similar statements about birth-rights in Parliament's *Book of Declarations*.[39] Parliament had declared 'That the law, and the ordinary course of justice, is the common birth-right of every subject of England'.[40]

Another text from the legal tradition, not quoted in Lilburne, makes clear how specific to those born within the realm the notion of birth-right was supposed to be: 'for the law is our birthright, to which an alien is collateral & a stranger, & therfore disabled to take any benefit thereby'.[41] Lilburne's vision of an essentially English inheritance of law is in accord with this.

Lilburne's use of old legal terms such as 'privilege', 'immunity', 'liberty', and 'franchise' is part of this project to unify the entitlements of English law. All of these terms denoted specific rights or exemptions granted piecemeal to individuals or bodies, and they were overlapping concepts. Cowell defines 'franchise' as 'a priviledge, or an exemption from ordinary jurisdiction, and sometime an immunity from tribute'. A 'libertas' (literally equivalent to 'franchise') 'is a priviledge held by grant or prescription, whereby men enjoy some benefit or favour beyond the ordinarie subject'. In defining privilege, he follows Cicero and others in seeing it as a 'privata lex' granted to one man. *Les Termes de la Ley* defines privileges as 'liberties and franchises graunted to an office, place, towne, or mannor, by the Kings great charter, letters patents, or act of Parliament'.[42] With all these terms, the inherited legal meaning was of specific privileges possessed by specific persons or institutions not through right but ultimately through grant. This is very far from the way in which Lilburne uses these terms.

The tenor of Lilburne's references to privileges, immunities, and franchises is that these are things due to all Englishmen. Lilburne refers to the 'priviledges' in Magna Carta being his 'Birth-right and Inheritance'.[43] He declares that 'Englishmen have some priveledges to stand for if they were not fooles'.[44] Since he has not impaired his own status as denizen and freeman of England, he 'ought to enjoy as great a priviledge in the enjoyment of the benefit of the law of England, as any free Denizon of England whatsoever, by what name or title soever he be called'.[45] Again, Lilburne 'ought by the fundamentall lawes of this Land, to enjoy the benefit of all the lawes, liberties, priviledges, and immunities of a free-born man'. The universality of these concepts is suggested by a reference to 'the liberties, immunities, and priviledges of all the Commons of England'.[46] *An Anatomy of the Lords Tyranny* was 'published to the view of all the Commons of England, for their information, & knowledge of their Liberties and Priviledges'.[47] In the same vein 'our Fundamentall Lawes and Liberties, Franchises and Priviledges' are mentioned in one breath.[48] It is not that some Englishmen have some privileges, some others. All are supposed to have the same privileges and liberties.

My argument, then, is that Lilburne's thought is rooted in a legalistic vocabulary, and can be seen to have developed largely through the medium of this vocabulary. In the course of its development, however, the fundamental logic of this language changed. The roots of the argument developed by Lilburne may lie in the set of notions described by Conal Condren as 'liberties of office': liberties tied to an office or status because they are necessary for the fulfilment of the duties inherent in that status. The legal 'privileges' and 'franchises' claimed by individuals as their particular rights may have been seen as liberties of this kind. However, if Lilburne is exploiting the logic of this kind of 'liberty', the status to which the liberty is tied is that of an Englishman, or sometimes simply a man – which, as Condren himself comments, 'is to extend the notion of an office to, or even beyond, its limit'. Condren may be right that such extensions of the relevant 'offices' testify to the power of the language in warding off potential charges of rebelliousness, but they surely also begin to nudge at more modern notions of liberty as having an absolute value, freed from dependence on social roles. Liberty of office may leave traces in the importance which Lilburne attaches to the status of Englishmen: if Condren is right, then the logic which leads Lilburne to tie his claims to a status, albeit a universalising one, is rooted in persistent political languages of the period.[49] Such universalising usages as Lilburne's, though, push this language to or beyond its logical limits. In Lilburne's writing, all Englishmen enjoy identical political 'privileges' – which effectively changes the meaning of 'privilege'.

IV

Lilburne, of course, was not dealing with an unmediated tradition of medieval legal terms. His materials were not 'raw' but embedded in already politically specific discourses. It is clear that the writings of Sir Edward Coke were a major source for Lilburne, and Lilburne's usage of legal terminology is undoubtedly influenced by the particular cast given to it by Coke and others in the early seventeenth century.

The tendency to generalise from unhelpfully specific medieval legal provisions is certainly not confined to the works of Coke and Lilburne. Weston describes the supposed Saxon laws as 'a farrago of items from which Stuart Englishmen fashioned legal and constitutional principles of wide application', and notes the way in which their application was extended by the framers of the Petition of Right – who of course included Coke.[50] Sacks has discussed the evolution of 'liberties' into 'the liberty of the subject', dating this shift in language to the late sixteenth and early seventeenth centuries, and linking it to a 'process of conceptual expansion' of other terms, particularly 'monopoly'.[51] Coke and Lilburne, I would argue, are particularly prominent figures in this history of expansive legal interpretation.

Modern scholarship on Coke has demonstrated that, however authoritative his pronouncements on the ancient laws of England were later taken to be, his legal writings were far from being neutral collations of the materials of the common law. Apart from his tricks of misreporting cases and inventing 'maxims', his very understanding of the nature of the common law implied principles of interpretation and generalisation that could not be neutral. If the common law was for Coke a system of artificial reason comprehending all that must be talked about in political life, as well as more narrowly legal matters,[52] then the new questions which might arise for the law's consideration would have to be answered using old materials: this meant, essentially, that they would have to be answered from principles taken to be exemplified in these old materials. This could be done unremarked upon, by a redefinition of vocabulary or the extension of the applicability of a maxim; it could be helped along by a newly coined 'maxim' or a tendentiously reported case; or it could be done in the name of the spirit or reason of the law.[53]

It is clear from Coke's parliamentary career in the 1620s, as well as his writing, that he became more and more concerned with asserting the law's control over, or at least bounding of, royal prerogative.[54] In his fostering of the Petition of Right we see him using expansive arguments from legal premises to reach conclusions quite different from those reached earlier in his career.[55] It is in the *Institutes*, parts II–IV of which were confiscated after his death and recovered and published by the Long Parliament for their own purposes, that Coke's most potentially radical legal interpretations are found.

Magna Carta prompted in Coke in the second part of his *Institutes* the same generalising impulses as it had during the framing of the Petition of Right. He invokes its authority to argue for the illegality of monopolies, on the grounds that the 'liberty of the subject' guaranteed by Magna Carta includes the liberty to follow any trade. (His definition of monopoly in the third part of the *Institutes* – as an institution by which persons or corporations other than the monopolists 'are sought to be restrained of any freedome, or liberty that they had before' – seems suspiciously well-suited to the workings of this extremely tendentious argument.)[56] Commenting on the famous chapter 29 of Magna Carta, which set out the legal limits on what could be done to a free man ('liber homo'), Coke not only extends the 'libertates' mentioned to specifics such as the right to trade, but also glossed the term, in one of its 'significations', as meaning 'the laws of the realme' *tout court*.[57] Similarly, he quotes an unexceptionable common-law maxim from Plowden's *Commentaries*, but then glosses it with a significant extra phrase – derived from Cicero – in his translation:

> *Le common ley ad tielment admeasure les prerogatives le roy, que ilz ne tolleront, ne prejudiceront le inheritance dascun*, the common law hath so admeasured the prerogatives of the king, that they should not take away, nor prejudice the inheritance of any: and the best inheritance the subject hath, is the law of the realme.[58]

A defence of the property of individuals – itself a great concern for Coke – is transformed into an assertion of an equal property of all subjects in the law. This glossed version of the maxim was transplanted from Coke's work to lend support to Lilburne's case.[59]

In spite of such examples, Coke has to be used carefully for Lilburne's purposes. There are limits to Coke's capacity to transform the connotations of legal language. Wende is right to point out the ways in which Lilburne follows Coke, but he seems to overlook the inconvenient aspects of Coke in much the same way as Lilburne himself. Thus, while Wende himself cites Coke to show that in the common law a 'freedom' is essentially a privilege enjoyed by some and not others, he sees as more important Coke's statements which imply that the law has to be equal for all and that it cannot privilege any individual or group. On the contrary, Coke says, for example, 'that ecclesiasticall persons have more and greater liberties then other the king's subjects'.[60] Lilburne, I would argue, makes a new and consistent egalitarian language out of these terms, where Coke merely redefines or glosses them in particular instances.

How well Coke's vision could nourish Lilburne's, and how subtle the changes were which could make Coke's language into truly Lilburnian language, can be seen in one example. Lilburne was trying to make out of the materials available in English law a unified set of rights which applied not haphazardly and individually but evenly as a package to a whole section of the population. Magna Carta is a central foundation for this set of rights. An ally of Lilburne's makes use of Coke for this purpose, declaring that:

> the Reasons ... why it [Magna Carta] is called *Charta Libertatum Regni*, The Charter of the Liberties of *England* from the effect, *Quia liberos facit*, It makes us Free-men, and for the same cause it is called (*communis libertas*, common liberty) and *Le charter des franchises*.[61]

The passage of Coke from which this is taken does not translate the Latin phrases.[62] Here the writer has chosen translations that are slightly more emotive than the Latin might suggest: the Latin phrase 'liberties of the kingdom' is translated as 'liberties of England'; the Latin phrase that could simply mean 'because it makes [us/them/people] free' becomes fixed as a statement of essential transformation in English – 'It makes us Free-men'. Together these translations recall Lilburne's key phrase, 'free men of England'. Coke and Lilburne's supporters agree: the 'liberties' and (a direct translation) '*franchises*' may be in the plural, but each man affected does not simply acquire a series of separate liberties – instead he is made a free man.

V

My discussion so far has focused on Lilburne's use of materials from the English legal tradition in shaping an inclusive and uniform conception of English citizenship. I believe this is the key to understanding the nature of Lilburne's political language, but it does raise further questions about his understanding of history and law.

Much has been written about the nature of Leveller theorising. Lilburne's writings raise a problem of legitimation. His arguments in defence of the liberties of free-born Englishmen imply much about the basis of those liberties, but explicit argument on the point is rare. On a couple of occasions he articulates a whole list of foundations for these liberties: they are 'our natural, rationall, nationall, and legal liberties, and freedoms', 'the rationall, natural, nationall, and legall liberties of my selfe and all the Commons of England'.[63] Thus reason, nature, the nation, and the law are all cited as sources of English commoners' liberties. This seems to suggest two different lines of argument: reason and nature belong most comfortably to natural law theory, while the nation and the law suggest an appeal to history, and specifically to the supposed ancient constitution of the English nation. Interpreters of Leveller writings have noted both aspects, but the overwhelming emphasis – with the honourable exception of Seaberg – is on natural law thinking.[64]

In Lilburne's case these two positions prove to be much less starkly opposed than the scholarship might suggest. There are certainly times when he appeals specifically to the law of nature, but it is appropriate that the most often-cited passage of this kind is found in a postscript to one of Lilburne's pamphlets, rather than in the main text. In the body of that pamphlet, as in his writing in general, Lilburne is far less explicit about the foundations of his case, and while he criticises some aspects of the common law, he appeals repeatedly to Magna Carta.[65] While at a stretch one might argue that the mixture of natural law and historico-legal language in Lilburne's writing is logically consistent – the common law is in his view simply not at odds with natural law – we can see that in fact there are much more subtle tensions and congruences running through and between his arguments from law and from nature. This suggests to me that his thinking really did occupy a space between the two extremes, rather than merely being channelled one way or another according to expediency.[66] Indeed, such blending of the different forms of argument is not confined to Lilburne or to Leveller writers.[67] Consideration of the nature of Lilburne's writings also militates against seeing his choice of argument and language as cynically tailored to his audiences: his publication, republication, annotation, and cross-referencing of his own works show that he considered his published writing as a single, ongoing oeuvre intended for an overwhelmingly consistent audience – precisely the inclusive audience of concerned free-born Englishmen. While utterances originally composed for particular contexts – law courts of varying degrees of perceived illegitimacy, either of the Houses of Parliament or their committees, private conversations with public figures – do certainly show the marks of their origins, they are embedded in Lilburne's editorial comments to his readers, and commended to readers for their use. Lilburne would like *all* the types of argument he uses to be absorbed into the thinking of all his readers.

At one pole, Lilburne appeals frequently to legal liberties, and often points out that these are national liberties because they exist under English law. He often implies that it is the English law itself which *confers* certain rights. Thus he remarks that he has published a specific collection of legal material so that people can read 'their chiefest freedomes, that the Statute law of England gives them'.[68] He backs up his assertions of his rights contained in the phrase 'I being a free man of England' by glossing 'England' with the phrase 'a Kingdome that professeth to be governed by law'.[69] More often it is the whole phrase 'free man of England' that is interpreted in terms of a right to fair treatment under the law. This is what underlies Lilburne's repeated insistence on his Englishness in *Innocency and Truth*. Lilburne's frequent references to specific statutes when contesting for a particular right – for example, annual parliaments[70] – support the view that the law itself was the primary source of the Englishman's rights. The constant references to the trope of the law as the 'birthright and inheritance' of Englishmen reinforce this impression.

These references to the law could be seen as broadly in line with Coke's celebrated 'ancient constitution' thinking, but historical legal arguments could take a variety of forms, and at the other end of the spectrum from a robust defence of current law as ideal there is the more romantic and aggressive historical vision of ancient Saxon liberties currently crushed under the 'Norman yoke'. To see where Lilburne falls on this spectrum – how far he sees ancient liberties as persisting in current laws, and how far they exist only as an ideal to be restored – we must ask what *kind* of law he appeals to.

Here Lilburne's meaning is often unclear. Sometimes he seems to be concerned with the law as it stands: thus 'the Law of England' is the 'birthright and inheritance' of royalist peers on trial 'in every punctilio of it'.[71] But generally the status of the laws that Lilburne appeals to is less clear. When he asserts that 'by the antient, good, just and unrepealed laws of England' parliaments should be held annually, only the fact that parliaments were clearly *not* held annually tells us that 'unrepealed' does not mean 'effectively in force'.[72] This must be true for many of the laws he sees as ideal. Lilburne's ambivalence about the existing law is clearly expressed in a pamphlet of 1649:

> And though the law of England be not so good, and so exact in every particular, especially in the administrative part of it, as I could, wish it were, yet till I can see a better, I for my part will make much of that which we have, as the principall earthly preserver and safeguard of my life, liberty, and property.[73]

Here it is unclear whether Lilburne is looking forward or back to a 'better' law – to an ancient constitution or to natural law to be implemented in the future. Lilburne's appeals to law often do not state the type of law he means, but where he distinguishes statute from common law he either calls on both or comes down in favour of statute.[74] Even when he appeals explicitly to 'common law', we might be wary about the precision of the term.[75] He also uses less technical terms to characterise the kind of law he appeals to: it is often 'known' or 'declared' or 'fundamental'. The law has different connotations in different contexts: sometimes it is important to distinguish what is written (and therefore 'known' and 'declared') from the unwritten law, with its inherent danger of arbitrariness;[76] sometimes to distinguish the 'tenour' or 'equity' from the letter of the law;[77] sometimes to imply that some provisions, even if in some sense 'laws', may not be 'fundamental' ones.[78] These categories and priorities do not map simply onto each other: written law may be preferable to unwritten, but the spirit may be preferable to the letter. These factors complicate any attempt to determine whether Lilburne's allegiance is primarily to the common law or to Parliament-made statute, to existing law of either kind, or to past or future ideal laws.

These shifting emphases do to some extent reflect the requirements of the argument in which Lilburne finds himself. Thus he can specifically argue that while common preservation is 'the ouldest Law' and can override normal laws in times of emergency, in safer times one should be satisfied with nothing less than 'the absolute benefit of the Law, and the common justice of *England*'.[79] This view is not actually incoherent, convenient though it might be; and the same can be said of other ambivalences in his language. In fact, even while arguing that much of the 'content and form' of Leveller writings, and especially the nature of the foundational arguments they invoked, was 'determined' or 'dictated' by 'rhetorical exigencies', Burgess concedes that it is not strictly incoherent to invoke both natural and positive law, as equity and reason could effectively reconcile the two. While Burgess suggests that the common lawyers' logic of equity is ignored or reversed in Leveller writing so that law can be corrected from outside the legal framework rather than from within it, I do not see such a clear distinction.[80]

Much of the breadth and ambivalence of Lilburne's view of law would not have been alien to Coke's thinking. He too could emphasise the intent of the law (its 'true sense and sentence') as a crucial principle of interpretation,[81] say that what is against reason is against law ('this is another strong argument in law, *Nihil quod est contra rationem est licitum*'),[82] and assert the importance of at least the penal law being known to those who would be punished under it.[83] Like Lilburne, he could confess a dislike of the law's being in French, and count this among the negative effects of the Norman Conquest: 'we would derive from the Conqueror as little as we could.'[84] He, too, was ambivalent about the relationship between the common law and parliamentary statute, and, like Lilburne, saw principles of interpretation and correction flowing between the two rather than simply in one direction – although clearly Coke's inclination was to assert the superiority of common law over statute, where Lilburne would make the opposite claim.[85]

Given Coke's commitment to the reason of the law – albeit, for him, an artificial reason[86] – Lilburne can be seen as developing Coke's legacy even when he apparently steps outside legal and historical arguments and appeals to God, nature, and reason as legitimators – and measures – of English law.[87] Certainly, Lilburne's tone is sometimes radical: thus, the freedoms given by the law of England are admitted to be 'very slender and short to what by nature and reason they ought to be'.[88] The law of England consists of all England's existing laws, *providing* that they are 'agreeable to the law Eternall and Naturall'. Those which do not fulfil these conditions are tellingly described as 'contrary to [the people's] Birth-rights and Freedomes' – a phrase which more often suggests the English law than a higher and more perfect one.[89] Lilburne himself can characterise the *fundamental* law of the land as 'the Perfection of Reason'[90] – since it is by definition that part of existing law which is in accord with nature and reason. When he quotes St Germain to the same effect, he also makes it clear that this means that non-fundamentals in law may be changed for the better.[91] Again, law can – and should – be interpreted on the assumption that the law-giver did not intend to enact something that went against reason.[92]

The instabilities in Lilburne's account of law and history are nicely summed up in his use of Magna Carta. Accounts of 'ancient constitution' thinking by Weston and Greenberg, and Seaberg's work on the Levellers, suggest that the line between the common-law ancient constitution and the Norman yoke can be a thin one: much can depend on whether the 'Confessor's Laws' are maintained through prescription, as well as on the nature of the Norman Conquest itself. Magna Carta could be seen as an assertion of ancient rights, an example of prescription, and the authors of *Englands Birthright* perhaps hint at the thesis that Magna Carta and other statutes merely 'declare' the common law when they talk about 'knowne and declared' laws.[93] But when, under pressure from Leveller colleagues, Lilburne does criticise the common law as Norman, Magna Carta can be slotted into the category of statute. He admits that 'though there may be some veines issuing from former originals, yet the main stream of our Common law, with the practice thereof, flowed out of Normandy'. This shows clearly that he does, when forced to think about it, accept that the law was in large part Norman; it also contradicts Seaberg's argument that Lilburne sees this Norman corruption of the law as extending only to procedure and not to the provisions of the law itself.[94] Yet Lilburne then immediately rescues those elements of law that he most often appeals to as expressing English liberties: 'in the harshness of my expressions against the Common Law, I put … a cleare distinction of it, from the Statute Law'. The statute law, he says, is flawed, but contains 'gallant Lawes' such as chapters 28–29 of Magna Carta, the Petition of Right, and the Act abolishing Star Chamber. Magna Carta still, however, falls short of Edward the Confessor's laws, 'which the Conquerour rob'd England of'.[95] The excellence of the three statutes Lilburne mentions might easily have been justified by their alleged conformity with the ancient principles of the common law.

Lilburne does, of course, employ natural law ideas as well as common law thinking. Natural law thinking is present, alongside the common law, in his work from as early as 1646 (in *The Freemans Freedom*, discussed above.) Some of his later works, such as the two parts of *Englands New Chains* in 1649, might support the view that Lilburne's thought increasingly engages with natural law over time. Yet natural law never eclipses English law, precisely because Lilburne's version of English liberties can be vindicated by natural alongside national law. Even when making reference to the more universal laws of God, nature, and nations, and talking about what human nature itself requires, Lilburne's attachment to the legal tradition of England is not eclipsed. On two occasions, rather than grounding the specifics of English law in overarching natural and divine law, he reverses that relationship. Thus the best elements in the Petition of Right and Magna Carta 'are of universall concernment to all the sons of men, under any just Government in the world'.[96] As late in his career as his *Apologeticall Narration*, written in exile in 1653, he can talk about 'all English men or people being all borne free alike, and the Liberties thereof equally entayled to all of them alike', and then go on to subordinate the divine law to this English law: 'And suitable to these most righteous Maximes of the Law of England, are the most glorious and righteous dealings of the Soveraigne Lord of Heaven & Earth.'[97]

One final example – again relatively late in the development of Leveller thinking, in May 1648 – confirms that Lilburne really does seem happy to invoke 'rationall, natural, nationall, and legall liberties' alongside each other without feeling the need to rank them:

> it is not only my undoubted naturall right, by the light and Law of nature; yea, and by the ancient common Law of *England* to plead my owne cause my selfe, if I please, but it is also the naturall and undoubted right of every individuall Englishmen [*sic*], yea and of every man, upon the face of the Earth, in what Countrey soever; and therefore, Sir, I demand from you, liberty to speake freely for my selfe, not only by the Law of nature, but also by the ancient Common Law of England.[98]

VI

We have seen, then, that Lilburne's constant invocation of 'free-born Englishmen' carries a strong political message with it. Certainly Lilburne uses 'English' as a moral shorthand, declaring himself to be 'a true bred Englishman', 'a true-hearted Englishman', 'Englands Cordiall Freind', 'a true and real-hearted *Englishman*', 'As much an Englishman as ever', and '*A faithful* English-man'.[99] Lilburne often urges his audience to act by appealing to their sense of their own Englishness, and implying that an Englishman *ought* to have certain qualities. Sometimes this implicit message is reinforced by a quite explicit use of 'English' or 'Englishman' as a normative term. Thus Prynne's charges against Lilburne are described as 'unsufferable slanders, wicked, bloody and un-English-man-like provocations'.[100] The expression may be whimsical, but it is typical of Lilburne's conceptual world. Similarly, Lilburne's way of praising Wildman's pamphlet *Truths Triumph* is to call it 'his late masculine english peace'.[101] Again, it is 'every knowing English eye' and 'every unprejudiced and truly English heart' which are appealed to as the proper judges of the government of the country. It was 'old English valour' which was shown by the army's actions at its rendezvous of 4–5 June 1647. London citizens wanting to defend their goods and liberty by not paying tithes must 'play the Englishman'.[102] Adjectives are often added to the word 'Englishman', intended, in Lilburne's discourse, not so much to indicate that certain Englishmen are *also* 'honest', 'true hearted', etc, as to suggest that these are the qualities that *all* Englishmen ought to have. This is clear from Lilburne's proposal in *The Additional Plea* to appeal to 'all that have honest, english hearts'.[103]

Lilburne's imagined audience is made up of these 'true hearted', 'true bred' and 'honest' Englishmen. For example, he appeals 'to every true hearted Englishman that desires a speedie end of these warres';[104] publishes information for the benefit of 'all true hearted English-men';[105] and addresses only those 'True bred Englishmen, that have a life to lay down, for the defence of your just Liberties and Freedomes'.[106] He recommends books that 'are worth every honest English mans buying' in order to know about government,[107] and wants to replace monopolisers with 'honest Englishmen … that love the Fundamentall lawes, and the common and just liberties of the Nation'.[108]

The drive of this language, then, is at inclusivity. It implies only the most general limits to the membership of the polity: Lilburne appeals to all adult English males, and, if some are excluded by their lack of true-heartedness, that is for them to judge. Lilburne's writings themselves may even be the diagnostic tool: it is true-hearted Englishmen who will respond to them in the way that he hopes.

Lilburne's language, and provisions in other Leveller texts, hint that there are circumstances under which Englishmen who are not 'true-hearted' must be formally deprived of their legal liberties. In asserting that he retains his English liberties because he has not done anything that would disfranchise him, Lilburne implies that others could forfeit their liberties by their actions. Even the suspicion of treasonable behaviour does not justify disfranchisement from the protection of the law: due process must be used to decide such cases – that is, after all, what the law is for.[109] One can only forfeit one's English liberties by actions directed at the foundations of those liberties. These are not spelled out in Lilburne's works, but the provisions of the various joint Leveller programmes suggest that royalism or acting against a future constitution established through an *Agreement of the People* would count. Essentially, what is implied here is a Leveller version of treason, appropriate to a state reconstituted on Leveller principles; that the Levellers were aware how many of their fellow Englishmen might qualify as traitors on such terms is clear in their provisions for indemnity, oblivion, and the eventual readmission of past royalists, and initial non-subscribers to the *Agreement*, to political life. Even when inclusiveness is not immediately practicable, they aspire to achieve it in the long term.[110]

It is worth noting that even this account of the forfeiting of citizen rights does not settle the question of the foundations of those rights. While most of the time it is the benefit of English legal protections that is seen as forfeited by treasonable action, Overton writes that 'mankind must be preserved upon the earth, and to this preservation, all the Children of men have an equall title by Birth, none to be deprived thereof, but such as are enemies thereto'. The parallelism of this natural law case with the provisions of a positive, national law is clear when Overton goes on to redefine treason in natural law terms, as 'a destruction to humane society'.[111] Indeed, this type of forfeiting of rights could be seen as occurring at precisely the point where, even for a legalistic writer, the laws of England are left behind and those of nature come into force: by stepping treasonably outside the laws of England, one puts oneself into a state of nature, outside the protection of this law; one also violates natural law in so doing, as it is natural law which requires us to live under law – English or other – in the first place. For Overton, natural law corrects narrower, national definitions of treason; for Lilburne, the two can run alongside each other.

The Leveller oeuvre suggests some exclusions that are more difficult to reconcile with Lilburne's inclusive language. It is well known that, at certain points in their career, the Levellers, or people associated with them, were prepared to countenance the exclusion of 'servants' and almstakers from the franchise. However narrowly these categories are defined, they are still exclusions.[112] Lilburne's writing does not, I think, address this problem. The inclusive thrust of the writing does, however, tally with the hints to be found in Leveller proposals that they see the political nation as extending beyond heads of household only. The second, most compromised, Leveller *Agreement* did restrict the franchise to 'Housekeepers', and stipulated in detail that they should not be 'servants to, or receiving wages from, any particular person', and that, far from being almstakers, they be contributors to poor relief. Given these detailed restrictions, and the fact that at other points in the third *Agreement* the words of the second are carried over verbatim, it is surely significant that the *Agreement* of 1 May 1649 reverts to the formula of 'all men of the age of one and twenty yeers and upwards' except servants, almstakers and, for the time being, royalists.[113] The disappearance of the 'householder' requirement must be significant, even though the exclusion of servants remains. This exclusion is in some tension with Lilburne's language, which implies an appeal to *all* English men. In fact, the document which most explicitly applies Lilburne's language to the franchise is *The Case of the Armie*, which gives the vote to 'all the freeborn at the age of 21. yeares and upwards ... excepting those that have or shall deprive themselves of that their freedome'. No other exclusion is here stated or suggested than 'delinquency': one might exclude oneself by one's acts, but no freeborn man (maleness is not spelt out, but was perhaps easily assumed in an army context) was excluded on grounds of status.[114]

Lilburne's language suggests a wish to include all men, but gives a strong impression of excluding women. His masculine language – he even uses 'masculine' as a term of praise for writings he approves of[115] – may not entirely exclude English women from being 'free-born' or 'true-hearted', and women are sometimes mentioned alongside men as being entitled to protection under the law, but clearly women are not the prime examples of English citizen qualities in Lilburne's mind. Why this should be is a difficult question, but I think that for Lilburne the exclusion of women from the polity is not necessarily a function of a view about political dependence on household heads; rather, it is a more basic understanding of all males – household heads or not – as political beings in a way in which women are not. Lilburne's language of political struggle can be very martial, and he regards women as unlikely candidates for this kind of political valour.

VII

We have seen that Lilburne's language constitutes an appeal and a reminder to his male English readers to consider themselves as Englishmen and to act as such, and that the main force of the language is precisely its inclusiveness. Lilburne is robustly redrawing the boundaries of the political nation. The significance of this in terms of contemporary political thinking is demonstrated most clearly at the Putney Debates of October–November 1647. There, Ireton argues that some relatively narrow property qualification for the franchise should be retained. The civilians, agitators, and Colonel Rainborough argue instead that all those who live under a government should put themselves under that government – which they interpret to mean that it is Englishness which is the significant qualification for the franchise. Mendle is rare in taking this theme of the debates seriously, arguing that 'Putney … was in good measure a debate over who really constituted the English nation'.[116] Nobody, however, is disputing that the rank and file of the army are English, just as no one is disputing that all Englishmen are free-born. The question is whether English or free-born status are in any way relevant to inclusion in the political nation. Ireton says not. He explicitly argues that, for this purpose, there is no difference between an Englishman and a foreigner: 'the same reason doth extend' to both cases. For Sexby, this claim is simply insulting. Perhaps the angriest speech of the whole debate is his assertion that it was precisely for those English rights, which according to Ireton were nonexistent, that he and his fellow soldiers had fought: 'We have engaged in this kingdom and ventured our lives, and it was all for this: to recover our birthrights and privileges as Englishmen; and by the arguments urged there is none … I wonder we were so much deceived.'[117]

The question remains of the actual content of the political rights of the free-born Englishman. One might think that both in Lilburne and in the Putney Debates there is a strange gap: the English rights so crucial to assert take so much effort in the asserting that there is little energy left for thinking out the substance of those rights. In the Putney Debates and the *Case of the Armie* there is a commitment to government by consent through a franchise extended to fit the boundaries of the political nation as army and civilian radicals saw it. Even this is not generally spelt out by Lilburne. In *Englands Birth-right* it is suggested that, ideally, 'every freeman of England … would bestow his service one yeere at least, freely for the good of the Civill State', those who 'want outward means' being paid for this service.[118] Such sweeping proposals for the content of egalitarian citizenship disappear as the Leveller movement grows in sophistication, and this must surely be because the Levellers' formal proposals for overhauling the constitution, including franchise and local office-holding arrangements, are taken to imply the practical level of participation. Again we see how comfortably Lilburne's language of Englishmen's rights and duties sits alongside the natural-law consent theory more characteristic of the Leveller movement as a whole. Lilburne urges Englishmen to actively defend their rights; but, once established, English customary rights, as provided for under common law, are maintained simply by their exercise. Englishmen would thus fulfil their obligation to defend their rights precisely through the voting and holding of office provided for in Leveller constitutions. These actions would also be the expression of their continued consent to government.

There is evidence for this view in Leveller references to the significance of voting and petitioning. The franchise is interpreted – sometimes within the same sentence – in terms both of the ancient right of Englishmen and of consent theory. For Lilburne, the House of Lords was attempting 'to rob us of our native and undoubted liberties and rights (which is to chuse and impower all our law-makers, and to be bound by n[o] law imposed on us, by those that never were chosen & betrusted by us, to make uo [sic] lawes)'.[119] Similarly, Lilburne combines consent theory with a belief in the pre-existing constitutional right of freemen when he argues that the actions of corporations and the 40s. franchise itself disenfranchise people 'that by name are free-men of England' and who, under the present system, 'shall have no vote at all in chusing any Parliament man, and yet must be bound by their Lawes, which is meer vasalage'.[120] The Leveller petition of January 1648 set out its demands for the widening of the franchise in terms of ancient rights and the 'Birth-right of all English men':

> Whereas it hath been the Ancient Liberty of this Nation, that all the Free-born people have freely elected their Representers in Parliament, and their Sheriffs and Iustices of the Peace, &c. and that they were abridged of that their native Liberty, by a Statute of the 8. H. 6. 7. That therefore, that Birth-right of all English men, be forthwith restored to all which are not, or shal not be legally disfranchised for some criminal cause, or are not under 21 years of age, or servants, or beggers.[121]

While the franchise presented here is more limited than an adult male franchise, reflecting the concessions made at Putney, the thrust for its widening is expressed by giving it – in theory – to 'all the Free-born people', 'all English men', *before* then excluding certain categories. The franchise in shrieval elections is also claimed as a rightful possession of free-born Englishmen: in 1649 Lilburne complains that, under the new regime, selection of sheriffs has been entrusted to a few factious men 'while the right owners (the people) are rob'd of their free and popular elections of them'.[122] Petitioning, too, can be seen as part of the political rights belonging to the people: in *Englands New Chains Discovered*, Lilburne lists the denial of petitioning as a fundamental contradiction of the consent theory of government which the new Rump has itself now espoused: 'to so small an account are the people brought [in having their petitions scorned], even while they are flattered with notions of being the Original of all just power'.[123] Perhaps, too, Lilburne's insistence on the Leveller version of the second *Agreement of the People* (which, unlike the Officers' version, required voters to have subscribed to the *Agreement*) underlines the importance of voting as a continuing expression of the consent of the political nation to government under the constitution they had approved.[124]

This consonance between Lilburne's legal thinking and consent theories is not accidental. Claims of political status resting purely on natural right could become threatening and uncontrollable, as they were for Ireton at Putney; being able to domesticate that political status by limiting it to 'free-born Englishmen' gave radicals a way of countering Ireton's fears of anarchy. It also gave adult English males compelling reasons for, and ways of, thinking themselves into the role of active citizens of England, giving or withholding their consent to the actions of their governors – according to their traditional rights.

I have talked about Lilburne's 'free-born Englishman' as a citizen, and shown how the materials of that citizenship are assembled from traditional language of English law. Pocock suggests that English subjects' traditional rights, properties, and obligations could not in themselves make an individual into 'an active citizen or a political animal'.[125] While it would be wrong to see the Levellers' writings, which are in quite a different idiom, as an early flowering of the classical republicanism of the 1650s,[126] Lilburne's remaking of the English materials surely marks one stage in this transformation. As Pocock says, what is already there in England is a set of relatively uncontested ideas about the rights, duties, property, and obligations of individual Englishmen. Citizenship does not consist of this alone: these elements must be remade, or overlaid, by an idea that can animate these individuals' sense of themselves as citizens in relation to a state. Lilburne's language of Englishness did much to bring that about.

At the Putney Debates, whereas Ireton could not concede to Englishmen any direct connection to the state – meaningful status in the nation could only be achieved via *local* ties of property or status – the radicals had a way of connecting individuals directly with their nation and polity. That this was the key argument of the debates must surely be due to Lilburne's influence. For Lilburne, the content of citizenship could largely be taken as read; what 'liberties and privileges' actually *were* did not need to be spelt out. It was more effective simply to accuse opponents of 'incroaching', 'engrossing', 'invading', or 'usurping' Englishmen's privileges and liberties, as if the content of those liberties was self-evident. The real task facing Lilburne was to make those liberties and privileges into citizenship. The content of that citizenship might begin to be articulated under pressure – as it was by others at the Putney Debates – but the important thing was to establish that Englishmen, as Englishmen, had political status.

Notes

1 This article originally appeared in *The Historical Journal*, Vol. 47, Issue 4, December 2004, and is reproduced here by kind permission of Cambridge University Press.
2 Quentin Skinner, 'History and ideology in the English revolution', *Historical Journal*, 8 (1965), pp. 151–78; J.P. Sommerville, 'History and theory: the Norman conquest in early Stuart political thought', *Political Studies,* 34 (1986), pp. 249–61. John Sanderson, *'But the people's creatures': the philosophical basis of the English civil war* (Manchester: MUP, 1989), p. 7, sees the historical and theoretical arguments as fused in parliamentarian argument and separated out only by the Levellers.
3 See section V of this chapter.
4 Roger Howell and David E. Brewster, 'Reconsidering the Levellers: the evidence of the *Moderate*', *Past and Present*, 46 (1970), pp. 68–86, emphasises the diversity and range of Leveller thought.
5 'Radical' is of course a modern term of evaluation; I use it to express the Levellers' formal, theoretical innovation – their changing of structures of thought – harnessed to their practical hopes of changing the form and bases of government. See J.C. Davis, 'Radicalism in a traditional society: the evaluation of radical thought in the English commonwealth 1649–1660', *History of Political Thought*, 3 (1982), pp. 193–213, especially pp. 201–3, for constructive comments on the issue. Conal Condren, 'Radicals, conservatives and moderates in early modern political thought: a case of Sandwich Islands syndrome?', *History of Political Thought,* 10 (1989), pp. 525–42, is a provocative dismissal of the applicability of the term to early modern thought.
6 Conrad Russell, 'The rule of law: whose slogan?', ch. 6 of his *The causes of the English civil war* (Oxford: OUP, 1990); Glenn Burgess, *The politics of the ancient constitution: an introduction to English political thought, 1603–1642* (Basingstoke: Macmillan, 1992). Burgess does not argue that the common law was the only language available for talking about politics,

but that it formed 'a self-sufficient language for the discussion of *domestic* political issues', controlling the limits of other jurisdictions and thus providing the crucial framework for the early Stuart consensus (pp. 99, 119). This emphasis on the comprehensiveness of the common-law mind owes much to J.G.A. Pocock, *The ancient constitution and the feudal law: a study of English historical thought in the seventeenth century* (Cambridge: CUP, 1987 edn.). For Pocock 'the belief in an immemorial law was not a party argument put forward by some clever lawyer as a means of limiting the king's prerogative: it was the nearly universal belief of Englishmen' (p. 54), although, in his 1986 'Retrospect' on the book, he places more emphasis on the instability of of the prewar Fortescuean consensus, which set 'two unrelated conceptions of authority ... side by side' (p. 306). M.A. Judson, *The crisis of the constitution: an essay in constitutional and political thought in England 1603–1645* (New Brunswick and London: Rutgers University Press, 1988 edn.; originally 1949), offers a fine survey of the elements of consensus, since stressed by revisionists, in the first three chapters on the shared beliefs of 'Englishmen' about their polity, but similarly suggests that the balance of liberty and prerogative was, or became, unstable.

7 Janelle Greenberg, *The radical face of the ancient constitution: St. Edward's 'Laws' in early modern political thought* (Cambridge: CUP, 2001); Derek Hirst, 'Revisionism revised: the place of principle', *Past and Present,* 92 (1981), pp. 79–99; J.G.A. Pocock, 'Languages and their implications: the transformation of the study of political thought', in his *Politics, language and time: essays in political thought* (Chicago: University of Chicago Press, 1989 edn.). J. P. Sommerville, *Politics and ideology in England 1603–1640* (London: Longman, 1986) tends to suggest that ideological conflict in early Stuart England is to be located in a conflict between discrete languages expressing discrete theories.

8 Pauline Gregg, *Free-born John: the biography of John Lilburne* (London: Harrup, 1961), p. 63.

9 Robert C. Johnson et al. (eds.), *Commons Debates 1628*, (6 vols., New Haven: Yale University Press, 1977–83), III: entries for 23 April to 2 May, for example.

10 All pre-1700 works were published in London unless otherwise stated. Lilburne, *Coppy of a Letter ... to James Ingram and Henry Hopkins* (1640), p. 4; *Copie of a Letter ... to Prynne* (1645), pp. 2–3.

11 See Don M. Wolfe, *Leveller manifestoes of the Puritan revolution* (New York: Nelson, 1944), pp. 265, 374 for examples of complaints against being 'subject(ed)' to arbitrary powers.

12 Keith Thomas, 'The Levellers and the franchise', in G.E. Aylmer (ed.), *The interregnum: the quest for settlement* (London: Macmillan, 1972), pp. 73–75; Peter Wende, '"Liberty" und "property" in der politischen Theorie der Levellers', *Zeitschrift für historische Forschung,* 1 (1974), pp. 147–73; Iain Hampsher-Monk, 'The political theory of the Levellers: Putney, property and Professor Macpherson', *Political Studies,* 24 (1976), pp. 397–422; C.B. Macpherson, *The political theory of possessive individualism* (Oxford: OUP, 1962), pp. 120–29; Frost, *A declaration of some proceedings*, in William Haller and Godfrey Davies (eds.), *The Leveller tracts* (Gloucester, Mass.: Peter Smith, 1964), pp. 116–17, and cited in Thomas, p. 75.

13 Thomas, 'The Levellers and the franchise', pp. 73–75; David Sacks, 'Parliament, liberty and the commonweal', in J.H. Hexter (ed.), *Parliament and liberty* (Stanford: Stanford University Press, 1992), pp. 85, 290n1; Sir Edward Coke, *The second part of the Institutes* (1642), p. 45.

14 Lilburne, *Londons liberty in chains* (1646), pp. 41–43.

15 Lilburne, *An impeachment of high treason* (1649), p. 38.

16 Lilburne, *Londons liberty in chains*, p. 10.

17 Steve Rappaport, *Worlds within worlds: structures of life in sixteenth-century London* (Cambridge: CUP, 1989), p. 42.

18 Lilburne, *Londons liberty in chains*, pp. 38–41.

19 Norah Carlin, 'Liberty and fraternities in the English revolution', *International Review of Social History,* 39 (1994), pp. 223–54; Alan Houston, '"A way of settlement": the Levellers, monopolies and the public interest', *History of Political Thought,* 14 (1993), pp. 381–420, at p. 397.

20 Lilburne, *The legall fundamental liberties*, in Haller and Davies, *The Leveller tracts*, pp. 436–37; he is referring back to his *Innocency and truth justified* (1646), pp. 46ff., and to his writings on London.

21 Sir Thomas Smith, *De Republica Anglorum*, ed. Mary Dewar (Cambridge: CUP, 1982), pp. 64–77.
22 Lilburne, *The copy of a letter ... to a freind* (1645), p. 2.
23 Lilburne, *The grand plea of Lieut. Col. John Lilburne* (1647), p. 1.
24 Coke, *The first part of the Institutes* (1639), 129a.
25 John Rastell, *Les Termes de la Ley* (1629 edn.), p. 134.
26 John Cowell, *The interpreter* (1637 edn.), s.v. 'Denizen'.
27 Henry Cockeram, *The English dictionarie* (1626; 2nd edn.).
28 Cowell, *The interpreter*, s.v. 'Enfranchisement'.
29 Cowell, *The interpreter*, s.v. 'Villein'.
30 Lilburne, *Innocency and truth justified* (1646), p. 67.
31 Anon, *Englands birth-right justified* (1645), p. 29.
32 Lilburne, *Londons liberty in chains*, pp. 52–53.
33 Lilburne, *The charters of London* (1646), p. 39: reading as in the errata.
34 Wende, '"Liberty" und "property"', pp. 158ff.
35 Lilburne, *The juglers discovered* (1647), p. 12.
36 Lilburne, *The charters of London*, p. 1.
37 Lilburne, *The copy of a letter ... to a freind*, p. 2.
38 Coke, II *Institutes*, p. 56; Lilburne, *Innocency and truth justified*, p. 64.
39 Lilburne, *Innocency and truth justified*, p. 55.
40 Lilburne, *The resolved mans Resolution* (1647), p. 24.
41 Rastell, *Les Termes de la Ley*, s.v. 'Disabilitie'.
42 Cowell, *The interpreter*; Rastell, *Les termes de la ley*: s.v. terms cited.
43 Lilburne, *The copy of a letter ... to a freind*, p. 2.
44 Lilburne, *Innocency and truth justified*, p. 16.
45 Lilburne, *Innocency and truth justified*, p. 67.
46 Lilburne, *Londons liberty in chains*, pp. 71–72.
47 Lilburne, *An anatomy of the Lords tyranny* (1646), title page.
48 Lilburne, *The charters of London*, p. 1.
49 Conal Condren, 'Liberty of office and its defence in seventeenth-century political argument', *History of Political Thought*, 18 (1997), 460–82, at pp. 470–72.
50 Corinne Weston, 'England: ancient constitution and common law', in J.H. Burns and Mark Goldie (eds.), *The Cambridge history of political thought, 1450–1700* (Cambridge: CUP, 1991), p. 385.
51 Sacks, 'Parliament, liberty, and the commonweal', pp. 93–101; p. 99 quoted.
52 Alan Cromartie, 'The constitutionalist revolution: the transformation of political culture in early Stuart England', *Past and Present* 163 (1999), pp. 76–120, at pp. 87–88, 100; Glenn Burgess, *Absolute monarchy and the Stuart constitution* (New Haven and London: Yale University Press, 1996), pp. 166–71.
53 Christopher Hill, *Intellectual origins of the English Revolution revisited* (Oxford: Clarendon Press, 1997), pp. 224–25; Stephen White, *Sir Edward Coke and the grievances of the commonwealth* (Manchester: MUP, 1979), p. 226; Pocock, *The ancient constitution and the feudal law*, p. 268; Cromartie, *Sir Matthew Hale* (Cambridge: CUP, 1995), p. 19; J.W. Tubbs, *The common law mind* (Baltimore and London: Johns Hopkins University Press, 2000), pp. 174–75.
54 Burgess, *Absolute monarchy and the Stuart constitution*, pp. 200–1; White, *Sir Edward Coke*, pp. 219ff.
55 White, *Sir Edward Coke*, pp. 238–42.
56 Coke, II *Institutes*, p. 47; *The third part of the Institutes* (1644), p. 181. Hill, *Intellectual origins*, p. 208, citing Wagner's conclusions.
57 Coke, II *Institutes*, p. 47; Wende, '"Liberty" und "property"', p. 159.
58 Coke, II *Institutes*, p. 63; Cromartie, 'The constitutionalist revolution', pp. 102–3. The quotation from Cicero is given on the title page of Coke, I *Institutes* (1639): 'CICERO. Major haereditas venit unicuiq; nostrum a Jure, & Legibus, quam a Parentibus.'
59 This Coke passage is quoted verbatim in Anon, *Liberty vindicated against slavery* (1646).
60 Coke, II *Institutes*, p. 3. Wende, '"Liberty" und "property"', p. 159.

61 Anon, *Liberty vindicated against slavery*, p. 1.
62 Coke, II *Institutes*, proem, unpag.
63 Lilburne, *The charters of London*, p. 1; Lilburne, *The juglers discovered*, p. 5.
64 For natural law in Leveller writings, see David Wootton, 'Leveller democracy and the Puritan revolution', in J.H. Burns and Mark Goldie (eds.), *The Cambridge history of political thought, 1450–1700* (Cambridge: CUP, 1991); Iain Hampsher-Monk, 'The political theory of the Levellers', *Political Studies*, 24 (1976), pp. 397–422; Brian Manning, 'The Levellers and religion', in J.F. McGregor and B. Reay (eds.), *Radical religion in the English Revolution* (Oxford: OUP, 1984); R. Gleissner, 'The Levellers and natural law', *Journal of British Studies,* 20 (1980–1), pp. 74–89. For historical and legal argumentation in Leveller writings, see R.B. Seaberg 'The Norman Conquest and the common law', *Historical Journal*, 24 (1981), pp. 791–806; and Michael Levy 'Freedom, property and the Levellers', *Western Political Quarterly,* 36 (1983), pp. 116–33.
65 Lilburne, *The free-mans freedom vindicated* (1646).
66 Scholars who have suggested that Leveller writers use common law language strategically are G. Burgess, 'Protestant polemic: the Leveller pamphlets', *Parergon*, n.s.11 (1993), pp. 45–67, and *The politics of the ancient constitution*, pp. 90–93; Andrew Sharp, 'John Lilburne's discourse of law', *Political Science,* 40 (1988), pp. 18–33; Pocock, *The ancient constitution and the feudal law*, pp. 125–26.
67 Sharp, 'John Lilburne and the Long Parliament's *Book of Declarations*', *History of Political Thought*, 9 (1988), pp. 19–44, at p. 23, points out that Parliament similarly used arguments both from natural and from positive law. Greenberg, *The radical face of the ancient constitution*, ch. 5, while picking out the ancient constitution elements in parliamentarian thought, shows how they were integrated into arguments for resistance that might have looked familiar from other sources.
68 Lilburne, *The peoples prerogative* (1648), p. 5.
69 Lilburne, *Innocency and truth justified*, p. 32.
70 Lilburne, *The peoples prerogative*, p. 9.
71 Lilburne, *The legall fundamental liberties* (2nd edn., 1649), p. 70 [mispaginated as 52].
72 Lilburne, *The resolved mans resolution* (1647), pp. 19–22.
73 Lilburne, *A preparative to an hue and cry* (1649), pp. 1–2.
74 Both common law and statute appealed to: Lilburne, *A defiance to tyrants* (1648), sig. Av, marginal note; statute superior to common law: Lilburne, *The just mans justification* (1647), pp. 14–18.
75 An unqualifiedly positive reference to 'common law' (rather than 'English law'): Lilburne, *The lawes funerall* (1648), p. 9.
76 Lilburne, *The free-mans freedome vindicated* (1646), pp. 3, 7.
77 Lilburne, *The free-mans freedom vindicated*, p. 10; Lilburne, 'On the 150th page' in Andrew Sharp, ed., *The English Levellers* (Cambridge: CUP, 1998), pp. 3–4.
78 Lilburne, *The prisoners plea for a habeas corpus* (1648), unpag.
79 Lilburne, *The lawes funerall*, pp. 4–5.
80 Burgess, 'Protestant polemic', pp. 49–59.
81 Coke, *Le quart part des Reportes* (1635), unpag. preface.
82 Coke, I *Institutes*, 97b.
83 Coke, *Le quart part des Reportes*, unpag. preface.
84 Coke, *The third part of the Institutes* (1644), unpag. proem; I *Institutes* (1639), proem. Lilburne, *An impeachment of high treason* (1649), p. 48.
85 Burgess, *Absolute monarchy and the Stuart constitution*, pp. 175–92; Tubbs, *The common law mind*, pp. 154–59, 183–86; Cromartie, 'The constitutionalist revolution', pp. 97–99.
86 Tubbs, *The common law mind*, pp. 161–66.
87 Diane Parkin-Speer, 'John Lilburne: a revolutionary interprets statutes and common law due process', *Law and History Review,* 1 (1983), pp. 276–96, at pp. 278–79.
88 Lilburne, *The peoples prerogative*, p. 5.
89 Lilburne, *Londons liberty in chains*, p. 41.

90 Lilburne, *Londons liberty in chains*, p. 41.
91 Lilburne, *Rash oaths unwarrantable* (1647), p. 28.
92 Lilburne, *The legall fundamental liberties*, p. 54.
93 *Englands birth-right* (1645), p. 3. I suspect that this pamphlet is not by Lilburne alone. Weston, 'England: ancient constitution and common law', pp. 379–84; Greenberg, *The radical face of the ancient constitution*, pp. 19–32, 226–29; Seaberg, 'The Norman Conquest and the common law', passim.
94 Lilburne, *The just mans justification* (1646), p. 13; Seaberg, 'The Norman Conquest and the common law'.
95 Lilburne, *The just mans justification*, pp. 14–15.
96 Lilburne, *Rash oaths unwarrantable*, p. 28.
97 Lilburne, *L. Col. John Lilburne his apologeticall narration* (1652), p. 17.
98 Lilburne, *The lawes funerall* (1648), p. 3.
99 Lilburne, *The just mans justification*, p. 16; *The legall fundamental liberties*, p. 22; *Jonahs cry out of the whales belly* (1647), p. 7; *To his honoured friend, Mr. Cornelius Holland*, reprinted in *An impeachment of high treason* (1649), pp. 7, 9; *A letter ... to Mr John Price* (1651), p. 12.
100 Lilburne, *The copy of a letter ... to a freind*, p. 12.
101 Lilburne, *The peoples prerogative*, unpag. proem.
102 Lilburne, *The legall fundamental liberties*, in Haller and Davies, *The Leveller tracts*, p. 426; *As you were* (1652), pp. 14, 13; *A defiance to tyrants* (1648), p. 74.
103 Lilburne, *The additionall plea of Lieut. Col. John Lilburne* (1647), p. 24.
104 Lilburne, *The reasons of Lieu Col. Lilbournes sending his letter to Mr Prin* (1645), p. 7.
105 Lilburne, *The peoples prerogative*, title page.
106 Lilburne, *The freemans freedome vindicated* (1646), p. 1.
107 Lilburne, *Innocency and truth justified*, p. 52. The books are Pym's speech against Strafford, St John's speech for Hampden against ship money, and the judgments of Hutton and Crooks in the ship money case.
108 Lilburne, *Londons liberty in chains*, p. 57.
109 Lilburne, *The grand plea of Lieut. Col. John Lilburne* (1647), pp. 5, 13; *The copy of a letter ... to a freind*, p. 2; *The legall fundamental liberties*, p. 70; Hampsher-Monk, 'The political theory of the Levellers', p. 418ff.
110 The third *Agreement of the People*, of 1 May 1649, excludes royalists from the franchise and from office for ten years only; actions against the constitution established under the *Agreement* would be proceeded against as treason: Sharp, *The English Levellers*, pp. 170, 177. Lilburne's version of the second *Agreement* provides for a time lapse between subscribing the *Agreement* and being able to vote: Wolfe, *Leveller manifestoes*, p. 297.
111 Overton, *An Appeale from the degenerate representative body* (1647), in Wolfe, *Leveller manifestoes*, p. 178.
112 See Macpherson, and the works in response to him, cited above, n. 12.
113 Wootton, 'Leveller democracy and the Puritan revolution', pp. 432–33; Wolfe, *Leveller manifestoes*, pp. 297, 342; Haller and Davies, *The Leveller tracts*, p. 321.
114 Wolfe, *Leveller manifestoes*, p. 212. Wootton, 'Leveller democracy and the Puritan revolution', pp. 432–33; and Ann Hughes, 'Gender and politics in Leveller literature', in Susan D. Amussen and Mark A. Kishlansky (eds.), *Political culture and cultural politics in early modern England* (Manchester: MUP, 1995) both argue for the centrality of household heads to Leveller thinking.
115 Lilburne, *The peoples prerogative*, unpag. proem; *An impeachment of high treason*, p. 5; *The legall fundamental liberties*, in Haller and Davies, *The Leveller tracts*, p. 403.
116 Michael Mendle, 'Putney's pronouns: identity and indemnity in the great debate', in Mendle (ed.), *The Putney Debates of 1647* (Cambridge: CUP, 2001), p.125.
117 A.S.P. Woodhouse (ed.), *Puritanism and Liberty*, (London: Dent, 1992), pp. 67, 69.
118 G.E. Aylmer, *The Levellers in the English Revolution* (London: Cornell University Press, 1975), p. 62.
119 Lilburne, *A whip for the present House of Lords* (1648), p. 16.

120 Lilburne, *Londons liberty in chains,* p. 52.
121 Wolfe, *Leveller manifestoes,* p. 269.
122 Lilburne, *An outcry of the youngmen and apprentices* (1649), p. 2.
123 Lilburne, *Englands new chains discovered* (1649), p. [7]; J.P. Kenyon, *The Stuart constitution: documents and commentary* (Cambridge: CUP, 1966), p. 324 for the Rump's resolution of 4 January 1649.
124 S.R. Gardiner (ed.), *The constitutional documents of the Puritan revolution* (Oxford: Clarendon Press, 1906 edn.), pp. 363–64; Wolfe, *Leveller manifestoes,* p. 297. Obviously, the measure was also a pragmatic limitation of the franchise to those sympathetic to the Levellers' constitutional aims.
125 J.G.A. Pocock, *The Machiavellian moment* (Princeton: Princeton University Press, 1975), p. 335.
126 Samuel Glover, 'The Putney Debates: popular vs. elitist republicanism', *Past and Present,* 164 (1999), pp. 47–80, argues for the Levellers as republicans, but the argument rests on sparse and atypical examples.

2
LILBURNE, TOLERATION, AND THE CIVIL STATE

Norah Carlin

Few things were so important to John Lilburne as religious toleration. He adhered to this principle in its most radical and unqualified form, despite the reservations held by many of the Levellers' supporters among the separatist and sectarian religious groups, and in the face of opposition from the leaders of the Independent congregations in London. When he attempted a compromise on the issue, in the run-up to the debates in the Army Council at Whitehall in December 1648, it led only to political disaster. Lilburne's response was not further compromise but a return to the unqualified principle.

Once seen as a mark of the Levellers' secularism and rationalism, the importance they attached to religious toleration was largely neglected by historians in the late twentieth century, who dwelt instead on the strength of religious faith among the individual leaders, and the ways in which they felt Christianity justified their activism. 'Religious motivation' for a time took over from political theory as historians' key interpretation of the Levellers, at least in revisionist circles. But acknowledging that it is impossible to separate politics from religion in the thought of most seventeenth-century activists does not mean that all other aspects of their thought can be *reduced* to religion, in the way that their political choices have been reduced to economics in crude or caricatured versions of Marxism. Politics was not an alternative to religion in Leveller thinking but the other side of the same coin: their political theory of the church and state.

Lilburne and the other leading Leveller writers believed the civil state to be a natural institution, in essence common to all human societies. The purpose of this institution was the regulation of civil society, including the enforcement of moral laws, but it could lay no claim to any kind of authority over matters of religious belief or worship. They never accepted the view, put forward by both Luther and Calvin in the European Reformation and supported by many of the London Independent ministers, that Christian princes, city-states, or parliaments had the power or the duty to restrict or regulate religious belief and worship.[1] Although they fought for righteous and responsible rule, and tried hard to design a constitution that would be proof against both tyranny and corruption, the Levellers rejected the idea that the English nation, like that of Old Testament Israel, consisted of God's chosen people and must set up the godly rule of his saints on earth to fulfil his providential plan.

In one of John Lilburne's early pamphlets, *A Light for the Ignorant*, he says of the civil state:

> In this state or in these cities are the laws and ordinances of men, that the saints must obey in the Lord, for though in the time of Christ and his Apostles there were no Christian Kings, yet the Churches of the Saints were commanded to obey their Laws ... therefore the Apostle Peter distinguisheth them from the Divine, by calling them the Ordinances of men, due unto Caesar as divine obedience is unto God.[2]

Throughout this work, Lilburne applies this same definition to states and cities existing in his own time, though their rulers were now Christians. In a series of parallel passages, he describes the differences between the civil state and the 'true ecclesiastical state', which consists of multiple 'visible churches and bodies incorporated together in [Christ's] name and power', constituting separate 'bodies pollitique', each with its own officers and discipline, free from interference by the civil state.[3] Both these ideas were shortly to appear also in the work of Roger Williams, founder of the colony of Providence, Rhode Island, who visited London in 1643–44. In his *Bloudy Tenent of Persecution for Cause of Conscience* (1644), 'All Civil States with their Officers of Justice in their respective constitutions and administrations are proved essentially civil and therefore not judges, Governors or Defenders of the Spiritual Christian State and Worship'.[4] For Williams as for Lilburne, 'the Church or Company of worshippers (whether true or false) is like unto a Body or Colledge of Physitians in a Citie; like unto a Corporation, Society or Company of East-India or Turkey-Merchants', while the civil state is essentially distinct from these corporate bodies, its peace and welfare undisturbed by disagreements and quarrels within or among them.[5]

These theories of the natural state and corporate liberty were among the commonplaces of medieval and early modern political thought as taught in English universities, and no doubt echoed in many provincial grammar schools and parish congregations by graduate teachers and ministers.[6] They were seized upon by both Lilburne and Williams for new and potentially revolutionary purposes, however. Williams explicitly justified excluding the civil state from religious affairs by reference to the sovereignty of the people, who as 'natural men' could not convey to government a power they did not themselves possess.[7] The Levellers also adhered consistently to this view. It is difficult, if not impossible, to say whether they advocated toleration because they believed in the sovereignty of the people, or vice versa, though individuals among them may have come to prioritise these twin goals by different routes.

Other arguments deployed by Williams in *The Bloudy Tenent* are also to be found in Leveller writings, and featured prominently in the crucial debate on religion in the army council at Whitehall. God in the Old Testament is shown on many occasions urging his chosen people, the Israelites, to maintain a holy state which would follow his commandments and enforce obedience to his laws; Williams argued that these divine commands now applied to Christian churches, not Christian states.[8] Since the time of Jesus Christ, the struggle for true religion had been transferred from the material to the spiritual plane:

> It is the will and command of God, since the coming of his Sonne the Lord Jesus, that a permission of the most Paganish, Jewish, Turkish [Muslim] or Antichristian [Catholic] consciences and worships, be granted to all men in all Nations and Countries: and they are onely to be fought against with that Sword which is only (in Soule matters) able to conquer, to wit, the Sword of God's Spirit, the Word of God.[9]

The parable of the wheat and the tares, which will grow together until God's harvest at the end of the world so that no good corn will be pulled up with the weeds, is repeated many times in *The Bloudy Tenent*. The supremacy of the individual conscience is also a central theme: even the native inhabitants of America 'must judge according to their Indian or American consciences, for other consciences it cannot be supposed they should have'.[10] No metaphor is more frequent in this very repetitive work than 'spiritual rape', which happens when people are forced to practise and profess religions they cannot believe in.

The English debate on toleration continued throughout the 1640s, with many contributors on both sides. I wish here to concentrate on views of the Levellers, who were at the same time political activists who aimed to achieve their goal as part of a revolutionary political programme for England.[11] In 1645, a number of London religious radicals started meeting regularly at the Windmill tavern in London's Lothbury to organise against the plans of the Assembly of Divines at Westminster, which had been appointed by Parliament to advise on the further reformation of the English church, but seemed resolved to have any new ecclesiastical regime enforced by law as the old one had been. Those who met at the Windmill did not all share the same outlook: some wanted freedom for all congregations and sects, mainly so that the true saints of God would be free to form their own exclusive 'gathered churches', and most would have restricted toleration to Protestants. Those among them who were soon to coalesce into the group now known as the Levellers were distinguished by their willingness to take up Williams's arguments for a general toleration. In *The Araignement of Mr Persecution* in 1645, Richard Overton blamed both Catholics and Protestants for the religious wars of the preceding century. 'Though from Rome', he argued, 'the spirit of Persecution is conveyed into most sects of Religion.' The solution advocated by 'Mr State-Policy', a witness in this literary mock trial, is for the state to deprive all religions of coercive power:

> Since all by compulsion are to be forced to the Civill peace and publike unity, and all are to be defended and preserved under the publike freedome, one as well as an other, therefore to this end the Magistrate ought to bind all Religions, that no Religion have power over other, that all in the Generall have Toleration, and none in particular be offensive; for the Papist may be a Papist, the Protestant a Protestant, without the power of Compulsion, the deprivation thereof is in no wayes injurious to their Religion.

Then, he says, 'their Controversies would then be of another kind, fair and equall Disputes, and it is better and farre cheaper to provide words for Argumentation, then instruments of war for blows and bloodshed'.[12]

'Liberty of Conscience', personified as another witness, argues that 'Turks, Jewes, Pagans, and Infidels, [are] to grow and live together in the Feild of the World their Dominions until the Day of harvest'.[13] He condemns especially the persecution of Jews in Christian countries:

> This Incendiary [Mr Persecution] hath caused our Kings, and our Rulers, our Bishops, and our preists not to suffer a Jew by authority to live amongst them; how then can we complain of the vengeance that is at this time upon us & our children, that have been so cruell, so hatefull, so bloody minded to them and their children? we have given them the cup of trembling, surely we must tast of the dreggs.[14]

The persecution of the Jews, he urges, is a barrier to their conversion to Christianity; he asks, 'What hindreth their salvation and deliverance so much as persecution?' The expectation that the Jewish people would convert to Christianity before the end of the world – which might be very soon – was widely held among religious radicals and biblical scholars in seventeenth-century England. The recommended toleration of Judaism was therefore in one sense a temporary measure; but as it was not conditional, it would put a permanent end to the persecution and exclusion of the Jewish people. Once in power, Oliver Cromwell showed his support for this view by recognising the small Jewish community in London, tacitly allowing them to set up a synagogue for their worship, and admitting new Jewish migrants from abroad.[15] But although Cromwell is reported to have said on one occasion, 'That he had rather Mahumetanism were permitted amongst us, then [than] that one of Gods Children should be persecuted'.[16] he did not extend toleration to Catholics, telling an official of the English regime in Ireland that if he thought that liberty of conscience would include freedom to celebrate the Mass, he was mistaken.[17] Milton also, in his *Areopagitica*, clarified his eloquent defence of liberty of the press by adding, 'I mean not tolerated popery and open superstition'.[18] While Protestant states had good reason to defend themselves against Catholic attack, and Puritans had notoriously suffered persecution under Laud and his fellow bishops in England, yet it was possible for the London merchant Henry Robinson, in his *Liberty of Conscience*, to recognise that 'it was not their Popery or Prelacie (that was to themselves) which so much oppressed us, as their power'.[19]

Not only does Overton in *The Araignement* frequently deploy arguments and metaphors found in Williams's work, such as spiritual rape or the wheat and the weeds, but he explicitly recommends *The Bloudy Tenent*, along with William Walwyn's *Compassionate Samaritane*.[20] Walwyn, a friend of Henry Robinson's who first met Lilburne in 1644–45, probably at the Windmill tavern, had advocated toleration for Catholics as well as Protestant sects in his earliest known work a few years earlier.[21] In *Tolleration Justified, and Persecution Condemned* (1646) he went on to assert that even someone 'whose mind is so mis-informed as to deny a Deity' must be won over by reason and argument, since incarceration in the Bedlam madhouse or Fleet prison could not do the job: indeed, 'It was ever found by all experience, that such rough courses did confirme the error'.[22] God's truth and peaceful persuasion were powerful enough, he believed, to win over even the most wrong-headed, but at a time which God alone would determine for each individual – 'his season is not the same for all'.[23] Walwyn repeatedly defended the supremacy of the individual conscience, since 'whatever is not of faith is sin, and every man ought to be fully persuaded of that way in which he serveth the Lord … To compell me against my conscience, is to compell me against what I believe to be true, and so against my faith'.[24]

Like Lilburne and Williams, Walwyn insisted on the limitations of civil government, holding 'that only things naturall and rationall are properly subject unto government; And that things supernatural, such as in Religion are distinguished by the title of things divine … such things are not liable to any compulsive government'.[25] There may be debate about where all these writers drew the line between the natural and supernatural, and Walwyn believed that the state should tolerate only 'such opinions as are not destructive to humane [human] society, nor blaspheme the work of our Redemption'.[26] Clearly, the anti-blasphemy qualification was not suggested by Walwyn or any of the other contributors to this debate for the reason it is advocated by some people in multi-faith societies today. In a passage that has rather dubiously been interpreted as advocating toleration for Islam, Walwyn argues that the religions of 'Turkes and those that believe in strange gods, which are indeed no gods' persist only because they are enforced by state power, whereas the truth of Christianity has no need of such support.[27]

While this is all very different from modern secular liberalism, Walwyn's works advocate a tolerant and pacific version of Christianity that had not yet been experienced in England, though something resembling it existed for a time in Catholic Venice and Tuscany, as well as in the Protestant Dutch republic.[28] For Walwyn as for Overton, Christian love was the quality that must conquer all. Both believed in universal free grace, available to all people on earth, though evidently not all had the opportunity or the awareness to accept and be saved by it (the case of persecuted Jews, according to Walwyn, for example). Williams and Lilburne, on the other hand, were Calvinists who believed that Christ had died only for those whom God had predestined to salvation.[29] It is hardly surprising that no single theology of salvation united the Levellers, since even the most moderate of the religious radicals were campaigning for the toleration of theological differences among Protestants.

According to the Presbyterians' chief heresy-hunter, Thomas Edwards, Walwyn was 'a desperate dangerous man, a Seeker and Libertine'; but, although he described himself as 'a seeker after truth', he always remained an active member of his parish congregation and is not known ever to have belonged to any sect, or to have advocated freedom from the moral law, as Edwards's name-calling implied.[30]

Throughout the political turmoil following the end of the first civil war in 1646, all the manifestos and petitions supported or initiated by the Levellers demanded an end to religious compulsion, freedom for alternative Protestant sects, and liberty of conscience. The declaration of the New Model Army in June 1647 pleaded for:

> a provision for tender consciences … that such, who, upon conscientious grounds may differ from the established forms, may not (for that) be debarred from the common Rights, Liberties, or Benefits belonging to all, as men and Members of the Common wealth, while they live soberly, honestly, and inoffensively towards others, and peacefully and faithfully towards the State.[31]

Similar but more specific demands, for the repeal of laws compelling attendance at the parish churches and the use of the Book of Common Prayer, together with those banning private religious assemblies or 'conventicles', were put forward in a number of Leveller pamphlets over the same summer, while the proposed *Agreement of the People* brought to the general council of the army meeting at Putney in October expanded on the rationale behind these demands:

> That matters of religion, and the wayes of God's worship, are not at all intrusted by us to any humane power, because therein wee cannot remit or exceed a tittle of what our consciences dictate to be the mind of God, without wilfull sinne; neverthelesse the publike way of instructing the Nation (so it be not compulsive) is referred to their discretion.[32]

The use of the word 'dictate' here, together with other expressions regarding the compelling nature of conscience, has inspired some historians to argue that, for all the Levellers, the inviolability of conscience 'emphasised the creature's duty of obedience to its creator', and that it could even be regarded (in 1992) as 'God's fax machine'.[33] It is perhaps necessary to point out that, while Lilburne explicitly described his own submission to God's will *after* his realisation of personal salvation by the gift of faith, Walwyn was concerned especially to defend the conscience of individuals who had *not yet* received or acknowledged that direct communication from God. Up to that point, every person would have to make use of their own reason. His explanation of this is hardly compatible with the metaphor of a fax machine:

> it will be granted by all, whatsoever a mans reason doth conclude to be true or false, to be agreeable or disagreeable to Gods Word, that same to that man is his opinion or judgement, and so man is by his own reason necessitated to be of that mind he is.[34]

There is no evidence that the clause on religion in this first version of *An Agreement of the People* was found divisive at Putney, though that may be because the debate on the document's first clause, concerning the parliamentary franchise, was so heated, and the meetings were brought to an end before this matter could be discussed. George Masterson, a hostile observer who attended a Leveller meeting at Wapping in January 1648, came away with a copy of their latest petition intended for presentation to Parliament, which, like all those mentioned above, was principally about the reform of Parliament and the law. It also included a short clause pleading for the repeal of laws that legally required oaths (objectionable to some religious people) and enforcing the Book of Common Prayer, and for nothing to be imposed on anyone against their conscience.[35]

During the second civil war from April to September 1648, the Levellers suspended their petitioning activities, but returned to the fray with their 'Large Petition' of 11 September, undoubtedly their most successful and well-known address to Parliament. It included two clauses on freedom of religion, the fourth and 23rd of the petitioners' expectations that Parliament had not fulfilled:

> 4. That you would have exempted matters of Religion and Gods worship, from the compulsive or restrictive power of any Authoritie upon earth, and reserved to the supreme authoritie an uncompulsive power only of appointing a way for the publick, whereby abundance of misery, prosecution, and hart-burning would for ever be avoyded…
>
> 23. That you would not have followed the example of former tyrannous and superstitious Parliaments, in making Orders, Ordinances or lawes, or in appointing punishments concerning opinions or things super-naturall stiling some blasphemies others heresies; when as you know your selves easily mistaken and that divine truths need no human helps to support them: such proceedings having bin generally invented to divide the people amongst themselves, and to affright men from that liberty of discourse by which Corruption & tyranny would be soon discovered.[36]

Of the wave of petitions that followed this Leveller initiative, some addressed to Parliament by bodies of the 'well affected' in specific places, others by soldiers in the parliamentarian forces to Thomas Lord Fairfax as their commander-in-chief, many declared their general support for the Large Petition, but at this stage none followed the Levellers in calling explicitly for religious freedom. Up to the meeting of the army council of officers at St Albans in mid-November, the petitions were concerned with stopping the current negotiations with the king on the Isle of Wight, securing constitutional and legal reform, and bringing the king and his chief supporters to justice.

The army's Remonstrance to Parliament, which was drafted by Commissary-General Henry Ireton (Cromwell's son-in-law) and agreed by the council meeting at St Albans, was read in the House of Commons on 20 November. Though it included the demand for a new constitution, or *Agreement of the People*, and a favourable reference to the Large Petition of 11 September, it steered clear of the question of religious freedom altogether, and it does not seem that this issue had been discussed at all at St Albans.[37] After Parliament refused to consider the Remonstrance, the army leaders took action by removing the king from the Isle of Wight and, on 6 December, purging the House of Commons of those members who had voted to make peace with the king. Before they and their supporters in the purged Parliament formally decided whether and how they would proceed to the trial of the king, however, the council of officers reconvened at Whitehall on 11 December. Their agenda was to follow up the Remonstrance by approving a new *Agreement of the People* to be put before Parliament; a number of London ministers as well as some of the leading Levellers were invited to take part in an advisory capacity. This promising collaboration between the army leaders and the Levellers was permanently shattered, however, when the issue of religious freedom was debated three days later, determining the limited nature of the coming revolution.

Lilburne's lengthy and typically partisan account of the discussions preceding the debate was published in June 1649. According to his narrative, in late November some of the Levellers had had a 'large and sharp discourse' with Ireton, in which their principal differences centred on 'his desire in the too strict restraining of Liberty of conscience, and in keeping a power to the Parliament to punish where no visible law is transgressed'. (The second issue, though not relevant here, had an important bearing on the trial of the king.) An agreed text had, however, been thrashed out in a series of committee meetings comprising four nominees each from the Levellers, officers, 'gentlemen Independents', and MPs, though only one of these last, Henry Marten, ever attended.[38] Recent research on the manuscript records of the Whitehall debates has confirmed that the text of the committee's proposals on the table at Whitehall was the one published by Lilburne a few days after the debate, except for two words of the clause on religion, which Lilburne admitted he had removed from his publication in order to give 'the sense of us all but Ireton'.[39] It read:

> Wee doe not Impower our Representatives to continue in force, or make any Lawes, oathes or Covenants, whereby to Compell by penalties or otherwise, any person to any thinge, in or about Matters of faith, Religion or gods Worship, or to Restraine any person professing Christianity from the professing of his faith and exercise of religion according to his Conscience in any house or place (except such as are or shall bee set apart for the publique worship) neverthlesse the instructing part and the directing of the Nation in a publique way for the matters of faith, Worshipp, or Discipline (soe it bee not compulsive or expresse Popery) is referred to their discretion.[40]

The words that Lilburne removed were 'professing Christianity'. No earlier tract or petition produced by the Leveller leaders had suggested that toleration be extended only to Christians, and this was the first time they had compromised on this point.

Some historians attribute the Levellers' dissatisfaction with the debate at Whitehall on 14 December 1648 to theological differences, to a temperamental inability of Lilburne to get on with anyone else, or to the Levellers' anger that what they thought was an agreed text had been opened up to further amendment.[41] Although the last point featured prominently in Lilburne's complaint six months later, it is now clear that by 14 December there had already been three days of discussion and amendments to the electoral procedures and redistribution of constituencies in the first part of the *Agreement*.[42] The conflict over this clause may have been the last straw for the Levellers, but it looks more like it was the first item which exposed a fundamental difference of principle.

The content of this debate has often seemed tedious or puzzling to modern readers, with many participants seemingly going off at a tangent about the relationship between the Old and New Testaments, or between natural law and the Ten Commandments. Some of the major questions address the toleration issue clearly enough: should the magistrate have any power over religion, either compulsive or restrictive? Should the state tolerate 'only men that are members and servants of Jesus Christ'? Does the requirement that the state maintain civil peace imply a power to restrain religious minorities from following their consciences?[43] Other formulations are less familiar to us, such as the question of whether the state of Israel in the Old Testament is to be understood as a 'type' (or foreshadowing) of the civil power of the Christian state, or of the purely spiritual power of the Christian church – an important theme in Roger Williams's work also.[44] While this particular issue may perhaps be described as theological, the context in which it was debated at Whitehall was undeniably political. The essential reference point for other important issues – whether all rulers are under an obligation to enforce the first four of the Ten Commandments, which are concerned with offences against God; the relationship between the Ten Commandments and natural law; and whether it is possible to know God by the light of nature without divine revelation – is the last chapter of John Calvin's great 1559 compendium, *The Institutes of the Christian Religion*, which deals with civil government.[45] Many of the participants would also know Theodore Béza's history of its practical application in Geneva: Lilburne, for example, had read both Calvin and Béza while keeping his master's shop as an apprentice.[46] In Calvin's Geneva, the city council had not only enforced religious observance, but, on Calvin's advice, expelled Anabaptists and other heretics, and with his emphatic support burned to death Miguel Servet (aka Servetus), a refugee scholar from Catholic Spain, for denying the trinity.[47]

While Calvin's positive attitude to resistance and even rebellion against tyrannical rulers has often been seen by historians as progressive – and probably was an important encouragement to some of England's revolutionaries – this 'resistance theory' was inseparable from his belief in the civil magistrate's God-given duty to enforce correct religious belief and practice, and his insistence that the only legitimate dominion was founded in grace.[48] On civil authority and the first four commandments, Calvin had written:

> Even if Scripture did not teach us that the magistrate's competence extends to both Tables of the Decalogue, we could still learn it from the pagan writers. For there is not one of them who, when dealing with the duties of magistrates, law-making and the civil order, did not begin with religion and divine worship. By so doing, they all acknowledged that no polity can be well constituted, unless it makes duties owed to God its first concern, and that for laws to attend only to the well-being of men, while disregarding what is owed to God, is an absurdity.[49]

On the nature of the civil order for which magistrates were responsible, he had asserted that

> civil order has not only to do with men's breathing, eating, drinking and flourishing ... but what is more important, it prevents idolatries, sacrileges against the name of God, blasphemies against his truth, and other scandals against religion ... it prevents disturbances of the public peace; it allows each to remain safe and unharmed in the enjoyment of what is his; it makes possible innocent contacts among people; and it sees to the cultivation of upright conduct and decency. In short, it upholds a public form of religion among Christians, and humanity amongst men.[50]

It certainly looks as if this work, widely known among the participants in the debate at Whitehall, was the unacknowledged source of many of the arguments used by opponents of the clause proposing to restrict the magistrates' power over religion.

The conduct of the Leveller speakers in the debate was far from disruptive. Lilburne himself said very little after his initial statement, identifying failure to define the magistrates' powers as the cause of England's civil wars, was contested by Ireton.[51] After several contributors, including a number of army officers, had spoken of their concern that, whichever way it was voted on, many individuals would refuse to subscribe to the *Agreement* as a whole, Lilburne proposed that representatives of the opposing sides might be appointed to consider restating the question, in order to reduce the time spent on it in the council.[52] When later still Richard Overton, in the only intervention attributed to him, pointed out that such consultation had already taken place before the council met, and called for the question to be put to the vote – in which only the members of the council of officers were allowed to take part – he was supported by the calls of 'All', according to the minutes.[53] Debating conventions still familiar to us had long been in use in the London guilds and other corporate bodies; these 'points of order' were practical suggestions, and the Leveller speakers were not the only ones to make such points.

Ireton soon made his attitude to the Levellers very clear, despite what has been seen as his recent radicalisation.[54] In his response to one Captain Clarke, who spoke enthusiastically about the army's role in bringing nearer the possibility of establishing at last 'that freedome soe often spoken of, and that common right soe often desired', and explicitly invoked the Remonstrance's mention of the 11 September petition, Ireton effectively dissociated himself from the latter. 'When wee had desired the whole', he said, 'wee did nott insist upon every particle of itt.' Religion, he went on, was one of those things that should be left to a parliament elected after the aims of justice, a general settlement, and the dissolution of the current parliament had been achieved. The petition had been mentioned in the Remonstrance only 'because wee saw very many and great dreames of good thinges and therefore desired they would take itt into consideration with this Agreement'.[55]

The way in which Ireton then reformulated the main issue may have rendered it insoluble:

> The Question is now, whether you shall make such a provision for men that are conscientious, that they may serve God according to their light and conscience, as shall necessarily debarre any kinde of restraint on any thinge that any man will call religion. ... Truly, bringe itt to a restraint for [sic] the Magistrate to punish only men that are members and servants of Jesus Christ, all that are heere would give an aye to itt ... I thinke itt is our great duty and great interest to indeavour yett whether wee shall make our provision for that in such a way as shall give to all men their latitude, without any power to restraine them, to practice idolatry, to practice atheisme, and any thinge that is against the light of God?[56]

No wonder Lilburne at this point moved that the meeting return to the question of whether or not the clause should be in the *Agreement*, because Ireton's new angle made for prolonged and divisive debate. The meeting was now attempting, as Colonel Nathaniel Rich summed it up, to distinguish between 'things that are really religious and not pretended so'.[57] The debate undoubtedly reflected the scaremongering about the Ranters which had gone on in the press during 1648, and was to continue in response to the emergence of the Quakers in the following year.[58] The London Independent minister Joshua Sprigge's argument, that trust in God alone could protect the nation against being 'overrunne with idolatry and the grossest things that are',[59] did not prevent others seizing the opportunity to expound their favourite views on the magistracy of Old Testament Israel, the two tables of the biblical commandments, the light of nature, and the boundary between moral precepts and religious commandments. Another minister, Philip Nye – politically a strong supporter of toleration – got into deeper water by describing a case he had been involved in, of a man sentenced to death for bigamy who had claimed to be following his conscience, as the Old Testament allowed it.[60] The Leveller position – that the state as a natural institution could enforce only the moral laws evident to all humanity by the light of nature, and that what applied to one civil state must apply to all – was ably argued by John Wildman.[61]

The debate was adjourned without agreeing any amendments, and the Levellers took no further part in the proceedings at Whitehall. Despite Lilburne's later account of the harsh words and angry challenges he claimed to have exchanged with some of his opponents before leaving, his objections were not purely personal, for 15 colleagues joined him in signing and delivering a petition to Fairfax on 28 December which protested against the way in which the council had been constituted as well as the debate on religion.[62] The council continued to discuss and amend the *Agreement of the People*, however, and when they presented it to Parliament on 20 January it contained four lengthy and much qualified clauses concerning religion. These allowed for the state to provide not only a non-compulsive form of public worship, which must not be Catholic or Episcopalian, but also preachers to lecture against 'Heresy, Errour, and whatever is contrary to sound Doctrine'; and while it was proposed to permit all Christians to believe and worship as they pleased, provided that they did not disturb the peace, it was 'not intended that this liberty shall necessarily extend to Popery or Prelacy'.[63]

In the next three months the trial and execution of the king, the abolition of monarchy and the House of Lords, and the establishment of the English Commonwealth transformed the political situation. When Lilburne and other Levellers challenged the legitimacy of this new regime, they lost many of their former allies, including leading figures in the Particular Baptist sect, who accepted the toleration which included themselves.[64] Both Walwyn and Wildman were temporarily disaffected, but by May 1649 the Levellers had regrouped and issued a new manifesto, *An Agreement of the Free People of England*. This rejected all compromise on freedom of belief and worship, stating:

> That we do not inpower or entrust our said representatives [parliaments] to continue in force, or to make any Lawes, Oaths, or Covenants, whereby to compel by penalties or otherwise any person to any thing in or about matters of faith, Religion or Gods worship or to restrain any person from the profession of his faith, or exercise of Religion according to his Conscience, nothing having caused more distractions, and heart burnings in all ages, then persecution and molestation for matters of Conscience in and about Religion.

The only qualification, made in a subsequent clause, was to exclude from public office 'such as maintain the Popes (or other forraign) supremacy'.[65] This limitation had been imposed on English Catholics since the reign of Elizabeth, and was to be removed only in 1839.

Neither the Commonwealth nor the Protectorate that followed it from 1653 was a tolerant regime. When John Owen's sermon preached to the House of Commons on the day after Charles I's execution was published, it included a lengthy appendix denouncing those who advocated a general toleration, thundering against blasphemy and idolatry while defending the protection of Protestants wrongly labelled heretics – Muslims, Owen claimed, were the true heretics. Applying Calvin's arguments on the magistrate's responsibility for the 'two tables' of the Ten Commandments, and the identity of the natural law with all those commandments, he asserted that a godly ruler must not only outlaw 'the practice of any such worship as he is convinced to be an abomination unto the Lord' but also destroy all its 'outward monuments', a conclusion with which the destroyers of

Buddhist monuments in twenty-first-century Afghanistan would no doubt agree.[66] Cromwell was so impressed by Owen that he hired him as his chaplain before his Irish campaign later that year.[67] The ban on services using the Book of Common Prayer continued in force, the Heresy Ordinance of 1648 remained in place, and a new Blasphemy Act was passed in 1650. Two Catholic priests were hanged, drawn and quartered in the 1650s (compared with 24 in the years 1641–46) and fines were still imposed on lay Catholics, though Cromwell was friendly with several of them himself. Nor would Parliament agree to any formal toleration for Jews, despite the advocacy of Cromwell and others.[68] Hundreds of Quakers suffered corporal punishment and imprisonment, culminating in the boring of James Nayler's tongue after he had been whipped and stood in the pillory in 1656, despite Lord Protector Oliver Cromwell's opposition – a savage punishment carried out by order of a parliament elected under the wider franchise and in the redistributed constituencies adopted by the 1653 Instrument of Government.

After the restoration of the monarchy and bishops in 1660, the Clarendon Code imposed severe restrictions on Protestant dissenters, and the parliaments of Charles II and James II protested vehemently against attempts by those monarchs to grant relief to either Catholics or Protestant sects. The Toleration Act which followed the revolution of 1689 in England granted freedom of belief and worship only to Protestants (except those who denied the trinity), but dissenters from the Church of England were excluded from public office. The position taken by John Locke in his celebrated *Letter Concerning Toleration*, first published in 1689, bore many resemblances to that of the Levellers, though its religious temperature may be described as much cooler. Nevertheless, it explicitly denied toleration not only to atheism, but to any religion whose members, by belonging to it, 'do thereby ipso facto deliver themselves up to the protection and service of another prince'. Slyly avoiding naming Catholicism here, Locke gave Islam as his example of such a faith.[69]

Against this background, the importance of the Levellers and others who advocated unqualified toleration in the mid-seventeenth century can no longer be denied. They were not 'ahead of their time' but embedded in the religious and political discourse of their contemporaries, yet they were bold enough to advocate a basic but universal toleration in the form of what we would now call a level playing field for all religions. Can this be said to have any relevance for us centuries later? Was their civil state what we now call the secular state? The word 'secular' was available at the time but rarely used: just one speaker in the Whitehall debate used it, referring to the Catholic church handing over condemned heretics to be punished by 'the secular power'.[70] It was more widely used in Britain by the nineteenth century, when the National Secular Society was formed in 1866 to campaign for some aims that fit well with the Levellers' views: to abolish the requirement for elected Members of Parliament to swear on the Bible – in which they were successful – and for the removal of the Church of England's bishops from the House of Lords, which has yet to be fully achieved. The society also continues to campaign today for the abolition of faith schools and religious ceremonies in state schools, an aim which seventeenth-century tolerationists would not have supported, so long as all religious faiths were permitted to have their own schools. More dubious is its ongoing campaign against the methods of slaughtering animals prescribed by Judaism and Islam: not only is this susceptible to racist appropriation, but it would probably have been incomprehensible in the age of the Levellers, when methods of slaughter were a household choice in the countryside and guild regulations in the towns were mainly concerned with preventing nuisance and pollution arising from the presence of butcheries or shambles.

Even British secularism today bears little resemblance to the French concept of *laïcité*, a word whose original meaning simply excludes the clergy, and a concept which draws on a quite different historical heritage. Resentment of the power and wealth of the Catholic Church in eighteenth-century France gave rise to a violent campaign of 'dechristianisation' during the most radical phase of the revolution in 1793: the destruction of churches by rioters and attacks on priests and nuns culminated in the notorious mass drownings at Nantes, and a halt was called to it by the Jacobins who were then in power.[71] After relations between the French state and the Catholic Church were restored under Napoleon's Concordat of 1801, the memory of dechristianisation was largely suppressed, however. The origins of *laïcité* as the French know it now lie in the 1880s during the Third Republic, when the state school system was established as a means not only to take over education from the Catholic clergy, but to unify the linguistically and culturally diverse population of France through an ideology of patriotic citizenship with a strongly militaristic and imperialist slant.[72] At the time of writing, while the concept of secularism has been marginal to the problems of minority religious communities in British society, French *laïcité* is more controversial in its often aggressive attitudes towards not only the Catholic clergy but Muslims who are mostly by any consistent definition *laïcs*, or lay people.

Is the separation of church and state a better way of stating the aim of the Levellers and those who agreed with them? This is guaranteed in the Constitution of the United States by Article Six of 1789, which states that no religious test shall ever be required as a qualification for any public office, and the First Amendment of 1791, which rules out the establishment of any official religion and guarantees 'the free exercise' of religion without qualification. These are still in force today, though some later associated developments, such as the exclusion of religion from publicly maintained schools, are regularly challenged by evangelical Christians in many states. The French, however, understood the concept of separation very differently in 1905, when a law repealing Napoleon's Concordat severely restricted the freedom of the Catholic Church to organise, to own property, or to choose its own bishops. Complete separation has never come about in either England or Scotland, which have retained their present established churches for more than 300 years, or in Ireland, where twentieth-century independence got rid of the establishment of a minority religion, Anglicanism, only to replace it with a special relationship with the Catholic Church that has only recently been eroded. Yet while our institutions have not matched up with the Leveller ideas of equal treatment for all religions, more liberal attitudes towards different religious beliefs are prevalent today. It is a paradoxical legacy, but one which may help us to think more clearly about what we want for the present and the future in our own multi-faith societies.

Notes

1 William Twisse et al., *Certaine considerations to dis-swade men from further gathering of churches in this present juncture of time* (London, 1643), p. 2.
2 John Lilburne, *A Light for the Ignorant* (London, 1641), published anonymously in Amsterdam, 1638, p. 9.
3 Ibid., p. 7.
4 Roger Williams, *The Bloudy Tenent, of Persecution, for Cause of Conscience, discussed, in a Conference betweene Truth and Peace* (London, 1644), sig. A2v.
5 Ibid., p. 25.
6 Antony Black, *Political Thought in Europe, 1250–1450* (Cambridge: CUP, 1992), pp. 20–24; Antony Black, *Guilds and Civil Society in European Political Thought from the Twelfth Century to the Present* (London: Methuen, 1984), pp. 12–75; Anthony Pagden (ed.), *The Languages of Political Theory in Early-modern Europe* (Cambridge: CUP, 1987), pp. 3–6.
7 Williams, *Bloudy Tenent*, pp. 137, 195.
8 Ibid., pp. 202–4, for example.
9 Ibid., sig. A2.
10 Ibid., p. 137.
11 See Norah Carlin, 'Toleration for Catholics in the Puritan Revolution', in Ole Peter Grell and Bob Scribner (eds.), *Tolerance and Intolerance in the European Reformation* (Cambridge: CUP, 1996), pp. 216–30.
12 [Richard Overton], *The Araignement of Mr Persecution* (London, 1645), p. 29.
13 Ibid., p. 22.
14 Ibid., p. 23.
15 Christopher Hill, '"Till the conversion of the Jews"', in *Religion and Politics in 17th Century England* (Brighton: Harvester, 1986), pp. 269–300; David S. Katz, *Philo-Semitism and the Readmission of the Jews to England 1603–1655* (Oxford: Clarendon, 1982).
16 John Coffey, *Persecution and Toleration in Protestant England 1558–1689* (Harlow: Pearson, 2000), p. 148.
17 *Letters and Speeches of Oliver Cromwell*, ed. T. Carlyle (London: Chapman and Hall, 1888 edn.), vol. 5, p. 74.
18 John Milton, *Areopagitica; A Speech of Mr. John Milton, for the Liberty of Unlicens'd Printing, to the Parliament of England* (London, 1644), p. 37.
19 [Henry Robinson], *Liberty of Conscience, or the Sole Means to Obtaine Peace and Truth* (London, 1643), [p.6]
20 *Araignement of Persecution*, pp. 13, 22, 31.
21 Jack R. McMichael and Barbara Taft (eds.), *The Writings of William Walwyn*, (Athens, GA and London: University of Georgia Press, 1989), pp. 55–61. The two titles under which this tract was published, *A New Petition of the Papists* and *The Humble Petition of the Brownists*, were perhaps deliberately misleading.
22 Ibid., pp. 164, 239
23 Ibid., p. 239.
24 Ibid., p. 114.
25 Ibid., p. 29.
26 Ibid., pp. 94, 241.
27 Ibid., pp. 18, 239.
28 Carlin, 'Toleration for Catholics', p. 230.
29 Williams, *Bloudy Tenent*, p. 139; John Lilburn, *The Legall Fundamentall Liberties* (London, 1649), p. 20. Lilburne's words, '[God] had *particularly* washed and clensed my soul' would have been clear at the time as a statement of belief in Calvinist predestination.

30 Barbara Taft, 'Walwyn, William (*bap.* 1600, *d.* 1681)', in *Oxford Dictionary of National Biography*, Oxford University Press, 2004; online edn., Oct 2008 [www.oxforddnb.com/view/article/28661, accessed 2 Feb 2016].
31 *A Declaration: or, Representation from His Excellencie Sir Thomas Fairfax and the Army under his command* (London, 14 June 1647), p. 15.
32 *An Agreement of the People for a firme and present Peace, upon grounds of common-right and freedome* (London, 1647), p. 4.
33 David Wootton, 'Leveller democracy and the Puritan Revolution', in J.H. Burns and Mark Goldie (eds.), *The Cambridge History of Political Thought, 1450–1700* (Cambridge: CUP, 1991), pp 412–42; Andrew Sharp, *Political Ideas of the English Civil Wars 1641–1649* (London: Longman, 1983), p. 19; J.C. Davis, 'Religion and the struggle for freedom in the English Revolution', *Historical Journal*, vol. 35 (1992), pp. 507–30. An excellent critique of these views is Rachel Foxley, 'Freedom of Conscience and the Agreements of the People', in Philip Baker and Elliott Vernon (eds.), *The Agreements of the People, the Levellers and the Constitutional Crisis of the English Revolution* (Basingstoke: Palgrave Macmillan, 2012), pp. 117–38.
34 *Writings of William Walwyn*, p. 103.
35 *A Declaration of Some Proceedings of Lt Colonel John Lilburne* (London, 1648), pp. 26–34; Norah Carlin, 'Leveller organization in London', *Historical Journal*, vol. 27 (1984), pp. 955–60.
36 'To the Right Honourable the Commons of England, The humble petition of Thousands well affected persons inhabiting the City of London…', British Library 669.f.13[16]. This, the broadside version, is free from the misprints and wrong ordering of pages in the pamphlet-style one.
37 A full examination of the content of these petitions, often misrepresented as demanding the king's execution, is being prepared by the present author.
38 John Lilburne, *The Legall Fundamentall Liberties* (London, 1649, 1st edn.: British Library E.476[26]), pp. 31–35.
39 John Lilburne, *Foundations of Freedom, or an Agreement of the People* (London, 1648), p. 11; *Legall Fundamentall Liberties*, p. 35.
40 Frances Henderson, 'Drafting the Officers' Agreement of the People, 1648–9', in Baker and Vernon, *Agreements of the People*, pp. 163–94.
41 Carolyn Polizzotto, 'Liberty of conscience and the Whitehall Debates of 1648–9', *Journal of Ecclesiastical History*, vol. 26, pp. 69–82; Barbara Taft, 'The council of officers' *Agreement of the people, 1648/9*', *Historical Journal*, 28 (1985), 180–81; Murray Tolmie, *The Triumph of the Saints, The Separatist Churches of London 1616–1649* (Cambridge, CUP, 1977), pp. 179–80.
42 Henderson, 'Drafting the Officers' Agreement of the People' pp. 167–68.
43 C.H. Firth (ed.), *The Clarke Papers, Selections from the Papers of William Clarke, Secretary to the Council of the Army*, vol. 2 (London: Camden Society, 1894), pp. 73–132: frequently marred by editorial intervention, though less so than A.S.P. Woodhouse (ed.), *Puritanism and Liberty: Being the Army Debates (1647–9) from the Clarke Manuscripts* (London, 2nd edn., 1974), pp. 125–78. As there is no edition based on more recent readings of the manuscript sources, I have simply ignored everything which appears in square brackets in either of these publications.
44 Polizzotto, 'Liberty of conscience', and also 'What really happened at Whitehall? A new source', *Historical Journal*, vol. 57 (2014), pp. 33–51.
45 John Calvin, *Institutes of the Christian Religion*, Book 4, ch. 20. Many English translations are available in print and online; a good edition of the whole chapter, with notes on Calvin's own different editions, is in Harro Hopfl (ed.), *Luther and Calvin on Secular Authority* (Cambridge: University Press, 1991), pp. 47–86.
46 Lilburne, *Legall Fundamentall Liberties*, p. 21.
47 Alastair Duke, Gillian Lewis and Andrew Pettegree (eds.), *Calvinism in Europe 1540–1610* (Manchester: University Press, pb edn. 1997), pp. 15–25.
48 Quentin Skinner, *The Foundations of Modern Political Thought* (2 vols., Cambridge, 1977–8), II, pp. 3–108; J.W. Allen, *A History of Political Thought in the Sixteenth Century* (London,

1928), pp. 81–89; Harro Hopfl, *The Christian Polity of John Calvin* (Cambridge: CUP, 1982), pp. 51–52, 181.
49 Calvin, *Institutes*, Book 4, ch. 20 (9).
50 Calvin, *Institutes*, Book 4, ch. 20 (3).
51 Firth, *Clarke Papers*, vol. 2, pp. 78–83.
52 Ibid., p. 84
53 Ibid., p. 104.
54 David Farr, *Henry Ireton and the English Revolution* (Woodbridge: Boydell, 2006), pp. 118–37.
55 Firth, *Clarke Papers*, vol. 2, pp. 95–97.
56 Ibid., pp. 97–98.
57 Ibid., pp. 105.
58 J.F. McGregor, Bernard Capp, Nigel Smith and B.J. Gibbons, 'Fear, myth and furore: reappraising the "Ranters"', *Past and Present*, No. 140 (1993), pp. 155–94.
59 Ibid., pp. 99–100.
60 Ibid., p. 102.
61 Ibid., pp. 120, 131.
62 John Lilburne et al., *A Plea for Common-Right and Freedom* (London, 1648).
63 *A Petition from His Excellency Thomas Lord Fairfax and the General Council of Officers of the Army, to the Honourable the Commons of England in Parliament Assembled* (London, 1649), pp. 24–25.
64 Tolmie, *Triumph of the Saints*, pp. 181–84.
65 John Lilburne, William Walwyn, Thomas Prince and Richard Overton, *An Agreement of the Free People of England, Tendered as a Peace-Offering to this Distressed Nation* (London, 1649), pp. 5, 7; Brian Manning, *1649, The Crisis of the English Revolution* (London: Bookmarks, 1992), pp. 172–213.
66 John Owen, *A Sermon Preached to the Honourable House of Commons* (London, 1649), pp. 39–95, 78.
67 Richard L. Greaves, 'Owen, John (1616–1683)', in *Oxford Dictionary of National Biography* (Oxford University Press, 2004); online edn., September 2013 [www.oxforddnb.com/view/article/21016, accessed 18 Feb 2016].
68 John Coffey, *Persecution and Toleration in Protestant England 1558–1689* (Harlow: Longman, 2000), pp. 142, 157–59, 151–57.
69 [John Locke], *A Letter Concerning Toleration* (London, 1689), p. 47.
70 Firth, *Clarke Papers*, vol. 2, p. 94.
71 Daniel Guérin, *Class Struggle in the First French Republic* (trans. Ian Patterson, London: Pluto, 1977), pp. 138–51, 165–75.
72 Ian Birchall, 'The wrong kind of secularism', *Jacobin,* www.jacobinmag.com/2015/11/charlie-hebdo-france-secular-paris-attacks-lacite/, online only; accessed 16 February 2016.

3

WOMEN AND THE LEVELLERS

Elizabeth and John Lilburne and their associates

Ann Hughes

In June 1646, in prison in Newgate, John Lilburne praised his supportive wife, Elizabeth, whose petition to the House of Commons clearly demonstrated the illegality of his treatment. Elizabeth deserved 'exceeding commendations in so close following her husbands business, in his great captivity, with such resolution, wisdom and courage as she doth, whose practice herein may be a leading, just and commendable precedent for all the wives in England that love their husbands, and are willing to stand by them in the day of their trial'.[1] If Elizabeth was a shining example of loyal womanhood, she was nonetheless for John the 'weaker vessel' whose interests were subordinate and abilities inferior to his own. This seems clear from John's account of February 1647: 'I was led presently to take care, to do something for my wife as the weaker vessel, that so she might not be to seek in case she was called before them, and for that end, I drew her presently up a few lines, which I read unto her, and gave her instruction, that upon the very question they should ask her, she should give them her paper … unto which she readily assented, and set her name to it, which verbatim thus followeth.'[2]

Of course, our accounts of the Lilburnes' sometimes troubled relationship come from John's egotistical pamphlets; Elizabeth's voice is refracted through her husband's publications. For the first years of the Lilburnes' married life John was in the army, and for most of the time from August 1645 until John's death in 1657 he was either in prison or in exile. A so-called weaker vessel, Elizabeth was in fact clearly a resourceful and resilient woman. A heavily pregnant Elizabeth saved John's life when he was threatened with execution by the royalists at Oxford in spring 1643, petitioning Parliament to threaten reprisals if the cavaliers did execute Lilburne and carrying their resolution to Oxford to secure John's release. She frequently joined him in his later imprisonments, petitioned for his release or return from exile, and did her best to preserve her family in all its hardships. We should not underestimate the contributions of Elizabeth and the other brave 'Leveller wives' – Mary

Overton, wife of Richard, and Ellen Larner, wife of the radical printer William – who also appear in pamphlets with their husbands. They participated in the printing and circulation of radical literature, and the petitioning and agitation against the abuses of Parliament itself, thereby helping to bring a Leveller 'movement' into being between 1645 and 1647. There are petitions in their own names, no doubt representing their own perspectives – whoever drafted them – but they are presented as part of a family or household enterprise and the particular agency of the women is difficult to identify.

As we shall see, Leveller households are vividly represented in Leveller literature, with complex implications for gender relations within the movement. There were, however, more dramatic manifestations of female Leveller activism through collective petitioning by women in 1649, and renewed collective action in 1653. In their protests against the arrest of male Leveller leaders in March 1649, the women claimed spiritual equality and political rights: 'That since we are assured of our Creation in the image of God, and of an interest in Christ, equal unto men, as also of a proportionable share in the freedoms of the Commonwealth, we cannot but wonder and grieve that we should appear so despicable in your eyes, as to be thought unworthy to petition.'[3] This indicates the complexity of women's roles within the Leveller movement, and helps explain why historians continue to disagree over the ultimate implications of Leveller stances on relationships between men and women.[4]

John Lilburne in particular, but also other Leveller spokesmen like Richard Overton and William Walwyn, were adept at highlighting their own oppression as evidence of the tyranny of the House of Lords and other parliamentarian bodies. A pamphlet in Lilburne's support from June 1646, *The Just Man in Bonds or Lieutenant Colonel John Lilburne close Prisoner in Newgate*, made the point in its opening lines: 'Since this worthy gentle mans case is mine, and everymans, who though we be at liberty to day, may be in Newgate tomorrow, if the House of Lords, so please.' The Levellers have often been seen as radical individualists arguing for the political rights of the 'freeborn Englishman', and John Lilburne in particular often developed his arguments around very vivid (and egotistically titled) personal accounts of his troubles, from the early *The Christian Man's Trial* (1641) through *The Free-Man's Freedom Vindicated* (1646) and *The Resolved Man's Resolution* (1647) to *The Upright Man's Vindication* (1653). But this emphasis was qualified or even contradicted by equally strong presentations of the Levellers as a composite and inclusive movement, with its leaders presented in company with allies, friends, and, especially, with their families. Their publications, too, were sometimes coherent personal narratives, but more often compilations of various texts, bringing together associated campaigns for justice, and including petitions from wives and other family members. *London's Liberties in Chains discovered*, published by Lilburne from the Tower of London in October 1646, for example, included a call from provincial merchants for free trade alongside accounts of Elizabeth's petitioning on his behalf. Richard Overton's pamphlets included petitions from his wife and other kin: he had 'prepared a petition and appeal … in the behalf of my wife and brother to the

House of Commons, which for the better credence of our miserable condition, was presented by a competent number of women'. This stress on a female alliance rather than simply on an individual wife was echoed by John Lilburne, who described Elizabeth at the parliament 'peaceably waiting there with eight gentlewomen more of her friends, for an answer to her late petition, and for justice from the house about my illegal sufferings'.[5]

The household, inhabited by and defended by men and women, masters and servants, was, in Mowry's terms, 'a major imaginative space of Leveller radicalism'.[6] We need to be precise about the sort of households imagined in Leveller writings and inhabited, in normal times at least, by typical Levellers. Unless impoverished by dedicated service to the parliament, or shattered by arbitrary imprisonment, a characteristic Leveller household was one of real, if often modest, prosperity, including servants and apprentices, and holding its own against the richest and most powerful. John Lilburne's pamphlets identified him as a gentleman as well as a freeman, while William Walwyn used the label 'Merchant', and William Larner was 'A Free-man of England, and one of the Merchant-Taylors company of London'. In such households women were active companions to their husbands in everyday life; educating and supervising children, apprentices, and servants; involved in family businesses; and defending family reputations. A wife who was completely subordinated, or incapable of independent initiative was of little use. Furthermore, the Levellers emerged from radical Christian circles that took seriously the commonplace that men and women were spiritually equal before Christ. It is thus unsurprising that women had the practical experiences and intellectual resources that enabled them to claim active roles within the movement. But it is important not to take this optimistic picture too far, for the Levellers emerged within a society and culture that was profoundly convinced of the ultimate inferiority of women; deeply held beliefs on gender hierarchies were tested but not overthrown by the revolutionary upheavals of the 1640s. The Christian religion offered notions of spiritual equality and there were some heroic, if exceptional, examples of female activism in the scriptures, but more pervasive and influential was the creation story, which taught that woman had been created as a companion for man, and that the disobedience of Eve, the first woman, had brought sin into the world, depriving humanity of its original bliss. Many well-known scriptural texts taught that women should be silent and obedient. Notions of female inadequacy were reinforced by medical or scientific teachings that considered women's bodies to be more unruly then men's: women were 'by nature' more emotional and less rational than men, much less capable of sober self-control; hence again the need for them to be obedient to husbands and fathers. Early modern households were therefore sites of tension and negotiation, where men who were supposed to be superior were at the same time dependent on the active support of their capable but ultimately obedient wives. Some of these tensions are evident in the contrasting interventions and presentations of women and men in Leveller publications. It is impossible, given the surviving sources, to know whether there were further debates over the role of Leveller women in private, or in particular Leveller households; however, private correspondence among

Quaker men suggests disquiet at the prominence of women in the movement that John Lilburne joined in his last years, even as Quaker publications defended the right of women to speak publicly.[7] The Levellers were a collective and inclusive movement, but it was one where different elements had their place in an ultimately hierarchical structure. At the funeral for the Leveller army martyr Robert Lockyer, in May 1649, 'citizens and women' and 'youth and maids' followed his coffin in ranks carefully defined by gender and age. Thus loyal and active Leveller women were crucial to the character and persistence of the movement, but, in theory at least, they remained subordinate to the men.

Within this complex framework, the vivid descriptions in Leveller pamphlets of men and women in their households were crucial to the self-representation of the movement. They established the staunch, independent masculinity and political integrity of the male leaders: such men were worthy of the loyalty of their virtuous wives; and they were clearly superior to the aggressive, cowardly men who opposed them. When Leveller women were abused and honest Leveller households attacked, the increasingly tyrannical and arbitrary character of the House of Lords or the new republican regime was all too clearly demonstrated. Exposing the sufferings of Elizabeth Lilburne in Leveller publications offered ample evidence of the cowardice and tyranny of her oppressors. When Elizabeth joined John in prison in Newgate in August 1645, parliamentary officials, searching for evidence of illicit printing, rifled through and then stole the linen prepared for her impending childbed, the intimacy of this intrusion underlining its horror.[8] Little more than a year later, John described the 'late abuse' given to Elizabeth at Westminster while she waited for Parliament to answer her petition for John's release. Richard Vaughan, a London citizen on guard that day, tried to throw her down the stairs, and although her friends preserved her for the moment, he seized her again in 'a piece of unmanlike cruelty and barbarism' that 'renders him to be one of the malicious, basest, unworthiest and cowardliest of men, to use a gentlewoman in such a barbarous manner … a fellow more fitter to feed hogs and swine, then to be named a soldier, or ranked amongst the number of martial men'.[9] It was not necessary to spell out who was the proper, 'martial', valiant man implied in this account.

The related experiences of Mary and Richard Overton made similar points even more vividly. In a pamphlet of early 1647, Richard Overton described his own arrest and violent treatment, and then proceeded to describe the 'barbarous inhumanity exercised upon my wife, and upon the rest of my family', which culminated in an order to cast Mary 'into the most infamous gaol of Bridewell, that common centre and receptacle of bawds, whores and strumpets, more fit for their wanton retrograde ladies, than for one who never yet could be taxed of immodesty'. Mary bravely defied the City Marshall who had brought the order: 'to the utmost of her weak power made opposition and resistance against it, for in plain downright-terms (like a true bred Englishwoman brought up at the feet of Gamaliel) she told the Marshall she would not obey it'. In response, the 'Turkey-cock Marshall … bristled his feathers and looked as big and as bug as a Lord' and eventually 'with his valiant looks like a man of mettle assails her and her babe, and by violence attempt[s] to pluck the tender babe out of her arms, but she forcibly defended it, and kept it in despite of his Manhood'. In this dramatic encounter between the brave, chaste mother and the ineffective, violent, 'turkey-cock' marshall, the imagery echoes the depiction of Vaughan in Lilburne's account. Their false, bombastic, aggressive masculinity is demonstrated in their treatment of loyal women, and forms a stark contrast with the dedicated manhood of the freeborn Englishmen, Lilburne and Overton. The assaults on an honest household were prominently displayed on the title page of Overton's pamphlet, *The Commoners Complaint or A Dreadful Warning from Newgate to the Commons of England* (London, 1647), which summed up the treatment of Richard, his wife, and brother, with a particular focus on Mary: 'And in that most contemptible and villainous manner cast into the most reproachful, infamous gaol of Bridewell: And their three small children (as helpless orphans bereft of father and mother, sister and brother) exposed to the mercy of the wide world.'[10]

The stories of households assaulted by the agents of an increasingly tyrannical Parliament were effective emotional appeals as the movement gathered support, constructing an identity for the Leveller leaders as honest householders supported by active and loyal wives. Another central element in this portrait was that the arbitrary actions of the Parliament were depriving families of the protection of husbands and fathers, who would normally have been providing for them. The Parliament was turning on men who had sacrificed much in their service. Thus Elizabeth Lilburne's petition described herself as the 'Wife of Lieutenant Colonel John Lilburne, who hath been for above eleven weeks by past, most unjustly divorced from him, by the House of Lords, and their Tyrannical Officers, against the Law of God, and (as she conceives) the Law of the Land'. A further striking example comes from the account of the troubles of the family of a less well-known Leveller, the printer William Larner. When Larner was imprisoned for distributing a seditious pamphlet in 1646, he was soon joined by two loyal servants who refused to give evidence against him. Ellen Larner, his pregnant wife, petitioned for their release, pointing out that master and servants had served together in Parliament's army. She had fallen into a 'dangerous sinkness [possibly a misprint for sickness], to her great charge and damage' following the trauma of her husband's 'violent apprehension' and reminded the House of Lords that William, in prison, could not 'supply the extreme wants' of his London household, or 'relieve his aged father and mother who are past labour' and had been recently plundered by royalists in their Gloucestershire home. William's own petition asked the House of Lords not to expose his family to ruin by not allowing him to pursue his calling. His role as a provider was a central element in his identity, and it was tyranny to deprive him of it: 'For if I provide not for my family I am worse than an infidel; but woe be to them that are the causes thereof.'[11]

The practical defiance and determined petitioning of Elizabeth Lilburne and other Leveller wives were thus presented within a broader context of harmonious households where women played key but ultimately secondary roles. The more dramatic collective activities of women in 1649 and 1653 can also be seen, in part at least, within this framework. After denouncing the new republic with a tactless pamphlet, *England's New Chains Discovered*, four Leveller leaders, Lilburne, Overton, Walwyn, and Thomas Prince, were arrested by the regime and sent to the Tower. In two remarkable petitions, women who clearly identified with the movement demanded their release. 'Leveller' was a term of abuse given by their enemies, so that on presenting *England's New Chains* to the House of Commons in February 1649, Lilburne described his movement as 'a company of honest men, living in and about London, who in truth do rightly appropriate to the themselves, the title of the Contrivers, Promoters, Presenters and Approvers of the late large London petition of the 11 September last', while in their April petition the women similarly claimed to be well affected approvers of the major petition of 11 September 1648. They also claimed London-wide organisation: 'All those women that are approvers hereof are desired to subscribe it, and to deliver in their subscriptions to the women which will be appointed in every ward and division to receive the same, and to meet at Westminster Hall upon Monday, the 23 of this instant April 1649, betwixt 8 and 9 in the fore noon.'[12] The women alleged that their intervention was an exceptional response to outrageous tyranny, even as they claimed 'an equal share in the commonwealth': 'it is not our custom to address our selves to this house in the public behalf, yet considering, that we have an equal share and interest with men in the common-wealth, and it cannot be laid waste (as now it is) and not we be the greatest & most helpless sufferers therein.' Women's petitioning was not, in fact, unusual, as the examples of Ellen Larner, Mary Overton, and Elizabeth Lilburne themselves suggest, although this type of collective action was extremely alarming to the authorities. Insisting on the exceptional nature of their intervention enabled the women to hammer home their arguments about the extremities to which arbitrary power had brought them:

> That so great is our particular sorrow and affliction under the grievous weight of the public calamity and distress, that with longer patience we are not able to undergo the woe and misery thereof, or longer to sit in silence, for oppressions are too many and great for us, we are not able to bear them and live … if oppression make a wise man mad; how is it better to be expected from us that are the weaker vessel?

The women thus began, paradoxically but not unusually, by using an appeal to female weakness to justify a determined public intervention, and continued to legitimise female political agency with dramatic exemplars from scripture and history:

> this we know that for our encouragement and example, God hath wrought many deliverances for several nations from age to age by the weak hand of women: By the counsel and presence of Deborah, and the hand of Jael, Israel was delivered from the King of Canaan, Sisera, and his mighty Host, Judges 4, and by the British women this land was delivered from the tyranny of the

Danes (who then held the same under the sword, as now is endeavoured by some officers of the army) and the overthrow of episcopal tyranny in Scotland was first begun by the women of that nation.[13]

The women were treated with contempt by the House of Commons, which made no mention of the petition in their official journal. A subordinate was sent out to answer them, as one newsbook reported:

> the House gave an answer to your husbands, and therefore that you are desired to go home, and look after your own business, and meddle with your housewifery.[14]

It was this dismissive reaction that prompted a more determined petition claiming some independent political agency for women. As well as insisting on their equality under Christ and their 'proportionable share in the freedoms of the Commonwealth' (as quoted earlier), the women grieved 'that we should appear so despicable in your eyes, as to be thought unworthy to petition'. They had 'an equal interest with the men of this Nation, in those liberties and securities, contained in the Petition of Right, and other the good laws of the Land' and were 'by no means satisfied with the answer you gave unto our husbands and friends'. Their intervention was nonetheless connected with the defence of their violated households, as in the culmination of a series of rhetorical questions they demanded:

> Would you have us keep at home in our houses, when men of such faithfulness and integrity as the four prisoners our friends in the Tower, are fetched out of their beds, and forced from their houses by soldiers, to the affrighting and undoing of themselves, their wives, children, and families? Are not our husbands, or selves, our children and families by the same rule as liable to the like unjust cruelties … [The Parliament should not] slight the things therein contained, because they are presented unto you by the weak hand of women, it being an usual thing with God, by weak means to work mighty effects.[15]

The Levellers as a movement were defeated over the course of 1649, but London radicals, women and men, rallied to the defence of John Lilburne in the summer of 1653, when he was tried and imprisoned following his unauthorised return from exile. Two further petitions from groups of women called for him to be allowed the benefit of true legal process, and justified their intervention with renewed appeals to scripture and history, and to the ways in which God worked mighty means by weak women: 'nothing is more manifest then that God is pleased often times to raise up the weakest means to work the mightiest effects'. Like Esther in the Bible, these London women had had been encouraged to intervene with the mighty by the 'justness of the cause', and they recalled again the 'deliverance obtained by the good women of England against the usurping Danes'. Again they stressed that 'the thing is so gross, that even women perceive the evil of it', although here they reiterated their 'undoubted Right of Petitioning'.[16]

Whether representing individual households or collectively allying themselves with John Lilburne's trials, and with the broader 'affectors and approvers' of the Leveller programme, women were, as Melissa Mowry has written, 'practically and theoretically integral' to the 'movement's core commitment to collectivity'; and in particular, I would add, to the representation of the Levellers as a movement of households as much as individuals.[17] Women claimed a share in the freedoms and legal liberties that Levellers were fighting for; they had an undoubted right to petition and other forms of activism, especially in emergencies and when men could not or would not act. But the Leveller conception of full citizenship was clearly confined to freeborn Englishmen. There were divisions and tactical variations over how far the parliamentary franchise, for example, should be extended among men, but no one seemed to have considered that women should have full, formal political rights. Wives, like servants and apprentices, would ultimately be represented politically by male heads of households.

Returning more directly to John and Elizabeth Lilburne, there were darker elements to John Lilburne's understanding of women and politics. At times in the 1640s, and more consistently in the 1650s during his exile and imprisonments, John Lilburne criticised Elizabeth in print as lacking self-control or staunch political commitment. Echoing conventional understandings of women's weakness and irrationality, John contrasted his own consistent adherence to the cause with Elizabeth's unreliability. In 1647 he presented a marital conflict during the Lilburnes' appearance before a parliamentary committee. Seeing John arguing with one of the committee:

> my wife … burst out with a loud voice and said, 'I told thee often enough long since, that thou would serve the Parliament, and venture thy life so long for them, till they would hang thee for thy pains, and give thee Tyburn for thy recompense, and I told thee besides, thou should in conclusion find them a company of unjust and righteous Judges, that more sought themselves, and their own ends, than the public good of the kingdom, or any of those that faithfully adventured their lives therefore'. But I desired Mr Corbet [chair of the committee] to pass by what in the bitterness of her heart being a woman she had said unto them.[18]

In 1647 Elizabeth seems to have been urging him to moderate his commitment to the cause, but she at least did agree that it was a righteous cause. During John Lilburne's exile in the Netherlands in 1652–53, Elizabeth (again according to her husband's narratives) apparently urged John to make peace with Cromwell and with Sir Arthur Heselrig, his most bitter enemy, so that he could return, free, to England. John denounced her irrationality and gullibility in a series of pamphlets that served to underline, again, his own staunch, manly loyalty to his cause, while also revealing Cromwell's underhand attempts to corrupt him through a weak woman. 'The

General gives my wife good words (which makes her believe him infinitely to be her friend)', wrote John, but unlike his 'poor simple wife' he was undeceived, reminded instead that Machiavelli had advised rulers to dissemble.[19] In a published letter to Elizabeth, John wrote, with angry capitals for emphasis, that no one was:

> worthy the name of a MAN INDEED, that is not so morally honest and just in his ways, that thereby he is inabled upon serious consideration with himself, to live above all earthly fears whatsoever & not to pine or storm … But I must confess, thou art but a woman & in that respect but the weaker vessel and therefore, I must rationally allow thee the more grains of IMPERFECTION and WEAKNESS & the rather at this time, because of thy being with child.[20]

Elizabeth had, apparently, sent a letter that 'enjoinest me either to be quiet, or else never write a line more unto me'. As he elaborated in a later work, Elizabeth had wanted 'to have me again in England upon such sneaking terms as my soul abhors, and in my poor opinion no way becomes a man of a gallant, ennobled and heroic mind'. John was sure he could not be safe, 'so long as Cromwell's absolute tyranny lasteth'; and 'my poor wife out of her over-earnest desire in England to enjoy my company, hath made thereby her self a burthen to herself, and forced me to the greatest use of my brains and patience, that ever I was put unto in my life, to deal with her with that tenderness (with a salvo to my own peace) that doth become a man of conscience, gratitude and humanity'. John, had, in his words, dealt with Elizabeth as with 'a sucking babe', but she 'through childishness, weakenness, or womanishness' had persisted, and he had been forced to take so many pains 'in reading, studying and writing large epistles to her, to satisfy her with reason', that he almost went blind. He concluded that she was not acting like the wife of 'J. Lilburn' and resolved to 'never own her again as the wife of my bosom while I breathed' if she carried on.[21] In his own estimation at least, John, in contrast to the childish Elizabeth, was 'a single-hearted, honest, just, plain-spoken Englishman, that hath been valiant and courageous for the regaining and preserving their freedoms and liberties'.[22]

If Levellers did not escape the prevailing seventeenth-century assumptions about the nature of women, or the necessity of their ultimate subordination to men, we should not be surprised; neither should it lead us to underplay the significance of women's activism within the movement through judging it by modern standards. A final, enduring theme within John Lilburne's writings certainly echoes across time: the perennial and intractable question of how to combine political activism with familial or personal relations. While Lilburne and other Levellers wrote copiously about their families, friends, and supporters, they also insisted that commitment to their cause took priority over personal ties. I have quoted several examples of John Lilburne's accusations against Elizabeth that her desire to preserve her children and her household weakened her commitment to the cause and threatened to weaken his own. Throughout his political career, John

Lilburne insisted that his fight for English liberties overcame all other concerns, including life itself. In April 1647, he resolved 'to maintain with the last drop of his heart blood, his civil liberties and freedoms, granted unto him by the good, just and honest declared laws of England (his native country) and never to sit still, so long as he hath a tongue to speak, or a hand to write'. He would carry on until he had obtained his rights or was sent to Tyburn to be hanged, as Elizabeth had feared. John spelt out what this implied for his wife and children, 'unto whom I ought, and I hope I have and do, bear a husband and fatherly affection unto, yet alas, shall I for love of them sin against my soul, and be silent, when my conscience, from sound grounds tells me God would have me to speak'. In any case, those he opposed sought to destroy his wife and children as well as himself, and all he could do, when 'ordinary means fails', was 'commit my wife and children with a great deal of confidence to the faithfulness and care of God'. As a prisoner, John was 'stripped of all industrious means to provide for my wife and children, and much more in the road way by expenses to destroy them, then to lay up six pence for their future'.[23] In 1649, when recommending *England's New Chains*, John declared to the House of Commons that for his company of honest men, 'to the most of us, our wives, children, our estates, our relations, nay our lives, and all that are upon earth we can call ours, have not been so highly valued by us as our liberties and freedoms'.[24] And in March 1652 he reminded Elizabeth that, although 'thou and my sweet babes are as dear and precious to me as any such relations are to any many upon the earth', yet 'my own personal self, or my own personal being, is nearer and dearer to my individual self'. Precious to John Lilburne were first, 'my reputation, as a Christian and an honest and just man'; secondly, 'my inward peace with God and mine own conscience'; and finally, 'mine own life and the preservation of it ought in reason, justice and conscience, by me to be preferred before the preserving both thee and my children from begging'. John was alone, and in danger, in Holland, and his right to defend himself overcame all other considerations.

We can sympathise with the bravery that led John to persevere during a lonely banishment after the eclipse of the broader Leveller movement without discounting the exasperation or despair of Elizabeth as she read of her husband's resolution to accept 'the apparent hazard of exposing thee and my children by the lawless and arbitrary wills of some great men to be robbed of mine estate'. It is less easy to sympathise with his accusation that Elizabeth could not truly love him if she hoped only 'to enjoy an estate by me, for thy more handsome and plentiful living in the world'. John concluded with a characteristic evocation of principled, manly activism: 'should I be silent, after the plucking up all the laws and liberties of England by the roots, as in my sentence they are … have I not been in the field and shed or helped to shed the blood of my countrymen, for the liberties and freedoms of my nation; and shall I after that, at once by my silence, be consenting to the grubbing them all up by the roots and burying them in the grave?'[25] These fine words still resonate, but they evade real dilemmas and contradictions that we still grapple with.

Notes

1. John Lilburne, *Regall Tyranny Discovered* (London, 1647), p. 71. Elizabeth's petition is given in an appendix to this pamphlet, and was also published separately.
2. Lilburne, *The Resolved Man's Resolution* (London, 1647) pp. 2–3.
3. *To the Supreme Authority of England. The Commons Assembled in Parliament, The Humble Petition of divers well-affected women* (London, May 1649), BL 669 f. 14 (27).
4. For useful accounts: Patricia Higgins, 'The reactions of women with special reference to women petitioners', in Brian Manning (ed.), *Politics, Religion and the English Civil War* (London: Edward Arnold, 1973), 179–224; Ann Marie McIntee, '"The [Un]civill-sisterhood of Oranges and Lemons": female petitioners and demonstrators, 1642–53', *Prose Studies*, 14 (1991), 92–111. I draw here on my own work in 'Gender and politics in Leveller literature', in Susan D. Amussen and Mark A. Kishlansky (eds.), *Political Culture and Cultural Politics in Early Modern England* (Manchester: Manchester University Press, 1995), 162–88, and *Gender and the English Revolution* (London: Routledge, 2011). A critical view of my conclusions can be found in Melissa Mowry, '"Commoners Wives who stand for their Freedom and Liberty": Leveller women and the hermeneutics of collectivities', *Huntington Library Quarterly*, 77 (2014), 305–29.
5. Rachel Foxley, *The Levellers. Radical Political Thought in the English Revolution* (Manchester: Manchester University Press, 2013), especially ch. 3. Overton quoted in Hughes, *Gender and the English Revolution*, p. 58; for Lilburne see note 9 below.
6. Mowry, '"Commoners Wives"', p. 308.
7. Kate Peters, *Print Culture and the Early Quakers* (Cambridge: Cambridge University Press, 2005).
8. Mowry, '"Commoners Wives"', p. 310.
9. *London's Liberties in Chains discovered ... published by Lieutenant Colonell John Lilburn, prisoner in the Tower of London* (London, 1646), p. 33.
10. Overton, *Commoners Complaint* (London, 1647) pp. 17–19, and title page. Mowry, '"Commoners Wives"', pp. 323–26. Mowry notes that Overton omits the fact that it was the House of Commons, rather than the Lords, that consigned Mary to the Bridewell prison.
11. Elizabeth Lilburne, *To the Chosen and betrusted Knights, Citizens, and Burgesses, assembled in the High and Supream Court of Parliament* (1646); for the Larners: William Larner, *A Vindication of Every Free-mans Libertie* (London, 1646), and *A true relation of all the remarkable Passages and Illegall Proceedings ... Against William Larner* (London, 1646), quoted from Hughes, *Gender and the English Revolution*, p. 116; Mowry, '"Commoners Wives"', pp. 312–15.
12. *Englands New Chaines Discovered* (London, 1649) sig. B4r; *To the Supream Authority of this Nation the Commons assembled in Parliament, The humble petition of divers wel-affected women* (London, 1649), title page and p. 8.
13. *To the Supream Authority of this Nation*, pp. 4–5.
14. *Perfect Occurrences of Every Daie Journall in Parliament*, quoted in Hughes, 'Gender and politics in Leveller literature', p. 163.
15. *To the Supreme Authority of England. The Commons Assembled in Parliament* (London, May 1649). The Humble Petition of divers well-affected women, BL 669 f. 14 (27).
16. *To the Parliament of the Commonwealth of England. The humble petition of divers afflicted Women, in behalf of M John Lilburn Prisoner in Newgate* (London, 25 June 1653); *Unto every individual Member of Parliament: The humble representation of divers afflicted Women-Petitioners to the Parliament, on the behalf of Mr John Lilburn* (London, 29 July 1653).
17. Mowry, '"Commoners wives"', p. 306.
18. *The Resolved Man's Resolution*, p. 8.
19. *The Upright Mans Vindication or An Epistle writ by John Lilburne Gent. Prisoner in Newgate, August 1 1653* (1653).
20. L Colonell John Lilburne, *His Letter to his dearly beloved wife, Mrs Elizabeth Lilburne, March 1652* (1653, np).

21 *Colonel Lilburne Revived* (March, 1653, np), pp. 1–4 (second sequence).
22 John Lilburne, *As You Were* (1652), p. 9.
23 *The Resolved Man's Resolution*, pp. 8, 23.
24 *Englands New Chaines Discovered* (London, 1649), sig. B4r.
25 Lilburne, *His Letter to his dearly beloved wife*.

4

LILBURNE AND THE LAW

Geoffrey Robertson

In 2015, the Western world commemorated the 800th anniversary of Magna Carta, with its promises of trial by jury and the rule of law. The celebrations were wildly unhistorical: in 1215, Magna Carta had said nothing about juries and merely restated some traditional baronial privileges. It had little force or effect for four centuries and would have remained a medieval curiosity were it not for two extraordinary Englishmen. One was Edward Coke, a brilliant and bitter lawyer, sacked by the king as chief justice, who reimagined and reinvented Magna Carta as a set of liberties that had become a part of the common law. The other was John Lilburne, an unlettered agitator and polemicist, who, at the risk of his life in two treason trials, lodged Coke's learning in the hearts of the common people of England. It is no exaggeration to say: 'no Lilburne, no Magna Carta' – at least, no Magna Carta as we know it today.

Lilburne's contribution to the law came from his role as its most charismatic and courageous victim. It began in 1637, when he was hauled before the Star Chamber, the king's executive court, on suspicion of sedition – smuggling banned Puritan literature in to the country. When interrogated he refused to take the oath or to answer questions that might implicate himself or his associates, claiming that as a free-born Englishman he was entitled to a right not to incriminate himself. The court lacked the evidence to convict, so it sent him to prison for contempt, ordering him additionally to be whipped all the way from Fleet Street to New Palace Yard. The flogging was carried out viciously, in the sight of a large crowd that marvelled at his defiance of the court and greeted his bravery with cheers for 'Free-born John'. This was a moniker that stuck, and a cheer that, some years later, would be heard again and again.

When the king was forced to recall Parliament (he had prorogued it for 11 years, but then needed it back to supply money for his war against Scotland) it contained many Puritan MPs. They soon secured the release from prison of some well-connected Puritan preachers, but who would speak up for Lilburne? There came one voice, 'sharp and untunable', from an unknown MP with a 'swollen and reddish countenance'. This was Oliver Cromwell, making in his maiden speech a successful demand for Lilburne's release. It played well with the London mob, to whom Lilburne was already a legend. He had been honing his writing skills in prison, producing pamphlets attacking the bishops, the king's great supporters.

When Charles in 1642 declared war on Parliament, Lilburne enlisted in its army in time to fight at Edgehill. He was later captured at Brentford by Prince Rupert's men and carried off to the king's redoubt at Oxford. There, with other prisoners, he was put on trial for high treason – a grave breach of the law of war, by which soldiers cannot be punished for fighting on the opposite side. They were convicted and ordered to be executed, but Lilburne managed to smuggle a letter out of his cell to the Speaker of the House of Commons. Parliament was so outraged that it declared that, if the execution went ahead, it would order the hanging of royalist prisoners. But how could the declarations have reached Oxford in time to stop the execution, given there was no open line of communication between the two forces? Lilburne's heavily pregnant wife, Elizabeth, persuaded the Speaker to give her a letter authenticating the parliamentary declaration and set off on horseback to Oxford, reaching the royalist capital just in time. The king was forced to abandon his unlawful attempt to kill prisoners of war, and in due course Lilburne was swapped for a royalist prisoner. Lilburne probably fought at Marston Moor, and then left the army to take up the trade of a pamphleteer against corruption, in particular against corrupt MPs, mostly those in the Presbyterian faction who supported a deal with the defeated king. He libelled their leaders, for which they had him thrown into prison. He needed a good lawyer, so he called for John Cooke.

Cooke was an ingenious and determined young Puritan barrister, who became Lilburne's pro bono adviser and his 'get out of gaol free' card whenever he was detained in the Tower for sedition or libel. It was Cooke (led by John Bradshaw) who argued the famous case for the 'right to silence' when Lilburne, in 1646, persuaded the victorious Parliament to re-examine his youthful conviction for contempt of the Star Chamber by refusing to answer its questions. The House of Lords upheld his right not to incriminate himself – a right which still lives on throughout the British Commonwealth (although it has recently been much reduced in the UK) and is guaranteed by the fifth amendment to the US Constitution (hence some of Senator McCarthy's victims could avoid self-incrimination by 'taking the fifth').

In this period (1646–47) Lilburne's polemical output was both prolific and popular: he had the help of a fellow prisoner and gifted polemicist, Richard Overton, together with William Walwyn, Edward Sexby, and the young republican lawyer John Wildman, who had a savage turn of phrase and nerves of steel (which he showed when crossing swords with Ireton in the Putney Debates.) Lilburne kept his barrister, John Cooke, on call for advice on what the law might offer were it reformed. This Leveller group produced a flood of pamphlets: *England's Misery and Remedy*, *England's Birthright Justified*, *Protestation and Defence of Lieutenant John*

Lilburne, and *The Just Man in Bonds*. The more effort that Parliament made to suppress them, the more popular they became among soldiers who were asking, as taxes and prices rose, 'what have we fought for all this time?'

When the victorious Parliamentary Generals entered London in 1647, Cromwell and Fairfax went straight to the Tower, ostensibly to inspect its copy of Magna Carta, although Cromwell slipped away to talk to Lilburne in his cell – the Levellers were increasingly influential in the army. This meeting may well have been the spark for the Putney Debates, chaired by Cromwell in November to consider the Leveller manifesto *The Agreement of the People*. Lilburne may not have written this remarkable document – England's first draft of a bill of rights – and he was absent from the debates, preparing for an appearance before a House of Commons committee. But the *Agreement* expressed his answer to the question, 'what have we been fighting for all this time?' That answer was a charter, setting out the rights of every Englishman freely and fairly to choose representatives to a parliament with supreme power to pass laws and make war, but which would be constrained by a set of five fundamental and unalterable rights that could not be denied to any citizen:

1. Liberty of conscience in matters of religion ('The ways of Gods' worship are not at all entrusted to use by any human power').
2. Freedom from conscription.
3. A general amnesty to all who had fought on either side of the civil war.
4. All laws must be 'no respecter of persons but apply equally to everyone: there must be no discrimination on grounds of tenure, estate, charter, degree, birth or place'.
5. Parliament could pass no law evidently destructive of the safety or wellbeing of the people.

This was, in short, a draft constitution for a government as democratic as the times could conceive, comprising a sovereign parliament free of King or God and bound only by the inalienable right of all citizens to equality and religious liberty. It lacks Lilburne's literary flourish, although it expresses his wish to 'extract some principles of common freedom' that would be unalterable by Parliament ('things we declare to be our nature rights as the freeborn people of England'). It has echoed down the corridors of history, offering inspiration to the drafters of American constitutional documents and later to the Chartists; it provides the first blueprint for democratic parliamentary sovereignty, limited by certain inalienable human rights.[1]

Some Levellers, and Lilburne in particular, rather lost their nerve over the question of the king's trial. They had attacked Charles I vigorously and viciously, and had called for his removal but not for his trial or execution. In the crucial months of December 1648 and January 1649, it was left to Ireton and Cromwell to make the decision to put Charles on trial, without Leveller pamphleteering for or against. Lilburne left London to pursue a property dispute with Arthur Hesilrige in the north. However, his counsel, John Cooke, became the prosecutor and legal architect of the proceedings against the king (presided over by Bradshaw), who was accused of the crime of tyranny on an indictment that repeated some of the Leveller charges of abuse of power and war crimes. The Leveller irresolution can be put down to their scepticism of all power regimes: with the king gone, would Cromwell and the army leaders be any better? After the execution, they began again to sharpen their pens. Lilburne returned to London in February, and turned up unexpectedly at the High Court of Justice (the parliamentary tribunal which had convicted the King) during its proceedings against the leaders of his army. He was there as an adviser to Lord Capel, who had been insisting on his right to trial by fellow peers until Lilburne advised him to seek trial by jury, as his right under Magna Carta. It was the test run for an argument that Lilburne would use to obtain his own trial by jury a few months later.

Leveller fears of the 'new dictatorship' were soon expressed in Lilburne's *England's New Chains Discovered*, which blasted the Rump Parliament for refusing to submit to re-election, for censoring the press, and for undermining 'that great stronghold of our preservation' laid down (in Edward Coke's interpretation) by Magna Carta. It encouraged disaffection in the army ('We were before ruled by Kings, Lords and Commons; now by a General, Court Martial and House of Commons; and we pray you, what is the difference?'). Fairfax and Cromwell moved against Leveller agitators and followers, at Corkbush field and then at Burford; the pamphleteers were now 'the enemy within' and were arrested. Lilburne was sent for trial for the capital offence of high treason under the new Treason Act, which punished by death any who alleged that the republican government was unlawful. Lilburne had done exactly that, describing it as 'any army junto' run by 'tyrants, weasels and polecats'. At his first trial, later that year, his inspired advocacy established a set of defendant's rights which would begin the process of turning the English criminal trial from a foregone conclusion into a genuine adversarial occasion, where the possibility of a 'not guilty' verdict was guaranteed by an independent jury.

The treason trial of John Lilburne in October 1649 must be ranked as one of the most significant criminal trials in legal history. In the course of a three-day disputation with the judges, this brilliant and radical autodidact renegotiated the meaning of due process, of what fair play for a defendant required. Indeed, Lilburne's historic achievement through all his court appearances was to turn the English criminal trial into an adversarial process – hitherto, it had been largely inquisitorial: the defendant's guilt was assumed and he was given little chance to contest the evidence. Lilburne was a self-taught legal scholar but none the worse for it: a fine polemicist and an eloquent speaker, he had been a Star Chamber martyr, a courageous officer who had fought for Parliament, and a popular favourite both of the soldiers and the mob. He was not a defendant to trifle with, and the judges at his trial were well aware that they would be setting precedents for future treason trials. 'We are on trial for our lives too', they reminded him at the outset of the hearing.

Lilburne began with an eloquent demand that the court uphold 'the first fundamental liberty of an Englishman': that 'all courts of justice always ought to be free and open for all sorts of peaceable people to see, behold and hear, and have free access unto; and no man whatsoever ought to be tried in holes or corners, or in any place where the gates are shut and barred'. Judge Keble interrupted him with a smile: 'Mr Lilburne, look behind you, and see whether the door stands open or no.' The prisoner was somewhat deflated to see that it had just been opened, and hundreds of his supporters were filing onto the public benches even as he spoke. None the less, his outburst helped to establish the fundamental principle of open justice: the judges ruled that the court doors remain open at all times, 'that all the world may know with what candour and justice the court does proceed against you'.

Lilburne next mounted an attack on Bradshawe for hypocrisy. The judge was now president of the council and in that capacity had summoned Lilburne to its sitting at Derby House:

> I saw no accuser, no prosecutor, no accusation, no charge nor indictment; but Mr Bradshaw very seriously examined me to questions against my self: although I am confident he could not forget that himself and Mr John Cooke were my counsellors in February 1646 at the Bar of the House of Lords, where he did most vehemently condemn the lords of the Star Chamber's unjust and wicked dealing with English freemen in censuring them for their refusing to answer questions concerning themselves; and yet he dealt with me in the very steps that formerly he had bitterly condemned in the Star Chamber lords; yea, and there for refusing to answer his questions, committed me to prison for treason.[2]

Bradshaw had been acting as an investigator, not a judge, when he asked the questions, and Lilburne had not been gaoled for refusing to answer (his fate in the Star Chamber). But his protest was nonetheless pointed, and the court refused to permit the prosecutor, the new Attorney General Edward Prideaux, to force Lilburne to confirm that he was the author of the treasonable polemic. But this time, 'Freeborn John' was tripped up by his own love of publicity: he had personally presented the pamphlet to the Attorney General a few months previously, with the boast: 'Here is a book that is mine, the printing errors excepted – which are many.' Prideaux took a grim delight in proving Lilburne's authorship by calling his young law clerk to testify to the presentation.

Lilburne was charged with treason under the new Act, which had passed the Commons on 17 May, incriminating those who subverted the government or incited mutiny in the army. While it was being read, the Attorney General stepped up to chat with one of the judges – a common feature in criminal trials hitherto. Lilburne would have none of this and complained bitterly:

LILBURNE: Hold a while, hold a while. Let there be no discourse but openly. For my adversaries or persecutors whispering with the judges is contrary to the law of England and extremely foul and dishonest play.

ATTORNEY-GENERAL: It is nothing concerning you, Mr Lilburne.

LILBURNE: By your favour, Mr Prideaux, that is more than I do know.
JUDGE THORPE: I tell you, Sir, the Attorney-General may talk with any in the court, by law, as he did with me.
LILBURNE: I tell you, Sir, it is unjust, and not warrantable by law, for him to talk with the court or any of the judges thereof in my absence, or in hugger-mugger, or by private whisperings.[3]

Lilburne was confronting an English court with the unfairness of its traditional procedures – an unfairness that began to be recognised after the king's trial. He next challenged the rule that denied counsel to defendants on issues of fact. The Attorney General pointed out that allowing barristers to contest the prosecution evidence would delay trials, and the court with some reluctance declined Lilburne's request – although it did permit him to have a 'friend in court' sitting nearby, a solicitor named Spratt, the first of that profession ever to seek audience. His intervention on his client's behalf was firmly squashed ('What impudent fellow is that, who dares be so bold to speak in the court without being called to the bar?') but eventually the presiding judge accepted that Mr Spratt, the unsung precursor of solicitors' rights of audience (granted 350 years later), might be heard on points of law once the facts had been established. Lilburne, of course, was bluffing: he had no intention to yield the limelight to any lawyer, but his arguments for his right to have counsel to contest issues of fact and to cross-examine the witnesses read so powerfully (Lilburne, typically, edited and published the report of his own trial) that they were important in securing that reform in the next century.

Lilburne's trial achieved the consolidation of such defence rights as could be extrapolated from the recent proceedings against the king and the courtiers, supplemented with further rights drawn from the republican values for which Parliament had fought, i.e., fairness and equality before the law. The prisoner was to be treated with a measure of dignity and humanity, and the judges showed a dawning sense of pride that, by such principle, English law was comparatively much fairer than law in other countries: Judge Keble boasted that it was 'the righteousest and most merciful law in the world – this we sit here to maintain and let all the world know it'. For all this, the defendant was plainly guilty of the offence created by the new Treason Act. Lilburne therefore invited the jury to usurp the traditional role of the judges by deciding what the law should be, rather than what facts had been proved. In this, as the judges splenetically pointed out, he was totally wrong. But he got across to the jury the idea that the law should permit free speech, and that his acquittal would enable it to achieve this purpose.

Lilburne was playing for his life: he knew that the army grandees whose troops he had incited to mutiny wanted him dead, and that the judges, notwithstanding their fair procedural rulings, were time-serving at heart and would in due course direct the jury to convict. He begged for an adjournment – just an hour, to relieve and refresh himself and collect his thoughts for his final speech. The judges were unimpressed and ordered him to hurry up, but Lilburne had one last precedent to create:

LILBURNE: Sir, if you will be so cruel as not to give me leave to withdraw to ease and refresh my body, I pray you let me do it in the court. Officer, I entreat you – help me to a chamber pot!

The judges sat in stunned silence as a chamber pot was fetched by the sheriff; then, as the official report notes, 'When the pot came, he made water and gave it to the foreman', who passed it around the jury.[32] It was Lilburne's last and most important precedent: courts must ensure the comfort of the prisoners at the bar throughout their trial.

When it came time to sum up, the judicial mask of fairness and politeness slipped – as it often does in English criminal trials. Keble sent the jury out: 'If you have fully apprehended the dangerous things plotted in these books of Mr Lilburne's, you will clearly find that never was the like treason hatched in England.' The jurors asked 'that they might have a butt of sack to refresh them' – a request for alcohol, which was denied, as it has been to jurors ever since. They returned after an hour to acquit Lilburne on all counts, to the noisy acclamation of the packed Guildhall. He was conveyed back to the Tower, by soldiers who joined in the shouts of joy at his deliverance, and it was a fortnight before the Council of State judged it safe to discharge him. Cromwell, by now campaigning victoriously in Ireland, was astonished when he heard that Lilburne had been acquitted. Henceforth, the Commonwealth would try its common traitors before a more reliable mechanism – High Courts of Justice.

They need not have worried: the Levellers were finished as a political force, and Lilburne acknowledged as much. He buckled down to the new tyranny (as he saw it) and tried to restore his fortunes. He continued his dispute with Hesilrige over property in the north and settled in to a new occupation, running the first 'citizens advice bureau' from his home, conveniently situated in Old Bailey. He even applied to join an Inn of Court (the Inner Temple) to study as a barrister, but Prideaux churlishly led the clamour to refuse him admission.[4] In 1651 he made the mistake of returning to pamphleteering, albeit for his private interest, with a swingeing attack on Hesilrige, but his enemy was an MP and Lilburne was held in contempt of Parliament. For this crime there was no trial by jury; Lilburne was fined and ordered into exile by Hesilrige's MP friends. He departed, despondently, to the continent, following the path well-trodden by defeated English royalists.

The acquittal of John Lilburne may have irritated Cromwell, but it was the logical result of the revolution: justice and the Petition of Right had been a chief cause for which Parliament had fought. Lilburne repeatedly cited John Cooke's *King Charles: His Case* as proof that governments which influenced judges were guilty of tyranny – this had been a crucial part of Cooke's indictment against Charles I. The consequence was twofold: judges must display their independence, and prisoners must be accorded certain rights to a fair trial – in particular, since the law was no respecter of persons, they were to enjoy the same respect that the king had been shown at his trial. From the same crucible in which the republic was forged in 1649 emerged a set of precedents which began a new tradition of fairness (or at least fairishness) to the defence: the criminal trial was beginning its transformation from an 'inquisition for guilt' into a genuinely adversarial procedure, in which the possibility of innocence would be ever-present.

Lilburne endured banishment for two years until Cromwell lost patience with the Rump Parliament and dissolved it, replacing it with a Parliament of Puritans under the preacher Praise-God Barebone. Lilburne returned to England. The Commons had decreed his death should he return, but Lilburne plausibly argued that its dissolution had ended his liability for contempt of the House. He was arrested, nonetheless, and his old supporters came out onto the streets, including 6,000 women who signed a petition presented by their leader, the formidable Katherine Chidley, to a trembling Praise-God Barebone. Meanwhile, and despite his imprisonment, Lilburne managed to publish *A Juryman's Judgement* – an exhortation to his future jury to acquit him. Cromwell was wise to Lilburne's tricks and this time had a few of his own: on the eve of Lilburne's trial there appeared in print the testimony of government agents who had been tracking his meetings with royalist exiles. These revelations lost him some sympathy, but his supporters still crowded into court to applaud his jousts with the judges.

Lilburne's capacity to make legal history was undimmed. He invited the jury to pass judgment on the morality of the act of banishment rather than the more embarrassing factual question of whether he had breached it. The statute had set the stakes too high by decreeing death should he return, and the jury's verdict was a condemnation of the intemperate legislators: 'John Lilburne is not guilty of any crime worthy of death.' There were the usual rejoicings, even among his guards, but he was taken back to the Tower while the Council of State turned itself into the Star Chamber: it called each juror before it to demand an explanation. But the jurors had all met at the Windmill tavern and agreed on their answer: 'I gave the verdict with a clear conscience and I refuse to answer any questions about it.'[5] It was an unparalleled act of defiance: John Lilburne's juries carved out a new role for that body as an independent protector of the citizen against the state.

The Levellers had, finally, found one institution on which freeborn Englishmen could rely. Not the king, or Parliament, or the army, but this protected body comprising twelve representatives of the people who would not be cowered or corrupted in their brief exercise of power over fellow citizens. It was the Levellers' greatest achievement, through Lilburne's own courage in the dock, to lodge in the English (and American) civil soul a sentimental attachment to trial by jury that no government ever after has been able to dislodge.

Notes

1 See *Geoffrey Robertson Presents the Levellers: The Putney Debates* (Verso, 2007), pp. xix–xxi
2 'The Trial of John Lilburne', in *A Compleat Collection of State Tryals* (London, 1719), vol. 1, p. 584.
3 Ibid., pp. 593, 603.
4 Ibid., p. 626.
5 'The examination of the Jury that try'd John Lilburne at the sessions House, Old Bailey, 20 August 1653', in *A Compleat Collection of State Tryals* (London, 1719), vol. 1, p. 638.

5

JOHN LILBURNE AS A REVOLUTIONARY LEADER

John Rees

The overwhelmingly dominant image of John Lilburne transmitted from the past is of an ungovernable spirit. Lilburne is pictured as intemperate and constitutionally oppositional, his politics presented as much as a personality disorder as a rational response to the revolutionary crisis of the 1640s. Even an historian as sympathetic as Christopher Hill described Lilburne as 'notoriously volatile'. His sympathetic biographer Pauline Gregg recorded that Lilburne 'had been told many times he was wrong, quarrelsome, contentious, unruly'. And an earlier biography by M.A. Gibb described Lilburne as 'very Calvinistic in dogma', humourless, and with 'a talent for self-dramatisation'.[1]

Of course, this image of Lilburne was well established in his lifetime. Naturally his enemies perpetuated it: from the heresy-hunter Thomas Edwards, who could find nothing bad enough to say of 'contemptuous', 'insolent', 'upstart John', to the Earl of Manchester wishing he could hang Lilburne, to Oliver Cromwell trying to variously cajole or threaten his old friend out of his oppositional stance, there were plenty willing to testify to Lilburne's irreconcilability to any form of governance. But even Lilburne's close allies were capable of making the same point. Typically, it was Henry Marten that made the apt joke, 'That if there were none living but himself, John *would be against* Lilburne, *and* Lilburne *against* John'. By 1657 the same joke was being repeated as a popular rhyme and it has continued to be retold down the centuries.[2]

But there is more to the story of Henry Marten's joke, and it may lead us to a wider consideration of Lilburne's qualities as a revolutionary leader. Marten had reason to know of Lilburne's intemperance: while imprisoned in the mid-1640s, Lilburne had appealed many times for his freedom to the parliamentary committee that was headed by Marten. In his distress at the lack of progress, Lilburne hit out at his old ally in print. Marten was personally wounded by that attack and went so far as to compose a reply, although he did not have it printed. In the end, the dispute was quickly overcome and Lilburne even offered to have Marten's reply printed at his own expense. It was a generous admission of his own fault. But Lilburne went further by repeating Marten's joke, albeit without attribution, against himself in a self-deprecating moment in *The Just Defence of John Lilburne*. Thus it may well be that the popular repetition of the joke owes more to Lilburne's printed version than Marten's verbal original.[3]

Here we see a different side to Lilburne. He had been in prison for many months and could legitimately have expected that Marten might be able to set him free. So perhaps this is an example of Lilburne being slow to anger rather than of his intemperance. Certainly his offer to print Marten's attack on him shows generosity of spirit, and his repetition of Marten's joke reveals an ability to recognise his own faults and to laugh at them in print and in public. If this aspect of Lilburne's character can be seen in more than one light, perhaps others can as well.

Lilburne's oppositional stance

Lilburne's perpetual opposition to all forms of government that emerged during the English Revolution is well documented. He was actively opposed to every government from Charles I's monarchy, through the years of the Long Parliament, to the administrations of the Rump Parliament and the Cromwellian protectorate. Lilburne himself reflected on this history. In *The Innocent Man's Second Proffer* of 22 October 1649, Lilburne lists 45 of his own publications broken down under four sub-headings. The first 16 works, starting with *The Christian Mans Triall* and concluding with the second edition of *The Just Mans Justification* in 1646, come under the heading 'Since his first Contest with the Bishops in the yeare 1637'. The next 13 come under the heading 'Since my Contest with the Lords'. The next seven are listed under 'Since his Contest with Commons and Lords joyntly, being Committed by them both Jan. 1647'. The final nine publications are listed beneath the title 'Since his Contest with the Council of State March 28 1649'.[4]

This certainly does tell us that Lilburne was, and saw himself as, systematically oppositional. But it also reveals that he was adhering to an emerging set of political principles which the revolution came closer toward, but never fundamentally embodied in institutional form. Perhaps the underlying continuity of Lilburne's politics was never more clearly displayed than in the engravings that adorned the front of two separate pamphlets: Lilburne's *The Christian Mans Triall* of 1641 and Richard Overton's *Remonstrance of Many Thousand Citizens*, published in 1646. The first engraving is Glover's famous portrait of the young Lilburne at the time of his Star Chamber imprisonment. The second is the same portrait but with prison bars superimposed over the image and the legend 'The Liberty of the FreeBorne Englishman, conferred on him by the house of lords, June 1646'. What was the intended message here? Surely Overton was saying to his readers, 'Remember Free-born John Lilburne that you came to know at the time of his imprisonment at the hands of Charles's Bishops and the Star Chamber? Now look: he is similarly treated by the Parliament which claims to defend the liberties of the freeborn Englishman!'

In short, the message is one of political constancy: the very things we struggled for under Charles's rule are still not achieved after a bloody civil war.[5]

One of Lilburne's repeated rhetorical devices was to use Parliament's own *Book of Declarations*, the record of its acts and proclamations up to 1643, to demonstrate that it was resiling from its own best intentions and imprisoning those who were simply acting upon its own first principles. His own copy of the *Book of Declarations* contains marginal annotations that mark passages to be used for this purpose. From the moment he managed to get a copy while in Newgate prison in August 1645, he cited it systematically. The first reference was used in a broadsheet giving conditions under which it was permissible to disobey the law, arguing that no soldier should obey a commander who turned his cannon on his own troops and that by extension none were bound to a parliament that would harm its own citizens. It began with the words 'On the 150th page of the book called *An exact collection*' and went on to cite this page of the *Book of Declarations* extensively. Lilburne marked this page in his own copy. In 1647 Walwyn was to base his arguments on exactly the same passage. Lilburne was still using the same argument in his treason trial of 1649, citing the *Book of Declarations* in his defence. This ability to persevere for the original freedoms which Parliament had proclaimed at the start of the revolution was not by any means limited to Lilburne or his Leveller supporters. They were shared by much wider constituencies among the gathered churches, in the rank and file of the army, among women and apprentices in London, and also by many who thought of themselves as Independents. William Walwyn had some sense of this when he wrote of Lilburne that 'Time will show that he and the public are but one'.[6]

Lilburne's strategic sense

If revolutionary persistence were all that Lilburne possessed, it would be hard to imagine he would have had the political impact he did. He might have remained a visionary with a small number of followers, as the Digger leader Gerrard Winstanley became, but not the leader of an effective popular movement. Lilburne managed to transcend the limits of his own immediate group of collaborators because he had an acute ear for the possibilities of allying his cause with that of other discontented layers or groups within society. Such groups were often those with whom he shared experience, but shared experience alone is no guarantee of being able to articulate, generalise, and mobilise a particular constituency for political action.

Lilburne's first such attempt was made on the apprentices of London. He was one of them and in the early stages of the revolution they were, for the most part, mobilised in support of the parliamentary cause. From his first imprisonment, and before the meeting of the Long Parliament, Lilburne arranged for Katherine Hadley to smuggle an appeal to the apprentices out of his cell and to have it distributed among them at Moorfields. This action was credited, exaggeratedly, with causing an apprentices' riot against Archbishop Laud. On his release from prison Lilburne was one of the leaders of the pro-Parliament crowds that drove Charles from London in 1642.[7]

After his release from prison Lilburne was a member of John Spilsbury's gathered church, and his *The Christian Mans Triall* contained a foreword from William Kiffin, a key figure in the sectarian church network in London. Lilburne remained closely allied to the gathered churches throughout the 1640s, gathering active political support and funds from their congregations. He was, in Thomas Edwards's oft-repeated phrase, 'the Darling of the Sectaries'. He drew around him some of the most powerful figures of this movement, including Thomas Lambe, whose gathered church in Coleman Street was reputed to be able to draw a congregation of a thousand. Plenipotentiaries from the Lambe church could be found distributing Leveller material not only in London but around the country.[8]

The experience of the war and army service gave Lilburne another ready audience. At first as part of Cromwell's Independent grouping and later in his own right, Lilburne was at the heart of the radicalisation which was at first most evident in the Eastern Association and then became widespread in the New Model Army after 1645. At this moment Lilburne left the army, but he was ever after addressed by his military rank of Lieutenant Colonel and his initial reputation as a Puritan martyr was burnished by his wartime heroism, including facing down Prince Rupert at a treason trial in Oxford after he was captured at the battle of Brentford.[9]

The army revolt of 1647 was not a direct product of Leveller agitation, though the radical pamphleteering of the immediately preceding years was no doubt a secondary cause. But the revolt soon raised concerns closely related to those central to Leveller agitation. Lilburne was alert to the possibilities from the beginning. He and other Levellers still in the army bent their actions to this new constituency. They won new adherents, the most notable of which was Colonel Thomas Rainsborough, who visited Lilburne in the Tower during the Putney Debates and was to be the most effective soldier advocating their cause. But Rainsborough was far from the only soldier who came into the Levellers' orbit and, despite the reverse at Ware when the 1647 mutiny was crushed, the Levellers retained influence in the army until they were dismembered as an effective political movement in 1649.

London apprentices, gathered churches, and army radicals were three key areas from which the Levellers drew support – but there were others. Leveller sensitivity to the plight of prisoners is not surprising: Leveller leaders spent a lot of time in gaol, Lilburne more than any of them – one of his children was christened 'Tower', so frequently was he incarcerated there. Lilburne took up the cause of prisoners of debt, many of whom were involved in prison protests. One of their spokesmen, James Freize, became a convinced Leveller.[10]

When the commonalty of the London corporations decided to run radical Henry Wansey against the oligarchy's candidate, Lilburne was so enthused that he threw his whole weight into the campaign. When fenlanders fought enclosure, Lilburne took up their case. Those in legal difficulties frequently sought Lilburne out, and for a while he even considered setting up as a legal advisor.[11]

None of these struggles were conjured into being by Lilburne or the Levellers. If they had been, Lilburne would have been less of a strategic leader and more of a magician. His skill was that, while other leading figures looked up to the centres of power when they constructed political alliances, often compromising on their earlier pronouncements in order to do so, Lilburne looked to the social layers around or beneath him. He identified with their concerns and, in turn, shaped their political expression, drawing their most effective activists into, or closer to, the Leveller movement.

Collaborative leadership

For a man whose natural debating style was confrontational, Lilburne seems to have been able to work in a remarkably constructive way with his close collaborators. He was always generous in recommending the printed material of others. He thought long before disagreeing with Marten in print, and even when Walwyn, briefly, and Wildman, permanently, retired from Leveller activity in the crisis of early 1649, Lilburne said nothing in public. Overton, by way of contrast, wondered in print where 'Johnny Wildman' had got to.

More generally we might note that the Levellers were one of the few groups with a closely allied and publicly acknowledged leadership. They were referred to by friends and enemies as a collective. And while Cromwell and his allies were often noted to be related, part of the 'great cousinage', or were held together by the wider networks of army command and parliamentary power which they occupied, this could not be said of the Leveller leaders. They were more purely an elective affinity bound by common adherence to the political project.

Lilburne could not have won the obvious respect that he had from his collaborators if he were simply as argumentative as he is sometimes portrayed. But it may also be a tribute to the qualities of his collaborators that the movement sustained this collective leadership. Walwyn's emollient character no doubt was of great value in this respect. Wildman, who we catch in the Wapping meeting of January 1648 trying to restrain Lilburne from making public some particularly outrageous piece of gossip from Henry Marten, had a more careful lawyer's mind.

While that might be, Lilburne certainly commanded the loyalty of many of his closest collaborators over the entire length of his stormy political career. Katherine Chidley and her son, Samuel Chidley, and printer William Larner were there from the earliest days and were still supporters in the 1650s. Overton and Walwyn remained loyal over almost as long a period. Lilburne was still addressing Marten as a special friend even in letters from exile while Marten was part of the new republican government.

Political courage

What first made Lilburne a popular leader was his religiously inspired political courage. That Lilburne was physically brave is obvious. He endured whipping, torture, and beatings in prison for his first defiance of the Star Chamber in the late 1630s. He led the hand-to-hand fighting in Westminster during the 'December days' of 1641. He fought with acknowledged bravery at Edgehill, and rallied retreating troops at Brentford, where he was also captured. He was on trial for his life in the king's capital of Oxford, freed only by the direct threat that Parliament would execute royalist prisoners if he were killed. In all likelihood he fought in the carnage that was Marston Moor, and was wounded in other action. And he took Tickhill Castle only to be abused by the commander of the army for doing so. He was repeatedly imprisoned and mistreated by Parliament and again under the republic.

But more than physical bravery was required in these trials. Political fortitude was also imperative. He was offered his freedom and money if he would turn his coat by a group of lords acting on behalf of the king in Oxford. Lilburne was made a similar offer by Cromwell personally when he visited Lilburne in the Tower in 1647. He could have found easy employment in the Republic, as some Levellers did. But he refused. The stories that he had dealings with the royalists in exile are, as Jason Peacey shows elsewhere in this volume, exaggerated. Elizabeth, his wife and political partner, understandably begged him at the end of a long career of joint hardship to take an easier road. But he remained unbending.

Bravery and political constancy are only in part purely personal characteristics, however. Lilburne emerged and remained very much the spokesperson for a popular movement, and then for a specific political organisation. These are relationships that create certain dynamics, including certain expectations about behaviour. Lilburne was encouraged to and was expected to behave in certain ways by his audience, his wider network of supporters, and his close collaborators. His very prominence meant that causes, and the people promoting them, came to his door and insistently asked for certain courses of action to be taken. Lilburne could, of course, have broken these bonds at any point. But they existed and they encouraged braver responses. They also rewarded such responses with support that neared adulation at some points, even in the darker days of his treason trials. To this extent, Lilburne's bravery was not only a personal quality but a social function of the movement that he had done so much to create.

Lilburne as a writer

Lilburne was certainly a prolific writer. Printing was absolutely central to his ability to inform, motivate, and organise his supporters. But he was not a good writer. There are often brilliantly expressive and eminently memorable passages in Lilburne pamphlets, but there is also much that is discursive and repetitive. Lilburne often reproduced his authorities and sources at inordinate length, and his marginal notes alone would fill a sizeable volume. Lilburne's life was certainly full of vivid incident, retellings of which he relied upon very heavily to make a political point. A reasonable autobiographical sketch of Lilburne's life could be assembled from these passages, though often the same incidents are repeated across different publications.

William Walwyn, Richard Overton, and John Harris, to mention only three of the most prolific Leveller writers, were all masters of what Margot Heinemann described as the Leveller style. In Overton's and Harris's cases, this was a theatrical ability to dramatise political issues in the most vivid, almost play-script, manner. In Walwyn, it was something different: a clear, concise, understated, supremely logical command of political issues. Lilburne lacked any of this.[12]

But what Lilburne lacked in quality he made up for in quantity. He was the most prolific of the Levellers, and he was the pioneer of getting his views out to a wider public in printed form and of using petitions and pamphlets to mobilise his supporters. John Bastwick once complained that Lilburne's printed letters would bring odium on him 'throughout the Kingdome' because 'his Letter is now as publike as weekly newes, and in every bodyes hands'. This was, claimed Bastwick, the 'ordinary practice' of Lilburne 'and those in his society', who 'abuse such in tongue and in print' in this and 'his many other Pamphlets' which had caused divisions as far afield as Boston and 'through Lincolnshire'.[13]

We know from Samuel Chidley's account, and from evidence at his 1649 treason trial, that Lilburne took a careful and direct interest in the actual process of printing his work. Chidley recorded his own and Lilburne's battles with one particular printer who insisted on 'foysting in his own tedious stuffe' and 'whimes of his owne braine' into the text. This 'mad stuffe' would make 'honest Liburne very much vexe … and he would put it out again'. And we know from the transcripts of the Well-yard meeting in Wapping that Lilburne had an equally intense interest in the means of distributing petitions and pamphlets, including the raising of funds to make this possible. Lilburne reported to that meeting that 30,000 copies of the Levellers' latest petition were due to be printed the following day. The Levellers' supporters were to distribute them, including friendly soldiers who would help get them around the country. One Lazarus Tindall of Colonel Barkstead's regiment was ready to take 1,000 copies for the use of the soldiers. To fund this work, Lilburne told the meeting, money needed to be raised:

> That because the businesse needs must be a work of charge (there being thirty thousand Petitions to come forth in Print tomorrow, and it would cost money to send their Agents abroad, though honest souldiers now at White Hall would save them something in scattering them up and down the Counties) they had therefore appointed Treasurers, namely Mr. Prince and Mr. Chidly, and others, and Collectors (whose names as I remember, he did not reade) who should gather up from those that acted for them, of some two pence, three pence, six pence, a shilling, two shillings, half a Crown a week.

Certainly Lilburne was developing a democratic ideology unique in the parliamentary camp in its insistence on popular sovereignty. But he was also unique in developing organisational methods of propagating this ideology to a popular audience. And it is this combination of elements, no matter how rough-hewn his prose, that marks one of Lilburne's central contributions to the revolutionary era.[14]

Conclusion

The English Revolution was the first of the great social and political upheavals that have shaped the modern world. All those who brought about the revolution acted without precedent. They could not look back to Minutemen, Jacobins, Chartists, Communards, or Bolsheviks for inspiration or warning. Lilburne could not look to Robespierre, to Marx, or to Lenin. More than any revolutionary since, Lilburne had only such intellectual and practical guides as he could assemble in the midst of battle. For intellectual light he relied on the Bible, Magna Carta, English law as interpreted by Coke's *Institutes*, the theory of the Norman Yoke, and the record of the revolution's own decisions as recorded in the *Book of Declarations*. For a practical guide even this kind of heterogeneous material was not available.

Lilburne certainly had weaknesses. He was, when all allowances are made, argumentative and stubborn. He was a poor writer. But he was personally and politically courageous and honest. The crowd were not mistaken in calling him 'Honest John Lilburne'. He was strategically alert and knew how to bind emerging radical constituencies to his cause and to make his cause relevant to them. He worked collaboratively and generously. Above all he was a master at the popular use of print. Many revolutionary leaders have followed Lilburne. Few have invented as much as he did, nor carried themselves through similar difficulties with as much success.

Notes

1 C. Hill, *The Experience of Defeat* (London: Verso, 2016), p. 31; P. Gregg, *Free-Born John* (London: Dent, 1986), p. 343; M.A. Gibb, *John Lilburne the Leveller* (London: Lindsay Drummond, 1947), pp. 112–14.
2 T. Edwards, *Gangraena*, Pt. III, (London, 1646), p. 215; M.A. Gibb, *John Lilburne the Leveller* (London: Lindsay Drummond, 1947), pp. 112–14; J. Rees, *The Leveller Revolution* (London: Verso, 2016), p. 116; P. Gregg, *Free-Born John* (London: Dent, 1986), pp. 193–95, 292; J. Rushworth, *Historical Collections of Private Passages of State: Volume 2, 1629–38* (London, 1721), pp. 461–81; E. Bernstein, *Cromwell and Communism* (Nottingham: Spokesman, 1980), p. 162.
3 J. Lilburne, *The Just Defence of John Lilburne*, in A.L. Morton (ed.), *Freedom in Arms* (London: Lawrence and Wishart, 1975), p. 323. For Lilburne's original complaint, see J. Lilburne, *A Copy of a Letter Written to Colonel Henry Marten* (London, 1647), p. 669. f11[46]. See also J. Lilburne, *Rash Oaths Unwarrantable* (London, 1647), E393[39]; and H. Marten, *Rash Censures Uncharitable*, BL Add. MS 71532. For further discussion of this incident, see J. Rees, *The Leveller Revolution* (London: Verso, 2016), pp. 168–71.
4 J Lilburne, *The Innocent Man's Second Proffer* (London, 1649), Wing (CD-ROM, 1996) L2120.
5 J. Lilburne, *Christian Mans Triall* (London, 1641), E181[7]; R Overton, *Remonstrance of Many Thousand Citizens* (London, 1646), E343[11].
6 See the broadsheet 'On the 150th page of the book called *An exact collection*', 669.f.10[33]. Also A. Sharp, 'John Lilburne and the Long Parliament's Book of Declarations: A Radical's Exploitation of the Words of the Authorities', *History of Political Thought*, Vol. IX, No. 1 (Spring 1988). I am grateful to Sylvia and Barry Williamson, the daughter and son-in-law of Lilburne biographer Pauline Gregg, for the chance to study Lilburne's own copy of the *Book of Declarations*, which is in their possession. The full title of the *Book of Declarations* is *An Exact Collection of all the Remonstrances, Declarations, Votes, Orders, Ordinances, Proclamations, Petitions, Messages, Answers, and other remarkable passages*

between the Kings Most Excellent Majesty, and his High Court of Parliament beginning with his Majesties return from Scotland, being in December 1641, and continued until March the 21, 1643. W. Walwyn, *The Poore Wise-mans Admonition* (London, 1647), in A.L. Morton, *Freedom in Arms* (London: Lawrence and Wishart, 1975), pp. 119–34. The original is in the Thomasson Tracts at E.392[4]. M.A. Gibb, *John Lilburne the Leveller* (London: Lindsay Drummond, 1947) p. 127.
7 J. Rushworth, *Historical Collections of Private Passages of State*, Vol. 3, 1639–40 (London, 1721), pp. 885–946; P. Gregg, *Free-Born John* (London: Dent, 1986), pp. 77–78.
8 J. Lilburne, *Christian Mans Triall* (London, 1641), E181[7], p. 2; S. Wright, *The Early English Baptists 1603–1649* (Woodbridge: Boydell, 2006) p. 92 and p. 93 n. 65; M. Tolmie, 'Thomas Lambe, Soapboiler, and Thomas Lambe, Merchant, General Baptists', *Baptist Quarterly*, 27, 1 (January 1977).
9 *The Speech spoken by Prince Robert* (London, 1642), Wing R2308.
10 Richard Bell presented an excellent paper on prisoners of debt, James Freize, and the Levellers at the Institute of Historical Research: British History in the 17th Century seminar on 15 December 2016. On James Freize, see his *The Levellers vindication* (London, 1649), E.573[8]. Lilburne recommended this pamphlet as a 'most remarkable Epistle' in his *Strength out of Weakness* (London, 1649), p. 5, E.575[18].
11 Lilburne describes 'Major Wansie, a Watch-maker in Cornhill (a man that in these late wars, hath freely and gallantly adventured his life for the preservation of the present Parliament, and Englands Liberties)'. J. Lilburne, *Londons Liberty in Chains Discovered* (London, 1646), E.359[17], p. 21. For Wansey's military service, see TNA, SP 46/95/fo24. TNA, SP 46/95 f.16. TNA, SP 46/95 f.20. Wansey was originally from Warminster in Wiltshire, where he was also described as a watchmaker. K. Lindley, *Popular Politics and Religion in Civil War London* (Aldershot: Scolar, 1997), pp. 168–69, 394–98, 402. J. Rees, *The Leveller Revolution* (London: Verso, 2016), pp. 162–63.
12 M. Heinemann, 'Popular Drama and Leveller Style', in M. Cornforth (ed.), *Rebels and Their Causes: Essays in Honour of A. L. Morton* (London: Lawrence and Wishart, 1978).
13 J. Bastwick, *A Just Defence of John Bastwick* (London, 1645), E265[7], p. 32. Pagination is erratic so that pp. 32–33 come before a sheet of two pages numbered 20 and 17.
14 S. Chidley, *The Dissembling Scot* (London, 1652), pp. 7–8, E652[13]. T. Varax (Clement Walker), *The Triall of Lieu. Colonell John Lilburne* (London, 1649), pp. 1–4, 22, 27–28, 38, 41–47, 98 (sequentially this is p. 114, but the pagination becomes irregular at this point), E584[9]. P. Gregg, *Free-Born John* (London: Dent, 1961), p. 231. On the Wapping meeting, see *A Declaration and Some Proceedings*, W. Haller and G. Davies, *The Leveller Tracts 1647–53* (Gloucester, MA: Peter Smith, 1964), pp. 100–1.

6

PRINT AND PRINCIPALS

John Lilburne, civil war radicalism, and the Low Countries

Jason Peacey

If we know anything about John Lilburne, it is that, as one of the most important political radicals of the mid-seventeenth century, he was acutely conscious of being English, and of the need to defend the rights and liberties of freeborn Englishmen. As such, it might seem odd to suggest that we need to think again about Lilburne's Englishness, and yet this chapter focuses on a brief but intriguing episode in his life – the time he spent in the Low Countries between his banishment in January 1652 and his return to face trial and imprisonment in June 1653 – precisely in order to correct some pervasive misapprehensions about his attitudes during the republic, and to reassess the pride he took in his homeland. This episode is obviously well known, and yet it also tends to be glossed over rather briefly by Lilburne's biographers. It has not been analysed rigorously or understood entirely adequately, and the reason for subjecting it to closer scrutiny here is to shed new light on Lilburne, as well as on neglected dimensions of his ideas about political and constitutional reform, not least by placing his comments from this period in the wider context of seventeenth-century radicalism.[1] The problem with this particular chapter in Lilburne's life is not just that it has been used to develop a highly problematic argument that he was prepared to collude with royalists, but also that an opportunity has been missed to recognise that he – like others – learnt from his experiences of, and reflections upon, the Low Countries. As such, the aim of this chapter is threefold. First, it seeks to examine the evidence about his exile in the Low Countries, using royalist correspondence, republican propaganda, and Lilburne's own pamphlets to assess the nature and strength of his links with exiled cavaliers. Secondly, it seeks to explore the ways in which Lilburne responded to the challenges that he faced in the Low Countries by using pamphlets to address a variety of audiences, both English and European, and both friendly and hostile. Thirdly, it seeks to evaluate what light this period, and these texts, can shed on Lilburne's attitudes towards the Dutch republic, and towards its system of government. The argument is not just that it is possible to question the idea that Lilburne became some kind of 'royalist' after his banishment from England, but also that he found it necessary and useful to deploy printed pamphlets in rather unusual ways, and in order to address not just English radicals but also exiled royalists and his Dutch hosts. Ultimately, it is possible to suggest that even this most English of political radicals was inspired by the example that had been set by the Dutch republic, which served in important and overlooked ways as a model for constitutional reform in England, and that Lilburne also provides an example of the ways in which political strategies, and the uses of print, became much more complex and creative as political cultures of England and the Dutch republic became entangled in such rich and difficult ways.

I

Lilburne's experience in the Low Countries in the early 1650s is generally discussed in terms of his fraught relations with the republican regime, with Sir Arthur Hesilrige, and with Oliver Cromwell, in relation to both his personal affairs – the property he claimed had been taken from him – and his outspoken political position. It was this complex situation that resulted in Lilburne being accused of treason and then expelled from England, and is said to have led to his conspiring with royalists in order to kill Cromwell and overthrow the Rump.[2] However, while Lilburne certainly knew and consorted with royalist exiles – such links were discussed explicitly in Lilburne's own pamphlets – the surviving evidence needs to be handled with considerable care, not least in terms of royalist attitudes towards the Leveller leader and the role of republican propaganda.

First, while Lilburne's arrival in the Low Countries was observed with interest by leading royalists, it is not clear that he was universally welcomed or taken very seriously as a possible ally. Writing in late February 1652, therefore, Richard Watson explained that Lilburne and some of his 'tribe' had arrived on the continent, but his first thought was that the old Leveller was not to be trusted; he added that 'I have a jealousy that his banishment is but counterfeit, to give him an opportunity of doing mischief in Holland'. Sir Edward Hyde, meanwhile, could barely bring himself to pay Lilburne even back-handed compliments, explaining to Sir Edward Nicholas merely that Lilburne would make a better neighbour than the Earl of Roxburgh, of whom the king was said to have had a deservedly bad opinion.[3] In June 1652, moreover, Hyde expressed his reservations by noting that 'Lilburne is not without reputation with some great persons here, as well as with you', and that 'I am thought an obstinate fool for not understanding that he will ever be able or willing to do good'. Indeed, it soon became clear that Lilburne's royalist contacts were largely confined to the so-called 'Louvre group', an assortment of Catholics and pragmatists who pursued a controversial policy of joining forces with Scottish Presbyterians, and from whom Nicholas and Hyde sought to distance themselves. More particularly, they bemoaned the fact that it was men like the Duke of Buckingham who became particularly close to, and perhaps even 'governed by', the 'infamous John Lilburne', adding somewhat mischievously that

Buckingham was 'the fittest man for those transactions'.⁴ Buckingham, of course, was a highly unorthodox and unpopular royalist who had fallen out of favour with Charles II, and who devised all sorts of implausible schemes for uniting royalists with republicans – and indeed with France and Rome – against Cromwell. At the same time, however, he was also attempting to make his peace with Cromwell, and may even have spied for the English government. Later, he would consort with other dissidents and radicals in the late 1670s. It is thus significant that it was with Buckingham in particular that Lilburne held 'close consultations' in July 1652, resulting in the two men having 'some design in hand' to kill Cromwell, 'on whom Lilburne will be revenged'.⁵ Indeed, this relationship seems to have lasted, notwithstanding the reservations of Hyde and Nicholas. In May 1653, therefore, Nicholas suggested that Bishop John Bramhall was 'very great and intimate ... with the rogue Lilburne, who boasts very much of his friendship and power with the Duke of Buckingham', while in June 1653 Hyde explained to Nicholas that Buckingham had been 'much in council' with Lilburne at Calais, in the belief that Buckingham had 'no little interest' with the ex-Leveller.⁶

Secondly, it is important to recognise that the association between Lilburne and the royalists may have been prompted by – and certainly was exploited by – the Rump regime, and by its chief intelligencer and propagandist, Thomas Scott. Although the nature of Scott's operation in the Low Countries remains murky, it seems clear that spies were set to watch Lilburne in exile, and to report on his activities. During the early months of his banishment, therefore, stories about Lilburne appeared fairly regularly in the official newspaper, *Mercurius Politicus*, and Lilburne certainly claimed to have exposed more than one of the characters involved.⁷ Chief among these was Captain Wendy Oxford, who was accused of having been hired by Scott in order to bring about Lilburne's ruin, and who may even have been subjected to a mock prosecution in order to give him a fake Leveller identity, thereby enabling him to follow Lilburne around Europe.⁸ Lilburne bemoaned having had 'too much cause confidently to believe' that a plan had been hatched to get Oxford to accompany him into exile, 'the more securely to get me murdered in our travels together'.⁹ Indeed, the scheme seems to have worked, to the extent that royalist onlookers made the connection between the two men; Sir Edward Nicholas explained to Hyde in May 1652 that Oxford, 'when he first came from England, was a great companion of your friend Lilburne, but they of late seem to be fallen out'.¹⁰

Lilburne's interpretation of Scott's strategy was not entirely consistent over time, but it certainly involved the idea that Oxford was engaged in a variety of subtle schemes, not all of which were necessarily compatible. On one occasion, Lilburne suggested that Scott's aim was to use Oxford to fool royalists into believing that he supported their cause, thereby 'to gull and cheat the credulous cavaliers'.¹¹ On another occasion, he claimed that Oxford sought to convince exiled royalists that parliamentarians were 'traitors against the king', adding that his 'constant plotted dissembling devices' were intended to 'exasperate the body of the mad and ranting cavaliers in these parts to cut my throat'. Yet another theory was that Oxford's goal was 'to make the people of Holland believe my banishment was but a counterfeit, a juggling and dissembling fictious thing, out of design, that so I might be the more serviceable to the general, or my brother traitors at Westminster … [and] that so the people in Holland might beat my brains out as a rogue, and one of the generals or Parliament's chief spies'.[12] Whatever the reality of Oxford's mission, Scott's aim was certainly to discredit Lilburne at home. In March 1652 he may have been responsible for peddling stories that Lilburne had been made 'captain of a man of war for the states of Holland', with 'power and instructions to fire, sink or take any ships whatsoever, that shall be declared enemies to the United Provinces'.[13] Another story, from December 1652, lumped Lilburne together with men like Major General Edward Massey and Sir Marmaduke Langdale, and implied that all three had made approaches to the Dutch, with whom England was then at war, apparently in the hope of facilitating a Dutch victory, not least in order to further their hopes of restoring Charles II. The author of this report claimed that Lilburne was 'very active, and great is the concourse of people towards him', adding that he had 'set forth a declaration, touching the liberty of the people, and the freedom of nations, which gives ample satisfaction to the states'.[14]

Such stories, which have the ring of black propaganda, may have been circulated surreptitiously by the republican regime, and it is perfectly clear that Scott was willing to publicise intelligence gathered by English spies alongside information from Lilburne's intercepted correspondence. Some such evidence appeared in a tract called *Severall Informations and Examinations*, which was timed to coincide with Lilburne's trial in July 1653 and was dispersed throughout the army, and which did more than anything else to cement the idea that Lilburne had associated with exiled royalists.[15] It contained evidence, for example, from Isaac Birkenhead, one of the spies that Lilburne himself identified, who referred to 'very desperate enemies of all sorts to this commonwealth, with whom I observed Lieutenant Colonel Lilburne much to associate'. Birkenhead outlined not just Lilburne's 'great correspondencies' with England but also his links to Buckingham and Lord Hopton, to whom he apparently offered to destroy Cromwell and restore Charles II in return for £10,000. According to Captain John Titus, meanwhile, Lilburne had not only held meetings with Buckingham, but also boasted to Hopton of his many 'agents' in England, and of his ability to 'instigate the people against the parliament'. Yet another witness, John Staplehill, claimed to have seen Lilburne, his wife, and Buckingham 'very familiar' with each other at the Silver Lyon in Calais in June 1653, not least in conversation about Cromwell.[16]

That such allegations were hugely damaging is evident from the vehemence of Lilburne's response. On 15 July, therefore, midway through the legal proceedings against him, he replied to *Severall Informations* in a work called *Malice Detected*, claiming that 'no stone hath been left unturned, no stratagem unattempted, to render me odious, and fit for death, in the esteem of my friends, my jury, and the parliament'. Denying the allegations made against him, moreover, Lilburne claimed that Scott's spies had lied in order to curry favour with the regime, that the work was 'full of the most abominable falsities that ever proceeded from the wicked heart of the falsest man', and that 'its poison' was intended to 'insinuate itself into the understanding of men without any possibility of an antidote'. For Lilburne, however, the real significance of *Severall Informations* was that it was 'a stratagem of a new nature, and far unsuitable to the way of true Christians, to print against the prisoner under trial, such particulars as are altogether foreign, and nothing relating to the way of his indictment'.[17]

II

Given the prevalence of such claims about Lilburne's activity in the Low Countries, it is necessary to pick our way through the evidence with some care, and doing so makes it possible to develop a rather different picture of both his activity and his aims.

The place to start is with Lilburne's known movements after his banishment. This can be done in part through contemporary newspapers, whose editors capitalised on his notoriety, as well as through the observations of contemporaries and Lilburne's own statements. We know, therefore, that Lilburne was given 30 days to leave England on 15 January 1652, and that, although he found it difficult to travel without an official pass, he reached Dover at the end of the month, where he was reported to have made a public speech before embarking for Europe.[18] According to his own account, Lilburne arrived at Ostend on 8 February 1652, from where he apparently sent 'several letters of compliance … unto several of his clandestick friends here in England, wherein he much complains of the severity of his banishment, desiring them to use their endeavours for his restauration, accounting it a thing easy, and within their power'.[19] From there he apparently passed through Flushing, Rotterdam, and Middelburg before reaching Amsterdam in late February, where he settled in Holy Way Street, apparently in the house of Miss Mezar in Sheep's Alley.[20] Thereafter, it was said that he 'lyeth very private, not daring to adventure himself much abroad openly', and, in the absence of hard news, journalists may have resorted to using their imaginations. One editor claimed that 'those whom he trusteth most are some few acquaintances of his of the Jewish synagogue, who have privately entertained him', while Nedham added that 'the talk is that he is very busy writing, but what they know not'.[21] We can be somewhat more confident, however, that Lilburne presented a petition 'to the magistrates of this place' in the hope of securing their protection, and that he was able to correspond with his wife, Elizabeth, in England.[22] In the end, however, Lilburne did not stay very long in Amsterdam. As early as 15 April 1652 it was reported that he found 'but small encouragements to stay here, so that tis talked he intends to remove', and by May he was living in Vianen, 'that pleasant city of refuge', a few miles south of Utrecht and just outside the United Provinces.[23] Indeed, despite subsequent reports that Lilburne had returned to Holland, he probably spent the rest of his exile in the Spanish Netherlands, most obviously in Bruges, where he found a 'beautiful dwelling' through an English friend called Mr Lambert, and from where he departed for England, via Dunkirk and Calais, in late May or early June 1653.[24]

This is a rather skeletal picture of Lilburne's activity in the Low Countries, but it nevertheless helps us to explore the challenges that he faced. In part, these were financial, and Lilburne claimed that he was 'forced in a land of strangers, for many months together, to borrow … every penny that brought me bread', although Wendy Oxford claimed that he received weekly contributions from 'his brotherhood and faction in England'.[25] More obviously, Lilburne faced very real threats to his safety, and he not only suspected a plot to kill him as he first made his way to Amsterdam, but also felt threatened thereafter by 'the rudest sort of cavaliers', who apparently threatened to 'Dorislay' him, and who prompted his plea for protection from the Dutch authorities.[26] Lilburne claimed, indeed, that 'all my brains, valour and mettle hath been scarce able several times to preserve my life, from the murderous hands of the various plots, and their greatly deluded credulous accomplices'.[27] Such dangers are likely only to have increased as political tensions rose between the two republics during 1652, and Lilburne's departure from Amsterdam was a logical move once war broke out.

More importantly, such difficulties also provide the context for, and make sense of, Lilburne's writing and publishing during his exile, not least during a brief printed battle with Wendy Oxford. Lilburne was evidently 'very busy looking after a printing press' as soon as he arrived in Amsterdam, and in March 1652 he produced the *Letter to his Dearely Beloved Wife*. This was quickly followed by his *Apologetical Narration*, which appeared from the same press in April 1652, and by a tract called *As You Were*.[28] In Leiden, meanwhile, Oxford produced *A Prospective for King and Subjects*, which was dedicated to Charles II, as well as *The Unexpected Life and Wished for Death of the thing called Parliament in England*, which in turn prompted the appearance of Lilburne's *L. Col. John Lilburne Revived* (March 1653), Oxford's *Vincit Qui Patitur, or Lieutenant Colonel John Lylborne Decyphered* (April 1653), and then Lilburne's *Defencive Declaration*, the latter of which appeared in May 1653, shortly before he returned to London. Such works saw Lilburne accuse Oxford of printing with the 'advice or consent' of Thomas Scott, while Oxford denied that he was an English spy and claimed credit for prompting Lilburne's departure from Amsterdam. But more important than the trading of such blows is evidence of the strategy that Lilburne pursued in response to Oxford's machinations.[29]

First, Lilburne's pamphleteering involved continuing his propaganda effort in England, not least in order to reassure those allies who would doubtless have been alarmed by allegations regarding his flirtation with royalists, and not least by demonstrating that he continued to 'stand up against oppression, to propagate the Gospel, to preserve the liberty of the people, and to maintain the laws of the land in its purity without corruption or bribery'.[30]

According to evidence presented against him by Captain John Tutus, therefore, Lilburne boasted that

> I'll set my press on work (for which purpose I have bought one with a letter to Amsterdam, which cost me £30) and then I'll send my papers over into England, which by my agents shall be spread all over the nation, and by my

agents (for I have enough) my papers shall be brought into the army there … and as soon as these papers are spread they'll fly in the faces of their officers, so that with the help of my particular interest, the soldiery shall do all themselves, and I'll do nothing but sit in my chair and use my pen.[31]

Thus Lilburne's *Letter to his Dearely Beloved Wife* contained a familiar assault upon the republican regime, in which readers were invited to reflect on what safety there would be in England once Cromwell's will became law, and when 'he is faster riveted in his unlimited and a thousand times more than kingly power'. Lilburne railed, moreover, that 'the House of Commons may bear the name of things, but in reality it is but his screen, he alone himself as to man, being the alpha and omega of all their chief results'.[32] In his *Defencive Declaration*, meanwhile, Lilburne dealt explicitly with Scott's campaign against him. He drew attention to spies like Hugh Riley, whom he described as 'one of Mr Scot's great agents and negotiators beyond the seas', despite being 'a common reputed Irish rebel, and lately a piece of a quarter master general to Sir Charles Lucas in Colchester', and who, 'for his most villainous roguery, cheating, cozening, treachery and running from one side to another, hath several times hardly escaped hanging in Flanders'. Lilburne also described Oxford's wife – one of Scott's go-betweens – as little more than 'a common notorious reputed whore'.[33] More importantly, he also felt compelled to respond to allegations that he had become a cavalier, 'or at least a mighty great man with the chief leaders of the king's party here', which, he said, were being peddled by Scott and his agents, 'even at parliaments [and] committees'.[34] Indeed, this determination to deliver public explanations to his natural constituency – as 'a rational security to my person' – explains why Lilburne sought to ensure that the pamphlets he produced in exile were conveyed to London, in order that they might be reprinted and distributed by Hugh Peter, Henry Marten, John Lambert, and Robert Bennet. *Lilburne Revived*, therefore, was described as being 'for the use of England', while the *Defencive Declaration* not only appeared in Amsterdam, in May 1653, but was also reprinted, in an expanded form, in London.[35] As he explained after his return to England, moreover, Lilburne's aim in exile had been to make 'clear demonstrations' of his 'true affection to my native country', to 'its liberties and freedoms', and to 'the way of a commonwealth rightly constituted', even while he was 'daily struggling with the complotted designs of my death, by the barbarous, wicked and most vile agents of Master Thomas Scot'.[36]

At the same time, however, the fact that Lilburne printed such works in the Low Countries also indicates that he had an eye on other English exiles. This no doubt reflects his awareness that such people had access to a range of English texts: Lilburne referred to having seen in Amsterdam 'a printed Act of Parliament' relating to his banishment, 'expressed in the notablest of English newsbooks, called *Mercurius Politicus*', as well as to the fact that copies of Clement Walker's *History of Independency* were 'openly and avowedly' sold at the Hague.[37] In this context, Lilburne's most obvious target was local royalists, not least out of a concern for 'the safety of my life'.[38] He explicitly reacted, therefore, to the way in which

Oxford had 'writ and caused to be printed several books, with his name to them, proclaiming *in foreign nations*' that both the army and the Parliament were 'traitors against the king', and he recognised that 'the main and evident scope of all his said books and constant plotted dissembling devices and actions' was 'to exasperate the body of the mad or ranting cavaliers in these parts to cut my throat'. Lilburne also claimed that Oxford had 'constantly made it his work to incense the whole body of the king's party beyond the seas against me, constantly averring that I have been the only principal man that embroiled the three nations in war, that murdered the king, and altered the government into a commonwealth, and have destroyed the king, his queen and posterity', adding that, as a result, 'my life hath been in a constant and perpetual danger to be taken from me, especially by the rasher and madder sort of the king's party'.[39]

As such, it seems clear that Oxford's pamphlets, and the evidence gathered by Scott's spies, placed Lilburne in an extremely awkward position. On the one hand, failing to reply to them would be to 'tacitly grant the truth' of claims that were being made regarding his radical hostility to the Stuarts, and thus run the risk of provoking royalist assaults on his person. On the other hand, reassuring royalists that he was trustworthy might mean that he would 'lose my interest in England', which was 'the thing they so much desire'.[40] Being thus caught between a rock and a hard place, in the face of claims both that he had become a royalist and that he was a dangerous enemy to monarchy, Lilburne's pamphleteering represented an attempt to address a range of English readers, including both radicals at home and royalists abroad, and an attempt to 'counterbalance … two destructive evils and mischiefs against me, and my life'.[41] His solution, therefore, was to produce a carefully calibrated account of his relationship with those royalists he encountered in the Low Countries. Lilburne explained that it was this awkward situation that underpinned his decision to develop 'a friendly familiarity with the rationalest and principalest of the king's party', including Lords Percy, Hopton, and Culpeper, as well as Bishop Bramhall and the Duke of Buckingham, the latter of whom he claimed to have dined with at Oxford's chambers in Amsterdam, and with whom he claimed to be 'the most conversant'. At the same time, Lilburne was also at pains to deny that he was in league with such men, adding that his discussions focused largely on facilitating Buckingham's return to England.[42] Elsewhere, moreover, he stated that 'if John Lilburne being banished did hold affinity or correspondency with malignants being beyond the seas, yet he betrayed no trust reposed in, or unto him', adding that he could not be 'blamed for what he said or did beyond the seas'. Indeed, having been made 'an alien and stranger to England', and placed 'in the condition of an enemy', Lilburne claimed to have been released 'from all the obligations, duties and performances of an Englishman', and left 'free in himself to act for himself either with or against those that banished him, as he pleased'.[43]

What makes Lilburne's printing in the Low Countries all the more intriguing, however, is that at least some of the texts he produced in Amsterdam – including the *Apologetical Narration* – were printed, in a somewhat innovative fashion, in bilingual editions, with parallel texts in both Dutch and English.[44] As such, it can be assumed that Lilburne was also addressing a Dutch audience, and indeed he boasted of having sought to translate his texts into French and Latin for publication across northern Europe. In *The Upright Mans Vindication*, Lilburne explained that it was his confidence about Cromwell's intransigence that led him to get 1,000 copies of his *Defencive Declaration* published 'in these parts', in Dutch as well as English, and to get another copy printed in Latin, and a copy sent 'immediately' to Paris in order that an Anglo-French version might be 'speedily' produced.[45]

In other words, Lilburne was seeking to address a wider European audience, and here, too, his publishing strategy was complex but explicable. Consistently, therefore, Lilburne made clear that his writings were intended 'to apologize for himself *unto the Netherlanders*, by laying open the true state of his late fine and banishment eternal from his native countrie', to respond to the claims that were being made about his activities, and to reassure the Dutch about his intentions.[46] This was why the *Apologetical Narration* was 'directed to the people of the United Netherlands, the place of his present abode, wherein the judicious reader will observe diverse mysterious passages of state in reference to the present condition of affairs in England', and why it consisted, in large part, of yet another reworking of his autobiography.[47] Lilburne replied, therefore, to evidence that 'some imagine me here to be a spy for the commonwealth'. This, he explained, was not merely a problem in terms of threats from 'the mad or ranting crew of the cavaliers', who 'enquired' after him 'as a traitor and rogue', but also in terms of the reaction of his Dutch hosts, especially in the event of war.[48] In detailing his life story and the circumstances surrounding his banishment, Lilburne hoped to convince the Dutch 'that the parliament hath banished me in good earnest and intended it as the greatest mischief to me … and never in the least by the whole or any part of them intended it as a cloak or colour to enable me the better to be a spy for them'.[49] Lilburne later reiterated this point, by insisting that one of Wendy Oxford's aims had been 'to make the people of Holland believe my banishment was but a counterfeit, a juggling and dissembling fictious thing, out of design, that so I might be the more serviceable to the general, or my brother traitors at Westminster', and so that 'the people in Holland might beat my brains out as a rogue, an one of the generals or Parliament's chief spies'. As such, Lilburne's response to Oxford involved using 'discourses and print beyond the seas, to make it evident and apparent *to the people there* that my banishment was a real thing, and no fiction … and that I was so far from being a spy for the general'.[50]

What seems clear, indeed, is that Lilburne's determination to convince the Dutch of his honourable intentions was driven in no small part by the worsening relations between England and the United Provinces, in the wake of the failed proposals for closer union and the passage of the Navigation Act. That Lilburne was acutely aware of mounting tension is evident from a letter to his wife in March 1652, in which he explained his need to consider the possibility of a war, and it is thus notable that, in April 1652, Lilburne professed to the Dutch his desire for 'a quiet and peaceable abode in your land, while I walk honestly, civilly and peaceably, without meddling … with any of your affairs in the least'. It is also striking that Lilburne was prepared to go a long way in order to convince the Dutch of his Leveller credentials, and thus of his opposition to the republican regime, only a matter of weeks before the first skirmishes of the Anglo-Dutch War. Thus, while seeking to reassure the Dutch that he was a Leveller 'of propriety and magistracy' – pointing out that the name 'Leveller' was devised by Cromwell and 'his crafty son Ireton' at Putney, as part of the attempt to 'blast and baffle' their arguments, and to 'render their persons odious in the eyes of the people of England' – Lilburne also sought to ensure that key texts, from *Putney Projects* to the *Manifestation* (14 April 1649) and the final *Agreement of the People* (1 May 1649), were also translated into Dutch.[51]

Of course, the challenges involved in simultaneously addressing and convincing three distinct audiences were profound, and, in the context of worsening diplomatic relations between England and the United Provinces, Lilburne was not entirely successful. Indeed, it was his attempt to convince the Dutch of both his credentials and his intentions that ultimately helped to bring about his departure from Amsterdam. In reporting that Lilburne found 'small encouragements' to stay in Amsterdam in mid-April 1652, and that he 'intends to remove', *Politicus* rightly noted that this was a response to his having 'taken a course to disperse those books he calls his Apologie', only to have copies 'seized by particular order from the Burgomasters', much to Lilburne's surprise and consternation. According to *Politicus*, the aim was 'to let him know they could not permit him to print them here, their intention being to use all means to preserve amity with the state of England'. It seems clear that, in the tense weeks before the outbreak of hostilities, the Dutch could not afford to run the risk that Lilburne was a spy, or to be seen to protect so notorious an enemy of Cromwell.[52]

III

Such evidence suggests that we need to be cautious about overplaying Lilburne's 'royalism' in exile, while also recognising that he faced serious if understandable difficulties in the United Provinces – and not just because he thought himself 'too old' to learn the language.[53] At the same time, however, caution is also required in assessing Lilburne's response to this situation and to his Dutch hosts. Thus, while *Politicus* claimed that Lilburne became disillusioned and petulant, noting how he indicated that 'if they would not permit him to print here, he would go where he might have that liberty', the reality may have been somewhat different. Lilburne himself claimed to have 'acquiesced' to the ban on his printing, and to have refrained from publishing other works 'till such time' as he could 'obtain licence to print avowedly what in that kind I have to say'. Thus, while Lilburne claimed to have been forced to 'spend much money and time to travel and look out for myself, where safely to abide and print without offence', he also recognised that the Dutch decision was probably inevitable in the current diplomatic context, and his departure was more obviously provoked by his sight of Parliament's declaration of war against the United Provinces.[54] While the differences between this account and that offered in *Politicus* might be regarded as subtle, they are surely of vital importance for a more accurate assessment of Lilburne's attitude towards the Dutch republic.

What emerges, therefore, is that even though Lilburne expressed a desire to 'breath in England's air, in peace, security and quietness', and exclaimed that 'I long to see London', he also showed genuine respect for the Dutch Republic.[55] He referred to it as 'the common receptacle of wearied, tossed and banished men, being a place … of the greatest freedom that I have ever read or heard of', adding that Amsterdam was 'more famous for freedom, and flourishing thereby, more than all the rest'.[56] In March 1653, moreover, Lilburne made clear that, 'although I am very much an Englishman, yet I am … no enemy to Holland and its welfare, but desire with all my heart an honest and a just peace betwixt them and England'.[57] Indeed, Lilburne's subsequent writings made it perfectly clear not just that he still had much to teach England – and that this could only be achieved 'if you get me home in safety, and thereby free me from the murderous dealings of Mr Thomas Scot, and his cursed and blood-thirsty associates' – but also that such lessons were informed by his time in Holland. Indeed, Lilburne's comments were sometimes explicitly framed in terms of England needing to imitate the Dutch in order to emulate their glory and the fortunate situation in which Dutch citizens found themselves. From the Dutch, Lilburne learnt how to 'ease the people of three quarters at least of their present charges in taxes and excise'; he also sought to show how England could

> provide for all the old and lame people in England, that are past their work, and for all orphans and children that have no estate nor parents, that so in a very short time there shall not be a beggar in England, nor any idle person that hath hands or eyes, by means of all which the whole nation shall really and truly in its militia be ten times stronger, formidabler and powerfuller than now it is.[58]

This was explicitly aimed at the proud and passionate English reader, and those that 'love your own welfare, and the welfare and happiness of the land of your nativity'. It was such people who Lilburne implored to 'act vigorously, stoutly, industriously and unweariedly night and day for the preservation of your own interest, liberties and welfare'.

Such comments – which involved learning from, and emulating, a Dutch model – make even more sense when placed in the context of Lilburne's circle of friends and supporters, and indeed of seventeenth-century radicalism more generally. One pro-Lilburne statement from 1652, for example, demanded a 'publique banck' along Dutch lines.[59] More obviously, Lilburne's comments can usefully be placed alongside those of his friend, Hugh Peter, whose *Good Work for a Good Magistrate* set out ideas for social, economic, and educational reform, the unifying theme of which was that 'though Holland seem to get the start of us, yet we may so follow, as to stand at length upon their shoulders, and so see further'. Peter advocated new methods for setting the poor and sick to work, where 'Amsterdam is far advanced', and suggested following a Dutch model in relation to the execution of justice, the use of cheap loans, and the creation of banks. He also suggested remodelling London in order to improve the 'profit, pleasure and ease' of its inhabitants, as well as its economic fortunes: here, too, the model was Dutch. Peter suggested that the streets should be widened and paved, 'as in Holland', and made 'high in the middest with the gutters on both sides, and bricks on both sides next the houses, as in Holland', adding that houses should be remodelled 'as at Amsterdam'. London also needed to be made much cleaner: Peter found there 'most beastly dirty streets, the hurt of which is so great, as is strange, and what a world of work is daily made by the dirt and wet, in rotting of shoes and stockings, women's coats, fouling of houses, making clean of shoes, clothes etc'. Here, too, he noted that it was 'strange and not possible for merchants to live cleanly, and neatly, *as in Holland*, without cleaner streets'. In addition, Peter advocated better measures for preventing fire, with water pumps 'bored into the ground ... as in Holland', as well as new quays for ships in Southwark, 'as at Rotterdam'.[60] Earlier in the century, another radical pamphleteer – the prolific and controversial Thomas Scott – likewise advocated reflecting on the United Provinces and 'considering her ways' in order to 'learn to be wise', using the Dutch as 'tutors'. Scott explicitly argued that Dutch 'customs and orders' ought to be 'translated into our commonwealth', including their treatment of the poor (with almshouses 'maintained at the public charge of the state or the cities'), their tax system, their justice, their architecture, and indeed 'the general willingness of their hearts to advance any public work either for necessary use or ornament, wherein they are a people beyond comparison forward and liberal', and wedded to 'the common good'.[61]

More importantly, for both Peter and Scott, the 'virtuous emulation' that was being advocated extended to issues of 'politique government'. Scott, for example, observed 'a general freedom permitted and used, where general actions which concern all, and are maintained by all, are generally debated, argued, sifted and censured by all men without contradiction', and he noted that magistrates 'seek not the satisfaction of their own wills so much, as the general satisfaction of all, where it may be with the good of all'. He also explained his constitutional preferences: 'I should rejoice to see, instead of that monstrous head too big for the body, which hath cut itself off, by breaking asunder the fundamental laws and liberties of the state ... some prevention invented against change and disunion.'[62] For Peter, meanwhile, the example of the Dutch led to ideas such as the use of a ballot box to prevent corruption, as well as changes to the practice of elections:

> In the choice of a parliament man, if a thousand meet to choose, let these choose an hundred out of that number to choose for them, and the rest depart, the one hundred then out of themselves choose 20, to choose one for that service, and these upon oath to be faithful, if among these, two be in competition, then to balloting.

Indeed, Peter argued that:

> if these plain and just rules of God's word were observed, there would be no need of any deceitful, base and Machiavellian courses, to keep a commonwealth in peace and obedience, as may be seen in the Low Countries, where no people have more liberty than they, nor pay such great taxations, nor so little state anywhere used to preserve authority, and yet the people of so many nations, and religions live in the greatest peace, and plenty of the world, merely by good justice, mercy and religion.[63]

Such evidence might appear to take us some way from Lilburne. However, it seems clear that Lilburne and his fellow Levellers were much more beholden to the example of the United Provinces than historians have recognised. In Overton's *Remonstrance of Many Thousand Citizens* of 1646, for example, it was explicitly argued that the Dutch provided a model for how to maintain an army without the need for impressment; that the Dutch model worked because it was a republic; and that England should 'copy the Hollanders our provident neighbours'. As Overton explained, moreover, practical reforms were linked to constitutional models: 'if we would in many things follow their good example, and make this nation a state, free from the oppression of kings, and the corruption of the court, and show love to the people in the constitution of your government, the affection of the people would satisfy all common and public occasions'. Overton also made explicit reference to the Dutch model for Leveller ideas about representation and accountability, by arguing that 'we are your principals, and you are agents', and by suggesting that Parliament's power derived from the people's 'trust and choice'.[64] With this language of 'principals', Overton showed clear awareness of a Dutch political system whereby the authorities in the States General were beholden to provincial states, and whereby even provincial governments relied upon the consent of, and instructions from, their 'principals' in particular towns. As such, it is possible to argue that Leveller ideas were more or less directly modelled on the Dutch constitution, not least in terms of the kind of local self-government that the Levellers advocated in the so-called 'earnest petition', whereby:

> some chosen representatives of every parish proportionably may be the electors of the sheriffs, JPs, committee men, grand jury men, and all ministers of justice whatsoever, in the respective counties, and that so such minister of justice may continue in his office above one whole year, without a new election.[65]

IV

According to one of Thomas Scott's spies, Lilburne boasted that he had 'good intercourse with Holland'; it is now possible to reflect on what he meant, and what this means for our understanding of Anglo-Dutch political culture in the mid-seventeenth century.[66] It no longer seems possible merely to treat Lilburne's brief spell in the Low Countries as an awkward interlude, when he sought only to continue his English political campaigning, and when he dabbled with royalism. This is partly because, as scholars now recognise, 'royalism' is a problematic category. It seems clear not just that royalists were deeply divided over both principles and tactics, but also that many parliamentarians found themselves closer to a version of royalism as time passed, and that certain individuals changed sides more than once without really changing their political ideas.[67] In this situation, it is possible to accept that Lilburne's position was complicated by his experience of exile, and that, having concluded that the actions of the Rump regime – including the king's trial – were illegal, he was prepared to work with other enemies of the republic. Nevertheless, we should not place too much weight upon the strength of Lilburne's relationship with royalists in the early 1650s, just as we might need to reassess the links that emerged between royalist plotters and ex-Levellers during the protectorate. We should instead recognise that Lilburne's position in exile – and the tactics of Thomas Scott's spies – made it important for him not just to continue his attacks on Cromwell, but also to protect himself from 'ranting cavaliers', and to persuade the Dutch people of his good intentions, particularly as England and the United Provinces slid towards war.

It is this delicate situation that explains Lilburne's innovative use of bilingual print and Anglo-Dutch pamphleteering, which involved much more than merely exploiting the well-known opportunities offered by the Dutch system to produce pamphlets for audiences in England. Indeed, what is striking about Lilburne's tactics during the 1650s is not just his recognition of the need to speak to multiple English audiences, but also his willingness to address readers within and even beyond the Low Countries, far beyond the community of royalist exiles. More importantly, this outward-looking strategy was driven by more than just a pragmatic desire for self-preservation and the need to ingratiate himself with Dutchmen who may have suspected his motives. It was also linked to Lilburne's respect for Dutch society and Dutch political culture, and if Lilburne's reflections on what he encountered in the United Provinces were somewhat brief, they were nevertheless compatible with a strand of English radical thought – and with other Leveller texts – which regarded the United Provinces as an 'exemplar republic'. This theme has generally been overlooked by historians of republicanism and radicalism, who tend to focus on thinkers – like James Harrington and Algernon Sidney – who more or less explicitly rejected the Dutch model.[68] What Harrington and Sidney rejected, however, was precisely what the Levellers valued: a federal republic in which power was radically decentralised, and in which sovereignty was genuinely popular. Historians have only recently begun to appreciate the degree to which Leveller ideas were predicated on democratic local self-government, and it is thus important to emphasise that such ideas were influenced in no small part by observing the workings of the Dutch republic.[69] As such, it is possible to argue that while Lilburne and the Levellers may have been proud Englishmen, loyal to the liberties of freeborn Englishmen, they were also willing to respect, learn from, and emulate their European neighbours, and also to participate in the Dutch public sphere.

Notes

1. P. Gregg, *Free-Born John* (London: Dent, 1986), pp. 312–22; H.N. Brailsford, *The Levellers and the English Revolution* (Nottingham: Spokesman, 1983), pp. 611–15.
2. *Calendar of State Papers Domestic (CSPD) 1652–3*, pp. 415, 419, 423, 435; The National Archives (TNA), SP 18/37, fo. 258.
3. *Calendar of the Clarendon State Papers (CCSP)*, ed. O. Ogle et al. (5 vols, Oxford: Clarendon Press, 1872–1970), ii, pp. 121, 124.
4. *CCSP*, ii. 136; *State Papers Collected by Edward, Earl of Clarendon (CSP)* (3 vols, Oxford: Clarendon Press, 1767), iii. 74; Bodleian Library, Oxford (Bodl.), MS Clarendon 43, fo. 139; *The Nicholas Papers (NP)*, ed. G. F. Warner (4 vols, London: Camden Society, 1886–1920), i. 299, 301.
5. Bodl. MS Clarendon 43, fos. 217, 277–8, 303–4; *CCSP*, ii. 141, 146.
6. *NP*, ii. 13; *CCSP*, ii. 212–13; *CSP*, iii. 170; Bodl. MS Clarendon 45, fo. 442v; MS Clarendon 46, fos. 9-v.
7. *Mercurius Politicus*, 89 (12–19 Feb. 1652), p. 1424; *Politicus*, 90 (19–26 Feb. 1652), p. 1440; *Politicus*, 92 (4–11 Mar. 1652), p. 1472; *Politicus*, 97 (8–15 Apr. 1652), p. 1536; J. Lilburne, *A Defensive Declaration* (London, 1653, L2098); J. Lilburne, *Lilburne His Apologetical Narration* (Amsterdam, 1652, L2082), p. 45; *Severall Informations and Examinations* (London, 1653, S5255), pp. 2, 3, 6.
8. *Commons Journals (CJ)*, vi. 591–92; *CSPD 1651–2*, p. 287.
9. Lilburne, *Defensive*, p. 13.
10. *NP*, i. 299.
11. J. Lilburne, *L. Colonel Lilburne Revived* (Amsterdam, 1653, L2128), sig. a3.
12. Lilburne, *Defensive*, pp. 5, 14.
13. *Bloudy Newes from Holland* (London, 1652, B3270), p. 8; *A Declaration of the High and Mighty Lords* (London, 1652, N476), pp. 5, 8.
14. *A Declaration of the Proceedings of Major General Massey* (London, 1652, D748), pp. 3–5.
15. J. Lilburne, *Malice Detected* (London, 1653, L2141), pp. 1–2; *The Triall of Mr John Lilburn* (London, 1653, T2201), p. 33; *Politicus*, 161 (7–14 July 1653), p. 2580; *A Conference with the Souldiers* (London, 1653, L2098A), p. 2; *CJ*, vii. 284.
16. *Severall Informations*, pp. 1–4, 4–5, 13–14.
17. Lilburne, *Malice*, pp. 1, 3–4.
18. Lilburne, *Defensive*, pp. 2, 60–61; *Mercurius Bellonius*, 1 (28 Jan.–4 Feb. 1652), pp. 7–8; *Perfect Account*, 57 (28 Jan.–4 Feb. 1652), p. 456.
19. Lilburne, *Apologetical*, p. 61; *Bellonius*, 2 (9–16 Feb. 1652), p. 13.
20. *CCSP*, ii. 121; *Weekly Intelligencer*, 61 (17–24 Feb. 1652), p. 365; Lilburne, *Apologetical*, pp. 21, 72; J. Lilburne, *L. Colonel Lilburne his Letter to his Dearely Beloved Wife* (Amsterdam, 1652, L2136), sig. A4; J. Lilburne, *As You Were* (Amsterdam, 1652, L2084), p. 32.
21. *Perfect Account*, 60 (18–25 Feb. 1652), p. 480; *Politicus*, 90, p. 1440; *Politicus*, 92, p. 1472.
22. *Politicus*, 90, p. 1440; *Bellonius*, 4 (25 Feb.–3 Mar. 1652), p. 27; Lilburne, *Lilburne his Letter*, sig. A.
23. *Politicus*, 97, p. 1536; Lilburne, *As You Were*, p. 33.
24. *CCSP*, ii. 148; Lilburne, *Revived*, pp. 1, 12, sigs. A3, b-c4; J. Lilburne, *A Defencive Declaration* (Amsterdam, 1653, L2097); *Severall Informations*, pp. 1, 6; J. Lilburne, *The Upright Mans Vindication* (London, 1653, L2197), pp. 3–19, 20–22, 25–27.
25. Lilburne, *Defensive*, p. 4; W. Oxford, *Vincit qui Patitur* (London, 1653, O846).
26. Lilburne, *Revived*, sig. a3; Lilburne, *Apologetical Narration*, p. 21; *Bellonius*, 4, p. 27; Lilburne, *As You Were*, p. 9.
27. Lilburne, *Defensive*, pp. 5–6.
28. Lilburne, *Lilburne his Letter*, sigs. Av, A4; Lilburne, *Apologetical Narration*; Lilburne, *As You Were*, p. 5; *Severall Informations*, pp. 10–11.
29. W. Oxford, *A Prospective for King and Subjects* (Leyden, 1652, O844); W. Oxford, *The Unexpected Life* (Leyden?, 1652); Lilburne, *Revived*, sig. a3; Oxford, *Vincit*; Lilburne, *Defencive Declaration*. Oxford claimed that he had planned another reply to Lilburne, called 'The banished mans complaint, the other John Lylbornes Portraicture with a hue

and cry after him'. He also mentioned that his own printer was the same that Lilburne had known in Delft in the 1630s.
30 *Bloudy Newes*, p. 8.
31 *Severall Informations*, p. 6.
32 Lilburne, *Lilburne his Letter*, sigs. Av, A3v. See also: British Library, Additional MS 71533, fo. 8.
33 Lilburne, *Defencive*, pp. 6–7.
34 Lilburne, *Defensive*, pp. 5–6.
35 Lilburne, *Lilburne his Letter*, sig. A4; Lilburne, *Apologetical Narration*; Lilburne, *As You Were*, p. 5; *Severall Informations*, pp. 10–11; Lilburne, *Defensive*; Lilburne, *Revived*, p.10; Lilburne, *Upright Mans*, p. 27. This is not to say, of course, that such tactics were a great success; some copies were handed into the Council of State in April 1652, and imported copies were also seized by the authorities: *CSPD 1651–2*, pp. 204, 287; TNA, SP 25/66, fo. 533; *Weekly Intelligencer*, 69 (13–20 Apr. 1652), p. 427.
36 Lilburne, *Upright Mans*, pp. 26–27.
37 Lilburne, *Apologetical Narration*, p. 61; Lilburne, *Revived*, sig. a4v.
38 Lilburne, *As You Were*, p. 32.
39 Lilburne, *Defensive*, pp. 5, 14.
40 Lilburne, *Revived*, sig. a3.
41 Lilburne, *Defensive*, p. 14.
42 Lilburne, *Defensive*, pp. 15, 16–17.
43 Lilburne, *Upright Mans*, pp. 32–33.
44 For Lilburne's reference to these bilingual editions, see Lilburne, *Lilburne his Letter*, sig. A4; Lilburne, *As You Were*, p. 5.
45 Lilburne, *Upright Mans*, p. 26.
46 Lilburne, *Lilburne his Letter*, title page.
47 Lilburne, *Apologetical Narration*, title page.
48 Lilburne, *Lilburne his Letter*, sig. A2. See also Lilburne, *Apologetical Narration*, p. 21.
49 Lilburne, *Apologetical Narration*, pp. 63–64.
50 Lilburne, *Defensive*, p. 14. Later, Lilburne denied being legally banished, insisting instead that he had travelled as 'a freeborn Englishman, that might lawfully travel to any place about his occasions': *The Tryall of L. Col. John Lilburn* (London, 1653, T2195), p. 5.
51 Lilburne, *Apologetical Narration*, pp. 68–71; Lilburne, *As You Were*, p. 33.
52 *Politicus*, 97, p. 1536. In essence, this fits with Lilburne's account: Lilburne, *As You Were*, p. 33. Nedham, of course, mocked Lilburne by noting that his experience of 'arbitrary dealings in other countries' might make him 'think the better of his own'.
53 *Severall Informations*, pp. 11–13.
54 *Politicus*, 97, p. 1536; Lilburne, *As You Were*, p. 33; *Severall Informations*, p. 9.
55 Lilburne, *Upright Mans*, p. 26; *Severall Informations*, pp. 10–11.
56 Lilburne, *Apologetical Narration*, pp. 2, 21.
57 Lilburne, *Revived*, p. 12.
58 Lilburne, *Upright Mans*, pp. 20–22.
59 *A Declaration of the Armie* (London, 1652, D629), p. 5.
60 H. Peter, *Good Work for a Good Magistrate* (London, 1651, P1706), sigs. A3, A6, pp. 18–19, 39, 91–92, 102, 105, 106–7, 108.
61 T. Scott, *The Belgicke Pismire* (London, 1622), pp. 49, 50, 53–54, 72, 73–74, 75–80. This aspect of Scott's thought has generally been overlooked. See P. Lake, 'Constitutional consensus and Puritan opposition in the 1620s: Thomas Scott and the Spanish Match', *Historical Journal*, 25 (1982), 805–25; J. Scott, *Commonwealth Principles* (Cambridge: CUP, 2004), pp. 235–36.
62 Scott, *Belgicke*, pp. 51, 89–90, 96.
63 Peter, *Good Work*, pp. 30–31, 108–9.
64 R. Overton, *A Remonstrance of Many Thousand Citizens* (London, 1646, O632B), pp. 3, 16.
65 *A Declaration of Some Proceedings* (London, 1648, D625), p. 32.
66 *Severall Informations*, p. 9.

67 D. Smith, *Constitutional Royalism and the Search for Settlement, c.1640–1649* (Cambridge: CUP, 1994); J. McElligott and D. Smith (eds.), *Royalists and Royalism during the English Civil Wars* (Cambridge: CUP, 2007); J. McElligott and D. Smith (eds.), *Royalists and Royalism during the Interregnum* (Manchester: MUP, 2010).
68 Scott, *Commonwealth Principles*, pp. 135, 235–36.
69 J. C. Davis, 'Reassessing radicalism in a traditional society', in G. Burgess and M. Festenstein (eds.), *English Radicalism, 1550–1850* (Cambridge: CUP, 2007), pp. 338–72.

7
THE RESURRECTION OF JOHN LILBURNE, QUAKER

Ariel Hessayon

> A contentious, disloyal, commonplace man; little distinguished save by his ill nature, his blindness to superior worth, and the dark internal fermentation of his own poor angry limited mind, does not seem to me an apt hero.
> *Thomas Carlyle to Thomas Wise (Chelsea, 21 February 1848)*[1]

On Saturday 29 August 1657 John Lilburne, being 'very sicke and weake in bed', passed away while on parole at Eltham, Kent. His heavily pregnant wife, Elizabeth, possibly with their three surviving children, was with him during his final moments in a house he had recently rented so that she might be near her friends when she gave birth.[2] A Quaker source lamenting that he had died a prisoner, 'Beareing a Testimony for Truth', identified Lilburne's place of death as the 'Kings house'.[3] If so, then this was the royal palace at Eltham then in the possession of Colonel Nathaniel Rich, a parliamentarian army officer who had also purchased the royal parks and keeper's lodge at Eltham.[4] Lilburne had once railed against Rich, calling him a 'juggling paltry, base fellow', although by this time Rich – who had attended a Quaker meeting in Cheapside – had likewise been imprisoned by Cromwell for associating with Fifth Monarchist opponents of the Protectorate.[5]

As in life, so in death: the burial of this 'busie man' and 'factious spirit' was the cause of controversy.[6] On the morning of Monday 31 August his body was transported to the Bull and Mouth near Aldersgate. This inn was to be described after the Great Fire as 'large, and well built', and since March 1655 it had been used as the Quakers' principal London meeting place, also serving as the premises for their main publisher Thomas Simmons.[7] According to a contemporary journalist, as the day of Lilburne's funeral progressed so a 'medley of people' gathered at the Bull and Mouth, the majority of them Quakers. There was disagreement, however, as to whether the coffin should be covered with a black hearse-cloth that had been brought either by Lilburne's widow or by some of his old Leveller acquaintances.

The Quakers refused, insisting that the less pomp attended the proceedings the more opportunity there would be for piety.

So, at about five o'clock in the afternoon, Lilburne's bare coffin was brought out into the street, at which point an unidentified man attempted to cast a velvet pall over it. But to no avail: the crowd of Quakers would not permit it and hoisted the coffin on their shoulders, carrying it away without further ceremony to Moorfields, and from thence to the new churchyard adjoining Bedlam where Lilburne's body was interred.[8] An unsympathetic contemporary biographer considered the funeral route of this 'illiterate' latter-day 'Proteus' well-chosen since Lilburne had been partially blinded in one eye by a pike in Moorfields; and as 'his turbulent life came near to madness, so the place of his burial was near to the distracted crew'.[9] While Quakers eschewed funeral sermons, it seems words were spoken as part of the solemn obsequies.[10] The historian John Rushworth later added that there had been 4,000 mourners, although there is no way of knowing if this was an accurate estimate.[11] Even so, the event was reported in several contemporary newsbooks and pamphlets, and such was its significance that the Florentine agent in London included a brief account of this 'factious person who had a taste of all religions' but 'in the end died as a Quaker' in his weekly report.[12]

While one epitaph lamented the demise, 'after much wrangling', of 'this stout champion', another joked that 'John' and 'Lilburne' be buried separately lest they argue among themselves in the grave.[13] Similar quips that if the world were emptied of all but the Leveller leader then 'John would be against Lilburne, and Lilburne against John' were variously attributed to the regicide Henry Marten and the royalist judge David Jenkins.[14] His 'impetuous' contentious nature aside, even hostile seventeenth- and early eighteenth-century commentators were agreed that Lilburne had been a victim of Cromwellian tyranny, illegally tossed from one prison to another.[15] Thus the diarist and numismatist John Evelyn reproduced a medal commemorating the acquittal of that 'Stout and Couragious *Assertor*' who had withstood a famous trial 'under the late Arbitrary Usurper'.[16] Similarly, the author of *The History of King-Killers* (1720) conceded that:

> He may well be reck'ned at least half a Martyr for his long Imprisonment, Trials, and other Sufferings for the Fanatick Cause in General; and every Party under that Determination may claim a Share in him, he having been first a *Puritan*, then an *Independent*, next a *Leveller*, and lastly a *Quaker*.[17]

I

So what are we to make of the last phase of a religious and political struggle that had begun during the personal rule of Charles I, with membership of a separatist congregation and imprisonment for importing seditious books, and which ended during the Protectorate of Oliver with conversion to Quakerism and rejection of temporal weapons?

For contemporaries, the immediate question was of Lilburne's sincerity. So to allay the regime's concerns, his wife Elizabeth personally presented Cromwell with a letter intended to demonstrate that her husband had divested himself of Machiavellian stratagems and deceitful policies. Another copy of this missive was made for Cromwell's son-in-law and Lilburne's 'sometimes much familiar greatly obliging friend', major-general Charles Fleetwood. Yet at Whitehall, the seat of government, few seem to have believed him. Instead there arose 'many and great jealousies' at the 'strange politick contrivance' of Lilburne having turned Quaker. Indeed, Cromwell apparently feared that Lilburne was planning to foment rebellion. Lilburne did not help matters by initially refusing to sign a public declaration that he would not take up arms against the government – something that Quaker leader George Fox had done when in custody. For though Lilburne regarded Fox as a 'precious man', his 'particular actions' were 'no rules' for Lilburne to walk by. Moreover, Lilburne felt that if he compromised just to 'avoid further persecution' then he would become nothing but the 'greatest and basest of hypocrites'.[18]

Away from Whitehall, an Essex-based Puritan clergyman and committed opponent of the Quakers suspected that Lilburne was engaged in pretence, and insinuated that his was merely an outward profession of faith.[19] Likewise, one Thomas Winterton published 13 queries intended to demonstrate that Lilburne's supposed conversion was but a 'meer Imagination, and quaking delusion'.[20] Besides questions raised by his adversaries, all Lilburne's 'old and familiar friends' were 'much troubled' and 'offended' by him.[21] Some Quakers, too, had been made uneasy by Lilburne's sudden embrace of their faith and, to assure themselves that this was no superficial convincement, resolved to accept him as one of their own once he had shown willingness to receive their teachings.[22] Consequently, at his own 'earnest desire', Lilburne issued a public declaration of his genuine 'owning' and 'living in' the *life and power of those divine and heavenly principles, professed by those spiritualized people called* Quakers'.[23] This was *The resurrection of John Lilburne, now a prisoner in Dover-Castle*, published initially in mid-May 1656, and then again, within about ten days, in a second revised and expanded edition.

For the early eighteenth-century Dutch Quaker historian William Sewel, Lilburne's conversion merited detailed discussion. Although mistaken as to the place and date of his death, Lilburne's eventual embrace of the 'Doctrine of the Truth' was configured as the culmination of a spiritual journey undertaken by an extraordinarily bold if 'very stiff and inflexible' man.[24] In the same vein, Quaker minister and biographer Henry Tuke contrasted the turbulent partisanship and 'irritable disposition' that marked the greater part of Lilburne's life with the 'calmness and meekness of his latter days' following adoption of Quaker principles.[25] So, too, did another nineteenth-century Quaker biographer, who juxtaposed the 'turbulent', 'undaunted spirit' of this lover of liberty with the 'degree of calmness' Lilburne found on softening his stout heart and humbly submitting to the 'government of Christ'.[26] Yet whereas Quaker scholars regarded Lilburne's peaceable end as a fitting final chapter in the 'stormy career' of a 'great political agitator',[27] twentieth-century North American advocates of democratic government saw it as an experience of defeat. In the words of Theodore Pease, 'the warrior was displaced by the mystic'; 'the crusader became a Quaker' as 'years of imprisonment' seemed to have broken Lilburne's vitality. Instead of forcing 'the world into justice and righteousness', he found only the consolation of 'patience and long-suffering'.[28] Similarly, for Joseph Frank, 'Lilburne's physically and mentally tired escape into the refuge of Quaker mysticism' represented an exchange of 'outward liberty' for 'inner light and inner security'.[29] Pauline Gregg employed the same tone, suggesting that her subject had 'abandoned his efforts to change the outward face of society', and that 'the violence of his passion' may have 'found its antidote' in Quaker quietism.[30]

Conversely, for Marxist heresiarchs as much as orthodox Marxists and socialists alike, this last episode in Lilburne's life signified the continuation of native radicalism by other means. Hence for Eduard Bernstein, when Lilburne joined the Quakers 'this step did not constitute a humble submission to the authorities'.[31] Henry Brailsford said much the same: moving from the Levellers' political programme to the Society of Friends was a 'natural development'.[32] So, too, did Christopher Hill: 'Lilburne's acceptance of Quakerism in 1655 … was a very different act for the ex-revolutionary than if he had been convinced after 1660.' In Hill's view, Lilburne even 'outdid the Quakers … by renouncing "carnal weapons of any kind whatsoever"'.[33] And it has to be said that the image of an unbowed Quaker Lilburne is convincing, since he still had some weapons available – namely his spirit, pen, and mouth.

In the remainder of this chapter I will explore the last three and a half years of Lilburne's life. The standard biography is Gregg's *Free-Born John*, which, while still valuable, needs updating. So I have drawn on a far wider range of sources, notably newsbooks and letters. The focus is on Lilburne's contrasting experiences in Jersey and Kent. The dominant themes are habeas corpus, defiance, and suffering. To conclude I will offer an assessment of the wider significance of Lilburne's personal trajectory from Leveller to Quaker.

II

On Thursday 23 March 1654, Cromwell and the Council of State issued a warrant to Colonel John Barkstead, lieutenant of the Tower of London, to transfer Lilburne under armed guard to Portsmouth. From there, once wind and weather permitted, he was transported by ship to Jersey, where by the beginning of May he was confined at Mont Orgueil (Mount Pride).[34] This 'ill-seated' castle, nestled 'dangerously amongst wild sunken rocks' and overlooking the harbour of Gorey, had capitulated in October 1651 to parliamentary forces under the command of Colonel James Heane, who afterwards became Jersey's governor.[35] Lilburne's quarters, which afforded him the opportunity to walk in nearby paths, were the same lodgings where his former associate William Prynne had previously been kept close prisoner.[36] For his part, Barkstead was reimbursed £13-8s.-7d. in expenses;[37] a small price for the government to pay since, in removing Lilburne to the Channel Islands, they sought to place his body in a legal vacuum. Because the Channel Islands used ancient Norman laws and were dominions outside the English realm, it was arguable whether the writ of habeas corpus extended there. Accordingly, the government's intention was to prevent Lilburne seeking another trial and thereby causing them further embarrassment.[38] Moreover, following the dissolution of the

Barebones Parliament in December 1653, all prisoners committed by the Council of State during the life of that parliament had to be tried in the court of Upper Bench on production of an habeas corpus, or else released. Which is why in early February 1654 several 'eminent persons' were set free – including William Walwyn, who had been imprisoned in the Tower; and Captain John Streater, who had been committed to the Gatehouse for publishing seditious pamphlets.[39]

Evidently the Protector and his Council knew their man, since Lilburne's friends immediately set about obtaining a writ of habeas corpus in Upper Bench. Shortly after the commencement of Easter term, a messenger was despatched with the writ to Jersey. Although Colonel Heane received him politely, he nonetheless refused to release Lilburne. So instead, the go-between returned with news of Lilburne's health – he was apparently 'well and merry' – together with an account of his encounter with the governor.[40] This was published by Lilburne's supporters as *A Declaration to the Free-born People of England* (1654). Asserting that the law and courts of justice ought to be the keys for opening prison doors, it acclaimed the writ of habeas corpus as 'the water of life, to revive a free Englishman from the Death of Imprisonment'.[41] For good measure, sympathetic journalists added that Lilburne comported himself with '*abundance of patience and humility*', insisting that he sought nothing more than '*the restoring of every free born man of England, to its ancient Rights and priviledges, and the perfect purging of the Law from all abuses and corruptions*'.[42]

Lilburne may have been out of sight, yet he was still not out of mind. Reportedly he attempted to send a letter to his 'very much afflicted wife', but it was intercepted.[43] Consequently he seems to have been deprived of 'pen, ink, and paper'.[44] More startling were the 'strange and various' reports circulating that Lilburne had been tried and executed in Jersey. Although most newsbooks dismissed them as groundless, *The Faithful Scout* suspected a ploy – perhaps to gauge the extent of Lilburne's popularity, or else to make the government unpopular.[45] *The true and perfect Dutch-Diurnall*, on the other hand, published a purported copy of the last will and testament of Lieutenant Colonel John Lilburne, gentleman of London, aged 39:

> I bequeath my soul into the hands of the almighty, in whom I have put my trust, hoping by the merits of Christ Iesus, my only Lord and Saviour, that I shal be saved from hel and damnation. And that I shal be wrapt up unto the third heaven, prepared for all true believers. And for my body, in regard it hath indured a fiery trial, and hath been patient, and long suffering, It is my desire my friend Cornelius may have the burial hereof.[46]

This prompted a witty *Last Will & Testament*, which appeared in late May. It counselled that Lilburne's body should be 'carefully imbalmed' and 'decently wrapped in a double sheet of Lead' to prevent mutiny and earthquakes. Prynne was bequeathed Lilburne's brains and skull; the lips went to a sister to communicate 'holy salutations' to her fellow female saints; and the eyes to Argus (the many-eyed giant of Greek mythology), so that 'they may never more squint after the applause of people, nor the pomp, riches and glory of a transitory and fading world'. It concluded with a mock elegy:

> *All Faction ends in Death, Ambition, Pride,*
> *Death humbles all; had these with* Lilburn *died*
> *He had been famous, and dy'd full well,*
> *And scap'd his Anagram,* I burn in Hell.[47]

Mistaking rumour and parody for fact, the Venetian secretary erroneously conveyed news on 29 May that Lilburne, 'a man of singular ability and opposed to the present government', had been executed in prison without trial – supposedly because he possessed some manuscripts highly critical of the Protectorate. Cromwell, however, was not yet rid of this 'open enemy of his supremacy and of the tranquillity of the Commonwealth'.[48] Indeed, at the beginning of Trinity term, another attempt was made to get an habeas corpus in Upper Bench. It could not be granted, though, since it was determined that English law did not apply in Jersey. Hence there could be no appeal to the courts in Westminster, only to Parliament or the Protector.[49] For good measure, the Council of State instructed Heane that he was not to let Lilburne leave the island without special order.[50] On learning that he had been denied a second habeas corpus, Lilburne reportedly sent a remonstrance to Heane asserting 'the Rights and priviledges of a free born English-man, and that it is their sole and absolute birth right to claim and enjoy the benefit of the Law'.[51]

Following the summoning of the first Protectorate Parliament at the beginning of September 1654, a committee was established to investigate the use and abuse of habeas corpus and certiorari. On 4 November a petition submitted by certain Doctors of Civil Law on behalf of their profession was read in the House of Commons and then committed to the committee for consideration. Lilburne's case was most likely discussed since *The Faithful Scout* hoped for good tidings from Jersey.[52] On 10 November letters from Jersey were received certifying that Lilburne had disputed with an officer at Mont Orgueil who seemed to have belittled his 'present sufferings'. Recounting the story of some 'godly Martyrs' in Prague who, on the eve of their execution had been taunted by a 'great Papist' (the 'wretched Papist' was subsequently poisoned by his own cook), Lilburne drew on Isaiah 28:22 to warn 'it is not good for any to mock or scorn those which are in tribulation, lest their bands be made strong'.[53] Then, in mid-December, a number of 'well-affected' citizens petitioned Cromwell on Lilburne's behalf, imploring that 'long-suffering' gentleman's restoration to liberty. While one newsbook expected Lilburne's imminent return from banishment on taking an engagement to live peaceably and quietly, others doubted he would submit.[54] Even so, in early January a message was apparently sent to Lilburne outlining the conditions that would permit his return to London.[55] Lilburne's response was a letter to his friends asking them to make further entreaties on his behalf so that he might have 'benefit in the Law'.[56]

Little else is known of Lilburne's life on Jersey except that Heane was commanded to propagate the Gospel in the West Indies to weaken the 'power of the

Pope and Antichrist'. Heane, however, was killed in action at Hispaniola.[57] He was replaced by Colonel Robert Gibbon, who was appointed both Jersey's new governor and receiver general by patent on 14 March 1655.[58] Like his predecessor, Gibbon requested reimbursement for money spent on feeding and clothing Lilburne. The latter was very necessary since, at the beginning of winter, Lilburne still had only the summer suit he had worn at his trial at the Old Bailey, leaving him cruelly 'exposed to the extremity of cold'.[59] All the same, Lilburne was to claim he had been in 'great distress' and was attended to by a 'moral, honest, carefull, and industrious' old nurse called Elizabeth Crome.[60] Presumably not much had changed since Prynne had been kept close prisoner at this same remote location:

> *Mount Orgueil Castle* is a lofty pile,
> Within the Easterne parts of *Jersy Isle*,
> Seated upon a *Rocke*, full large & high,
> Close by the *Sea-shore*, next to *Normandie*;
> Neere to a *Sandy Bay*, where boats doe ride
> Within a *Peere*, safe both from Wind and Tide.
> Three parts thereof the *flowing Seas* surround,
> The fourth (North-west-wards) is firme rockie ground.[61]

The only noteworthy incident was in early April 1655 when it was reported that Lilburne had attempted to have a package smuggled into England but that the courier threw it overboard before being apprehended. This was subsequently embellished with news that the packet had been recovered and that a letter inveighing against Cromwell was seized at the same time.[62] It may be connected with a purported remonstrance by Lilburne concerning the *Law and Liberties of the People of England*, in which he supposedly declared that he loved Jesus and his country's liberties more than all his possessions, friends and relatives – even himself.[63] But the suggestion that he had finally 'made his Peace' and was expected home shortly was ill-informed.[64] Not for Lilburne the course of several cavaliers who in June resolved to take a new oath giving a 'further engagement to be true to the present Government'.[65]

On Wednesday 4 July 1655 Gibbon wrote to Cromwell from Elizabeth Castle off St Helier (just over five miles from Mont Orgueil). Here he recounted how the previous Saturday, accompanied by Lilburne's father-in-law, Henry Dewell (of Walton-upon-Thames, Surrey), he had ridden out to visit Lilburne. They had had a long conversation with him, but to little purpose. So on the Monday they tried once more. Yet Lilburne remained 'the very same man' as before. Despite the endeavours of his elderly father-in-law, he would not acquiesce to the state's authority. Instead, Lilburne insisted that his liberty could only be achieved through recourse to the law. When Dewell pressed him to stop trying to have all things his own way and to refrain from reproachful words, Lilburne replied that 'the lawe was his way' – but that he was prepared to submit to arbitration so as to settle his 'difference' with Cromwell. Gibbon, however, suspected that Lilburne would comply only if the outcome vindicated him, and indeed felt he had good cause to be freed of Lilburne, for he was 'more trouble' then ten like William Ashburnham (a royalist prisoner recently transferred to Jersey). Fortunately for Gibbon, Lilburne had proved amenable to a suggestion of which he wholeheartedly approved, namely removal to the Isle of Wight. In Gibbon's view, this was the likeliest way of subduing 'his spirit to be meek and quiet' since it was close enough to the mainland for some of Lilburne's 'soberest and wisest' friends to visit. And they might succeed where others had failed in persuading him to submit.[66]

On Saturday 7 July 1655 Gibbon wrote to Cromwell again, adding that he forgot to mention that Lilburne had requested that his own father, Richard Lilburne (of Thickley Punchardon, County Durham), be allowed to visit. Besides seeking guidance on the matter – Gibbon feared they might plot in secret if allowed to meet unsupervised – he also supplied further interesting details. Lilburne was being kept close prisoner because of his 'ill language' and threatening behaviour. He may even have attempted to persuade the garrison to his cause. This would chime both with a newsbook account and Gibbon's complaint against the 'many disorders' committed by his soldiers as well as the various troubles with which he had to contend. Moreover, Gibbon mentioned that he had offered Lilburne the opportunity to venture outside for the good of his health and spirit, but that Lilburne had refused if the condition was that he walked accompanied by his keeper like 'a dogg att his heeles'.[67]

A week later *The Faithful Scout* reported that Cromwell had ordered that the engagement and proposals be sent to Lilburne. Free-born John's signature would set him at liberty – 'a thing much desired', considering the heinousness of 'burying men alive in gaols'.[68] Then on Saturday 31 July 1655 both Lilburne's wife and father petitioned the Protector. Richard attempted to excuse his son's 'violent and unadvised expressions', claiming that, since he knew him better than anyone else, he was confident that Lilburne's 'distemper' stemmed 'only from restraint, hard usage, and afflictions'. Accordingly Richard requested the opportunity to speak with his uncontrollable son so that he might be persuaded to act peaceably and thus secure his liberty. For her part Elizabeth recounted the many 'greivous afflictions' she and her husband had suffered over the years, claiming that Lilburne's 'sences, health & life' were 'endangered' by the extremely 'severe' conditions of his imprisonment. Elizabeth therefore pleaded for leniency, insisting that her husband was not a violent man and that, if granted clemency, he would be neither aggressive nor abusive. She concluded by imploring Cromwell to end Lilburne's isolation and give him the opportunity to speak with his friends, alleging that he was no longer dangerous since his 'impatient spirit' was 'tyred and wearied out with long & sore afflictions'. In a dramatic gesture, she offered her life as surety, avowing that Lilburne at liberty would not disturb the state. These two petitions were read but no formal order issued.[69]

In late August Lilburne was reportedly 'in health' but still unlikely to gain his liberty, prompting *Certain Passages* to muse whether death was preferable to spending the rest of one's days in 'hard captivity'.[70] Yet by September something had changed: Cromwell interceded following Elizabeth's entreaties and endeavours to bring her husband back to England.⁷¹ That month it was reported that Lilburne was to be transferred to Dover Castle, where he would benefit from wholesome air and the comfort of his friends. Moreover, Cromwell told Elizabeth that John would be brought over on the next ship leaving Jersey.⁷² Accordingly on 11 October 1655 Captain Lambert Cornelius informed the Council of State while moored at Dover aboard the ten-gun frigate *Cornelian* that he had arrived on from Jersey with Lilburne and a cargo of several hogsheads of cider.⁷³ Although there was a common gaol in Dover Castle, not to mention a stinking dungeon under the bell tower called 'the Hole', one tradition located Lilburne's confinement to an 'old dilapidated tower' just outside the King's Gate and Bridge – probably Norfolk's Tower.⁷⁴ Towards the end of October a newsletter suggested that Lilburne had been moved there so that the authorities could keep a close eye on him.⁷⁵ Yet Dover may also have had another carefully considered advantage. It being a cinque port, there had been disputes as to whether it fell outside the bounds of habeas corpus. During the Stuart monarchy the answer was no, because habeas corpus was a prerogative writ. Even so, there may have been sufficient legal ambiguity to deny Lilburne trial should he pursue that course of action.⁷⁶

III

In *The Resurrection* Lilburne recounted that while imprisoned at Jersey he had lengthy discussions about the Quakers with Major William Harding of Weymouth, Dorset. Harding was one of several 'highflowne' army officers who had prevented the apprehension of Edward Sexby at Portland in February 1655, and was also a commissioner for compounding for Jersey. He treated Lilburne with 'kindness and tenderness' and their conversation had continued both aboard ship and at Harding's house in Weymouth, where Lilburne lodged en route to Dover.⁷⁷ Once at Dover Castle, Lilburne sent for a local shoemaker named Luke Howard to speak with him about religion. According to a Quaker source, Lilburne asked Howard:

> 'I pray, sir, of what Opinion are you?'
> L:H. answered, 'None'.
> Which struck him into that Silence for sometime, That he could not speake. And then he said to L:H., 'What must I say, & how must I speake?'
> L:H. answered, 'Thou mayest speak what is in thy owne Minde, & after thy owne Manner'. Who replied againe, 'You say, you are of noe Opinion.'
> L:H. said, 'I doe say soe, For really I am of no Opinion.'

Uncharacteristically at a loss for words, Lilburne begged Howard to visit him another time, which he did.⁷⁸ The problematic nature of this idealised account aside, Howard was himself a recent Quaker convert and only a few months old in the faith. He was formerly a Baptist who had been dipped by William Kiffin in the River Neckinger one icy February day.⁷⁹ Since Kiffin had a long standing association with Lilburne,⁸⁰ it is likely that Lilburne knew of Howard prior to his arrival in Dover and that he purposely sought his company so as to learn more about those people '*contemptibly and scornfully*' called Quakers. In a letter, dated

4 December 1655, to his wife Elizabeth, Lilburne called Howard his endeared 'spiritual, & faithful friend'. Furthermore, Howard was an 'understanding, spiritually knowing, & single hearted' Aquila to the poor, despised Priscilla that had instructed Lilburne when he was in 'great straits' during the Bishops' time. By implication Lilburne was therefore a latter-day Paul (Acts 18:1–3). Indeed, like Paul, Lilburne had 'fallen down' with 'astonishment and amazement' 'flat at the feet of Jesus' and was henceforth 'willing to be guided and directed by the heavenly wisdom of Jesus'. Yet he was also like the centurion Cornelius, standing ready '*to hear and obey all things that the lively voice of God speaking in my soul shal require of me*' (Acts 10).[81]

Before 10 November 1655, Lilburne possessed a two-volume collection of Quaker writings consisting of almost 1,700 printed pages. Most likely this had been supplied by Howard, with additional Quaker books sent to him by Harding. Within less than a month Lilburne had read '*extraordinary much of those two volumes*', so much so that this '*serious reading*' had been '*most convincingly, instructive*' for his soul. Three works merited particular mention. Firstly, a tract by that 'strong, or tall man in Christ' James Nayler, entitled *Something further in answer to John Jacksons book called Strength in weaknesse* (1655). Then, two pieces by that 'precious and divine soul' William Dewsbury, namely *The Discovery of the great enmity of the Serpent against the seed of the Woman* (1655) and *The Discovery of Mans Returne To his First Estate* (1654).[82] Interestingly, Lilburne reckoned Jackson an endeared friend of old acquaintance, a '*tall Cedar*' and 'a great professor of Religion'. He was also familiar with Jackson's *Strength in Weakness* (1655), which he had received by post from Elizabeth and which he considered the 'strongest and rationalest' response he had ever read in the controversies with his 'endeared freinds called Quakers'.[83]

Yet Lilburne's Quaker faith probably resulted in marital tension – especially since Elizabeth may have been a Baptist.[84] Having quarrelled with his wife at their last meeting in Dover Castle on 10 November and then reconciled, he instructed the publisher and bookseller Giles Calvert to send Elizabeth two bound volumes of 'precious' Quaker writings, with one intended 'principally for answering *Objections*'. On 21 November John wrote a letter to her, to which Elizabeth responded a week later from Whitehall. She concluded by exhorting her husband:

> *My Dear, Retain a sober patient spirit within thee, which I am confident thou shalt see shall be of more force to recover thee, then all thy keen mettal hath been; I hope God is doing a work upon thee and me too, as shall make us study ourselves more then we have done.*

Elizabeth also related how, on parting from John, she had endured a dangerous journey along the River Thames. At Whitehall she toiled ceaselessly to secure her husband's liberty, prompting John to request that she desist from needlessly expending her 'earthly strength'. He had now found 'a more clear, plain, and evident knowledge' of both God and himself, wishing only to be reunited with Elizabeth and his 'sweet' and 'dearly beloved' children. Nonetheless, the couple faced financial problems. To save money, John discharged his old nurse. He also '*contentedly*' subsisted on a diet of bread, cheese, and small beer. Yet for all their difficulties, John still loved his wife, avowing Elizabeth to be the 'greatest & dearest' of all his 'earthly delights and joyes'.[85]

On 5 December 1655 Lilburne wrote to his friend William Harding, informing him that he had been spiritually humbled. Henceforth 'the light of God' speaking in his soul would be his 'true teacher and guide'. Moreover, Lilburne was at present 'dead' not only to his earlier nature's 'reason, wit, wisdom, and desires' but also to his 'old bustling' ways.[86] Besides Harding, Lilburne corresponded with friends both old and new, notably an 'eminent' Quaker in London. By mid-December his conversion became more widely known. *Publick Intelligencer* reported that since he had 'put on the garb of a Quaker', Lilburne had 'fallen into a more tame humour'. Certain Quakers, however, considered his conversion hasty, and determined to accept him only once he had shown willingness to take up the cross with them.[87]

Meanwhile Elizabeth continued to plead her husband's case before Cromwell. Fearful of John's fate, this 'poor afflicted woman' implored him in a 'vehement manner' to sign an engagement that he would not bear arms against the Protectorate. But stubborn as ever, Lilburne refused. Even so, at some point he renounced 'all outward wars, and carnal sword fightings & fleshly bustlings and contests', declaring the 'spiritual Sword' to be the only weapon wielded by the 'glorious, conquering, spiritual King' against the 'powers of the Prince of Darkness', for 'carnal weapons' of any kind had no place in Christ's spiritual kingdom. Accordingly, from his 'innocent, and every way causeless captivity' in Dover Castle, Lilburne affirmed he would no longer use a temporal sword nor join with those that did so. Adding that he had received a 'new, or inward spiritual name' (Revelation 2:17), this protestation together with some correspondence was published by Calvert in mid-May 1656 as *The Resurrection of John Lilburne*.[88]

In a second revised and expanded edition of *The Resurrection*, Lilburne noted in a letter to his '*old beloved friend*' Elizabeth Honywood, dated 18 May 1656, that his wife and children – John, Elizabeth, and Benoni – had recently come to live in Dover. Elizabeth Honywood was the wife of Edward Honywood of Elmsted, Kent and the daughter of Lilburne's friend and ally Sir John Maynard.[89] Since one of Elizabeth Honywood's relations by marriage was a Merchant Taylor originating from Elmsted called Benoni Honywood, it is possible that John and Elizabeth Lilburne had reaffirmed their links with this family through the naming of their youngest son, Benoni, who had been born at Stoke Newington, Middlesex on 7 April 1654.[90] In this letter Lilburne also recounted how the Honywoods had made the roughly 15-mile journey from Elmsted to visit him at Dover, adding that his gaoler William Spicer was the brother of their neighbours Martha and Robert Gardner.[91] A further letter indicates that about the same time Lilburne became engaged in a religious controversy with Robert Barrington, Jeremiah Elfreth, and other members of a Baptist congregation meeting in Dover. Since Quakers denied the validity of the sacrament of Baptism, Lilburne consequently rejected water baptism as a mere 'empty, outside, vain, traditionall, humane, invented' form. Interestingly, responding to 31 'confused and ignorant' queries contained in some '*blasphemous Scriblings*' sent to him in a letter by Elfreth, Lilburne referred his disputant to an 'excellent and very much usefull' book by James Parnell called *The Watcher* (1655).[92]

Afterwards Lilburne was involved in a disputation at Dover Castle with Francis Duke, who accused him of erroneously maintaining six particular doctrinal positions:

> First, You deny the Trinity.
> Secondly, You deny the Scriptures to be the word of God.
> Thirdly, You deny there is any word of God, but that light which is in man.
> Fourthly, You affirm ... that that light in man, is as the light is in God himself, in whom is no darkness at all.
> Fifthly, You affirm, the Scriptures are true, as a witness-bearer, or declarer of that light in man, which you call Christ.
> Sixthly, You affirm Gods word, the light in man, was long before the Scriptures.

Duke concluded by suggesting that *The Resurrection* should be retitled '*The perverting of John Lilburn, in order to his destruction, if God in mercy prevent it not*'.[93] Similar charges were made by another antagonist, Thomas Winterton, who published 13 queries intended to demonstrate that Lilburne's supposed conversion was but a 'meer Imagination, and quaking delusion'.[94] On this occasion Lilburne was defended by an 'able and savoury soul', Richard Hubberthorne, who affirmed that Lilburne was plainly 'confident in his Religion' and that 'God owned him in opposing many of the unjust powers of the Nation'.[95]

Around August 1656, Luke Howard invited Lilburne to a Quaker meeting which was probably held in Howard's house. If a later account is reliable then it appears that the deputy governor of Dover Castle, Thomas Wilson, granted Lilburne parole so he could attend. Also present was George Harrison, a young man whose declaration and prayer Lilburne 'liked well', although 'his Wisdome was aboue it'. On leaving the meeting, Harrison ran after Lilburne, reproaching him for being 'too high for Truth'. These words stunned Lilburne, and he never forgot them, 'but liued & died in ye profession of ye Truth'.[96] Certainly by this time Lilburne had developed an extensive network of Quaker contacts. These included three 'deare & precious' friends: Luke Howard, John Higgins, and John Stubbs. Higgins was a former Baptist and was described as Howard's servant while Stubbs had been a soldier.[97] Another 'very faithfull & dearely' beloved friend was Henry Clark of Southwark, who had been present during Lilburne's trial at the Old Bailey in summer 1653 and who, as a keen continuator of John Foxe's *Acts and Monuments*, would list Lilburne among those who had cruelly suffered at the hands of persecuting bishops and clergy.[98] In addition, around March 1657, Lilburne met twice with Hubberthorne, who informed George Fox that he found Lilburne:

> zealus & forward for the truth. He hath a sight & comph'hention which is deepe. Hee sees that the truth comprehends all and hath in loue unto it & desire to ataine it.[99]

During spring 1657 Lilburne also encountered John Harwood of Yorkshire, who subsequently embarked for France but was soon imprisoned in the Bastille, from where he sent greetings to Lilburne and other friends.[100]

On 27 May 1657 Lilburne wrote to Margaret Fell from his lodging at John Cocks' in Woolwich, Kent. Evidently he had been granted parole and in this letter to his 'dearly beloved' and 'faithful' friend Lilburne named a host of Quakers: John Bolton, Edward Burrough, Henry Clark, William Dewsbury, George Fox, John Higgins, Luke Howard, Stephen Hubbersty, Richard Hubberthorne, Humphrey Norton, Thomas Rawlinson, Gerrard Roberts, John Slee, Amos Stoddart, and John Stubbs.[101] The purpose of Lilburne's letter was to request Fell's assistance in his dispute with Anthony Pearson. Originating from Lancashire and afterwards acquiring manors in Cumberland, Northumberland and County Durham, Pearson had served as a Justice of the Peace before becoming a Quaker. Besides visiting and corresponding with Margaret Fell, defending George Fox, and establishing a monthly meeting in Durham, Pearson also acted as secretary and estate manager for Lilburne's long-time adversary, Sir Arthur Hesilrige.[102] Lilburne accused Pearson of behaving in a wilful, wicked, headstrong, and plainly treacherous manner. According to Lilburne, some five or six years previously Hesilrige had forcibly seized Lilburne's lands in County Durham and then settled some tenants on them. Acting on behalf of his 'master' Hesilrige – and without Lilburne's authority or consent – Pearson had subsequently and in the most 'wicked' manner conveyed Lilburne's estate back to Lilburne's wife Elizabeth and their children, as though he had a real and unquestionable legal right to do so. Unsurprisingly Lilburne quarrelled with his family for acceding to the arrangement in what was a 'tormenting contest'. Moreover, extensive correspondence (nine letters from Lilburne, five 'wicked, foolish, false, rediculous, & contradicting' replies from Pearson) had failed to resolve the issue, prompting Lilburne to seek a meeting with Pearson in London. There, before an assembly of Quaker judges, he hoped that the truth would be heard and sin reproved.[103] Although there is no evidence of such an encounter, Lilburne was later reported to have preached in the Quaker manner on Sundays at Woolwich and Eltham.[104] Nonetheless, on learning that Lilburne had been granted parole by the deputy governor of Dover Castle, Cromwell issued a summons requiring Free-born John to return to captivity.[105]

Following Lilburne's death and burial, the copyright of two works was entered in the Stationers' Company register. One was a biography to be issued by John Stafford at 'The George' near Fleet Bridge, entitled *An exact and true narration of the life and death of that famous & most unsatisfied and unbounded person*. The other, for Richard Harper at 'The Bible and Harp' in Smithfield, was *A funeral exercise or sermon, spoken at ye solemnization of ye obsequies of that precious Saint and dearly beloved brother*.[106] There is no indication that either pamphlet was published, but in 1659 *Lilburns Ghost, With a Whip in One Hand, to Scourge Tyrants Out of Authority* was printed for the Fifth Monarchist bookseller Livewell Chapman.[107] That same tumultuous year, another writer called on brave and noble-spirited Englishmen to meet every Thursday or Sunday morning at Lilburne's tomb so that they might 'comfort and encourage' one another in doing the Lord's work and defending the '*Good Old Cause*'.[108] Elsewhere in Hampton, New Hampshire a Quaker was fined £10 for possessing two Quaker books, one of which was Lilburne's *Resurrection*.[109]

As for Lilburne's widow, she gave birth to a child named Bethia ('daughter of God').[110] On 4 November 1657 Elizabeth petitioned Cromwell in the hope that, out of 'tender pitty and compassion to her and her poore inosent children', he would repeal an act of Parliament of 30 January 1652 that had placed multiple fines on Lilburne's estate amounting to £7,000, of which £3,000 was assigned to the Commonwealth and £2,000 to Hesilrige. Because of his 'very greate tenderness' towards Elizabeth, Cromwell persuaded Hesilrige to return her the estate he had taken from her. Cromwell also granted Elizabeth a pension, without which she might have 'perished'.[111] On 11 February 1658 Elizabeth was granted letters of administration to oversee Lilburne's estate.[112] Then, following the Protector's death, she petitioned his son and successor on 21 January 1659. Here she lamented her 'manifold' extreme sufferings and almost continual sorrows for the past 17 years, as well as the unreasonableness of some tenants.[113] And for good reason, since a yeoman named William Huntington initiated proceedings against her in Chancery, alleging that Elizabeth had been 'plotting and contriving' to 'vex and trouble' him. The suit concerned a farmstead in Billingham, County Durham that had formerly belonged to Durham Cathedral. On the sale of the cathedral's dean and chapter lands, John Lilburne had purchased the reversion and inheritance, compelling Huntington to lease the property from Elizabeth for an annual rent of £18-15s.-7d. This long standing dispute had initially been referred to Hesilrige and Henry Marten for arbitration.[114] So it was doubtless with settlement in mind that, on 5 February 1659, Hesilrige initiated a motion on behalf of Lilburne's widow in the Commons. Accordingly Elizabeth's petition was read before the House and referred to a committee. After brief debate it was agreed to annul the act and discharge the fines on Lilburne's estate. This was resolved on 15 August 1659. In addition, Elizabeth's weekly allowance of £2 payable from the public exchequer was continued, temporarily supplemented with £100 paid by the Council of State. In exchange Elizabeth was required to deliver all papers in her custody relating to the matters for which the fines had been imposed. These were to be burnt.[115]

IV

Clearly Lilburne's health must have suffered from imprisonment in the Fleet, Oxford Castle, Newgate, the Tower of London, Mont Orgueil, and Dover Castle, since he died prematurely. On the other hand, given conflicting reports about his physical condition, it is possible that Elizabeth slightly overstated the extent of her husband's plight so as to secure him better treatment. But whatever the state of his body, Lilburne's spirit was evidently unbroken. Not for him a retreat into passivity during the last three and a half years of his life. On the contrary, Lilburne's activities reportedly ranged from preaching and disputing points of law and religious doctrine to quarrelling and reconciling with his long-suffering wife, not to mention writing. While the importance of publishing and petitioning for

Lilburne and his supporters has rightly been emphasised, more attention should be given to Lilburne's epistles – especially as a mode of communication during his various incarcerations. Indeed, his network of correspondents stretched from Dorset to Durham and the list of people he wrote to and/or received letters from is long: Elizabeth Lilburne, Major William Harding, Giles Calvert, Elizabeth Honywood, Robert Barrington, Jeremiah Elfreth, Mr Spire, Margaret Fell, Anthony Pearson, Roger Harper (probably of Harraton, County Durham), Martin Richmond (of County Durham), and several unidentified friends, possibly including Lieutenant Edward Tucker. Among the Quakers, these may have included his 'deare freind' George Fox and that 'savoury soul' Richard Hubberthorne.[116]

As to the wider significance of Lilburne's personal trajectory from Leveller to Quaker, there has been brief but lively debate. Thus Henry Brailsford thought it a 'natural development' that 'many of the Levellers found a spiritual refuge in the Society of Friends', while Christopher Hill assumed that 'many former Levellers became Quakers'.[117] These appear to be overstatements, however, and Barry Reay was doubtless closer to the mark when he found 'no evidence of any substantial continuity' between Levellers and Quakers.[118] For although Lilburne did not tread a solitary path, documented Leveller adherents turned Quaker are few and far between. The most likely is Christopher Cheesman, who had served as a cornet in Captain William Bray's troop and whose pamphlet *The Lamb Contending with the Lion* (1649) had been commended by Lilburne.[119] Another possibility is Edward Billing, who had served as cornet in Scotland before penning *A Word of Reproof, and Advice to my Late Fellow-Souldiers and Officers* (1659).[120] Then there was Captain George Bishop of Bristol, who had served as secretary to the Council of State's committee for examinations, and may be the Putney debater Captain Bishop.[121] A further possibility is George Fox 'the younger' in 'truth', who wrote several pieces in 1659 addressed to the parliament and army.[122] Yet his namesake condemned 'Levelling' as an earthly practice: those 'who goe under a colour of Levelling we deny'. Elsewhere Fox pronounced the 'word of the Lord' unto those called Levellers:

> you had a flash in your minde, a simplicitie, and your minds run into the earth and smothered it, and so got up into presumption, and you would [have] had unity and fellowship there, before life was raised up in you, so that withers, and much of it is withered as it is manifest and with the light, that is condemned, in which light is the unity of both those conditions.[123]

Just as Fox denounced the Ranters in manuscript, print, and person, so was he keen to disassociate Quakers from Levellers. And for good reason, since hostile observers regarded Quakers as the scummy residue of Levellers, Diggers, Seekers, Ranters, atheists, and whatnot.[124] Hence John Ward, vicar of Stratford-upon-Avon, concluded that 'severall levellers setled into Quakers'.[125] More specifically, Quakers were accused of promoting community of goods and being 'down-right Levellers' who 'affirmed that there ought to be no distinction of Estates, but an universall parity'.[126] 'Magistrate, People, Husband, Wife, Parents, Children,

Master, Servant': all were supposedly alike for the Quakers.[127] Accordingly an MP denounced Quakers as a 'growing evil' espousing a 'plausible way; all levellers against magistracy and propriety'.[128] In the same vein, writing from Perth to General George Monck in April 1657, a senior army officer explained that he had discharged one of his subordinates because he had become a Quaker. This 'sottish stupid generation' were 'blasphemous herritickes' who would corrupt the rank-and-file with their 'levellinge principle' since they neither valued the scriptures, ministry, magistracy, nor anything else.[129] Little wonder that, when examined on the charge of blasphemy in January 1653, James Nayler was asked: '*Wast thou not at Burford among the Levellers?*'[130]

Though Lilburne rejected the pejorative term Leveller,[131] it is noteworthy that, to my knowledge, no one explicitly linked him with the Levellers during the last three and half years of his life. Even within a few years of his death there are only a handful of references.[132] When Cromwell recalled in a speech to Parliament on 4 September 1654 that the 'magistracy of the nation' had been 'almost trampled under foot, under despite and contempt, by men of Levelling principles', he was invoking the ghost of a defeated movement; an alarming alternative to his Protectorate.[133] Yet it is also a reminder that Lilburne was still feared – not so much as the former leader of a fragmented faction but as a charismatic, uncompromising figure with an extensive network of supporters who would never bend the knee to Cromwell. Puritan, Leveller, Quaker, backwards and forwards, the same Free-born John.

Notes

1 Friends House Library, London, Portfolio 40/109, printed in *Journal of Friends Historical Society*, 27 (1930), pp. 25–26, and in *The Carlyle Letters* online [http://carlyleletters.duke-upress.edu//content/vol22/#lt-18480221-TC-TWJR-01].
2 *Mercurius Politicus*, no. 379 (27 August–3 September 1657), p. 1597, reprinted in *Cromwelliana: A Chronological Detail of Events in which Oliver Cromwell was Engaged; from the Year 1642 to His Death, 1658* (1810), p. 168; Anon., *The Selfe afflicter lively described in the whole course of the life of Mr. John Lilburn* (1657), p. 12; The National Archive: Public Records Office (TNA: PRO), SP 18/157A, fol. 129a; *Callender of State Papers Domestic (CSPD) 1657–58*, p. 148.
3 Kent History and Library Centre, N/FQz/2, p. 13, printed in Norman Penney (ed.), '*The First Publishers of Truth'. Being early records (now first printed) of the introduction of Quakerism into the counties of England and Wales* (1907), p. 145.
4 TNA:PRO, E 317/Kent/18; TNA: PRO, E 121/2/11: Kent, no. 19; TNA: PRO, C 54/3745 no. 28, mem. 5; Daniel Lysons, *The Environs of London* (4 vols., 1796–1800), pp. 394–403; Ariel Hessayon, '*Gold Tried in the Fire': The Prophet TheaurauJohn Tany and the English Revolution* (2007), p. 202.
5 Quoted in Ian J. Gentles, 'Rich, Nathaniel (*d.* 1700x02)', *ODNB*; FHL, William Caton MSS III 66, fol. 156.
6 Sir Henry Ellis (ed.), *The obituary of Richard Smyth*, Camden Society (1849), p. 25; John Dauncey, *An exact history of the several changes of government* (1660), p. 200.
7 John Strype, *A Survey of the Cities of London and Westminster*, www.hrionline.ac.uk/strype/TransformServlet?page=book3_121, Maureen Bell, 'Simmonds, Martha (*bap.* 1624, *d.* 1665)', *ODNB*.
8 *Mercurius Politicus*, no. 379, pp. 1597–98; *The Publick Intelligencer*, no. 98 (31 August – 7 September 1657), pp. 1874–75; Anon., *Selfe afflicter*, pp. 12–13.

9 William Winstanley, *England's Worthies* (1660), pp. 522–25; John Lilburne, *The resolved mans Resolution* (1647), p. 11; Pauline Gregg, *Free-Born John: A Biography of John Lilburne* (1961; reprinted, 2000), pp. 116, 153.
10 G.E. Briscoe Eyre, H.R. Plomer and C.R. Rivington (eds.), *A Transcript of the Registers of the worshipful Company of Stationers from 1640 to 1708* (3 vols., 1913–14), vol. 2, p. 151.
11 John Rushworth, *Historical Collections of private passages of state* (8 vols., 1721), vol. 2, p. 468; cf. R[obert] B[urton] [pseud. = Nathaniel Crouch], *The history of Oliver Cromwel* (1698), p. 108.
12 Archivio di Stato di Firenze, Florence, Mediceo del Principato, 4204, fol. 823r-v, Giovanni Salvetti to Giambattista Gondi (London, 21 September 1657). I am very grateful to Stefano Villani for the reference and to Lorenza Gianfrancesco for the translation.
13 Anon., *Selfe afflicter*, p. 14.
14 James Howell, *Paroimographia Proverbs* (1659), p. 7 [fourth century]; James Howell, *A new English grammar* (1662), p. 151; Rushworth, *Historical Collections*, vol. 2, p. 468; Anthony Wood, *Athenae Oxonienses* (2 vols., 1691–92), vol. 2, col. 102; *Biographia Britannica* (6 vols., 1747–66), vol. 5, p. 2961.
15 Winstanley, *England's Worthies*, p. 525; Dauncey, *Exact history*, pp. 200–1; James Heath, *A brief chronicle of the late Intestine War in the Three Kingdoms* (1663), pp. 3–4; Slingsby Bethel, *The world's mistake in Oliver Cromwell* (1668), pp. 11–12; Edward Hyde, *The history of the rebellion and civil wars in England*, ed. W. Dunn Macray (6 vols., Oxford, 1888), vol. 5, pp. 307–8.
16 John Evelyn, *Numismata* (1697), pp. 170–71.
17 Anon., *The History of King-Killers* (1720), vol. 2, p. 75.
18 John Lilburne, *The resurrection of John Lilburne, now a prisoner in Dover-Castle* (2nd edn., 1656), p. 9; H. Larry Ingle, *First Among Friends. George Fox & the Creation of Quakerism* (New York, 1994), pp. 121–22.
19 John Stalham, *The reviler rebuked* (1657), pp. 280–81.
20 Thomas Winterton, *The chasing the young Quaking Harlot Out of the City* (1656), title-page, pp. 17–19.
21 Lilburne, *Resurrection*, p. 1.
22 Worcester College, Oxford, MS Clarke 27, fol. 150r, printed in Charles Firth (ed.), *The Clarke Papers*, Camden Society (4 vols., 1891–1901), vol. 3, p. 62.
23 Lilburne, *Resurrection*, p. 1.
24 William Sewel, *The History of the Rise, Increase, and Progress of the Christian People called Quakers* (1722, 3rd edn., Philadelphia, 1728), pp. 120–23; cf. John Whiting, *A Catalogue of Friends books; written by many of the People, called Quakers, from the beginning or first appearance of the said people* (London, 1708), p. 91.
25 Henry Tuke, *Biographical Notices of members of the Society of Friends* (2 vols., York, 1815), vol. 2, pp. 93, 100, 106; cf. FHL, Temporary MS 745/HR3 [Robson MSS], pp. 48–54, 'Biography of John Lilburne', which was largely derived from Tuke's account.
26 Anon., *Brief memoirs of early Friends. No. 4. John Lilburne* (York, 1847), pp. 1, 4, 5–6, 11 [FHL, vol. 370/46 no. 23].
27 Joseph Smith, *A Descriptive Catalogue of Friends' books* (2 vols., 1867), vol. 2, pp. 110, 123; William Braithwaite, *The Beginnings of Quakerism to 1660* (1912; 2nd edn., revised Cambridge, 1955; reprinted, York, 1981), pp. 186, 366–67, 561, 572.
28 Theodore Pease, *The Leveller Movement: A Study in the History and Political Theory of the English Great Civil War* (Washington, DC, 1916; reprinted, Gloucester, MA, 1965), pp. 355–56.
29 Joseph Frank, *The Levellers: A History of the Writings of Three Seventeenth-Century Social Democrats (Lilburne, Overton and Walwyn)* (Cambridge, MA, 1955), pp. 241–42.
30 Gregg, *Free-Born John*, pp. 341, 343.
31 Eduard Bernstein, *Cromwell and Communism: Socialism and Democracy in the Great English Revolution* (1895), trans. H.J. Stenning (1930; reprinted, Nottingham, 1980), p. 231 n. 2; see also Mildred Gibb, *John Lilburne the Leveller. A Christian Democrat* (1947), pp. 334–36.
32 H.N. Brailsford, *The Levellers and the English Revolution* (1961; 2nd edn., ed. Christopher Hill, Nottingham, 1983), pp. 15, 637–39.

33 Christopher Hill, *The World Turned Upside Down. Radical Ideas during the English Revolution* (1972; Harmondsworth, 1984 edn.), p. 240; Christopher Hill, *The Experience of Defeat: Milton and some contemporaries* (1984), pp. 32, 131, 138.
34 *CSPD 1654*, pp. 16, 33–34, 44, 46, 50, 54, 433, 470; *Certain Passages of Every dayes Intelligence*, no. 13 (7–14 April 1654), pp. 99, 106; Frances Henderson (ed.), *The Clarke Papers volume 5: further selections from the papers of William Clarke*, Camden Society, fifth series, 27 (Cambridge, 2006), pp. 170, 173; Anon., *Selfe afflicter*, p. 12.
35 Edmund Toulmin Nicolle, *Mont Orgueil Castle. Its History and Description* (Jersey, 1921), pp. 60, 71–72, 78–81.
36 *Certain Passages* (7–14 April 1654), p. 106; *A Perfect Diurnall*, no. 4 (22–29 May 1654), p. 32.
37 *CSPD 1654*, pp. 446, 452.
38 Paul Halliday, *Habeas Corpus. From England to Empire* (Cambridge, MA, 2010), pp. 263–64, 267–68.
39 *CJ*, vii, 358; William Style, *Narrationes Modernae* (1653), pp. 96, 397; Anon., *Clavis ad aperiendum Carceris Ostia. Or, The High Point of the Writ of Habeas Corpus discussed* (1654); *CSPD 1653–54*, p. 344; *Certain Passages of Every dayes Intelligence*, no. 3 (27 January–3 February 1654), p. 18; *Certain Passages of Every dayes Intelligence*, no. 5 (10–17 February 1654), p. 38; Samuel Gardiner, *History of the Commonwealth and Protectorate, 1649–1656* (4 vols., 1894–1903; reprinted, Adlestrop, 1988–89), vol. 3, pp. 16–17.
40 *The Moderate Intelligencer*, no. 174 (12–19 April 1654), p. 1378; *Certain Passages of Every dayes Intelligence*, no. 15 (28 April–5 May 1654), p. 130; *A Perfect Diurnall*, no. 3 (15–22 May 1654), p. 22; *The true and perfect Dutch Diurnall*, no. 15 (15–22 May 1654), p. 340; *Perfect Diurnall* (22–29 May 1654), p. 32.
41 Anon., *A Declaration To the Free-born People of England* (1654), pp. 6–7. The London bookseller George Thomason dated his copy 23 May 1654.
42 *The Moderate Intelligencer*, no. 176 (26 April–3 May 1654), p. 1396; *The Faithful Scout*, no. 177 (28 April–5 May 1654), p. 1399; *The Weekly Post*, no. 177 (2–8 May 1654), p. 1339; *The Moderate Intelligencer*, no. 177 (3–10 May 1654), p. 1400.
43 *Weekly Post* (2–8 May 1654), p. 1399; *Moderate Intelligencer* (3–10 May 1654), p. 1400.
44 O. Ogle, W.H. Bliss, W.D. Macray and F.J. Routledge (eds.), *Calendar of the Clarendon State Papers preserved in the Bodleian Library* (5 vols., Oxford, 1869–1970), vol. 2, p. 351.
45 *Several Proceedings of State Affairs*, no. 241 (beginning 4 May 1654), p. 3834; *The Faithful Scout*, no. 178 (5–12 May 1654), p. 1407; *Certain Passages of Every dayes Intelligence*, no. 16 (5–12 May 1654), p. 138; *The true and perfect Dutch-Diurnall*, no. 15 (15–22 May 1654), p. 340.
46 *The true and perfect Dutch-Diurnall*, no. 15 (8–15 May 1654), pp. 117, 118.
47 Anon., *The Last Will & Testament of Lieutenant Col. John Lilburn* (1654), pp. 1–8. Thomason dated his copy 27 May 1654. The anagram had featured in an acrostic based on Lilburne's name preserved in Thomason's hand; 'The Anagram of John Lilburne. O I burne in hell' [Thomason E. 702(9)], dated June 1653.
48 *Callender of State Papers, Venetian, (CSPV)1653–54*, p. 217; cf. Ogle, Bliss, Macray, and Routledge (eds.), *Calendar of the Clarendon State Papers*, vol. 2, p. 365.
49 *Several Proceedings of State Affairs*, no. 244 (25 May–1 June 1654), no pagination; *A Perfect Diurnall*, no. 5 (29 May–5 June 1654), p. 33; *The Perfect Diurnall*, no. 234 (29 May–5 June 1654), p. 3576; *The Weekly Post*, no. 182 (6–14 June 1654), p. 1428; *A Perfect Diurnall*, no. 239 (3–10 July 1654), p. 80; *The Weekly Intelligencer*, no. 24 (4–11 July 1654), p. 317.
50 *CSPD 1654*, pp. 195, 208.
51 *The Weekly Post*, no number (18–25 July 1654), p. 1500.
52 *Commons Journal (CJ)*, vii, 382; *The Faithful Scout*, no. 204 (3–10 November 1654), p. 1637; *The Perfect Diurnall*, no. 257 (6–13 November 1654), p. 3934;
53 *The Weekly Post*, no. 204 (14–21 November 1654), p. 1642.
54 *The Weekly Post*, no. 205 (12–19 December 1654), p. 1673; *Mercurius Fumigosus*, no. 29 (13–20 December 1654), p. 226; *The Faithful Scout*, no. 206 (15–22 December 1654), p. 1682.

55 *The Weekly Post*, no. 209 (9–16 January 1655), p. 1672; *The Weekly Post*, no. 210 (16–23 January 1655), p. 1667.
56 *The Faithful Scout*, no. 216 (23 February–2 March 1655), p. 1728.
57 TNA: PRO, Prob 11/251 fols. 327r–28v; I.S., *A brief and perfect Journal of The late Proceedings and Successe of the English Army in the West-Indies* (1655), p. 15.
58 Thomas Birch (ed.), *A Collection of the State Papers of John Thurloe* (7 vols., 1742), vol. 3, p. 231; *CSPD 1655*, p. 161; *CSPD 1655–56*, pp. 6, 13; *CSPD 1656–57*, p. 62; A[braham] B[ecket?], *Articles of Impeachment Exhibited against Col. Robert Gibbons and Cap. Richard Yeardley, Late Governors of the Isle of Jersey* (1659); Charles Le Quesne, *A Constitutional History of Jersey* (1856), pp. 341–50.
59 *CSPD 1654*, pp. 372, 456; *CSPD 1655*, pp. 126, 128; *CSPD 1656–57*, p. 62; *Weekly Post* (12–19 December 1654), p. 1673;
60 Lilburne, *Resurrection*, pp. 6, 8.
61 William Prynne, *Mount-Orgueil* (1641); William Prynne, *A new discovery of free-state tyranny* (1655), pp. 10–11, 27, 34.
62 *Mercurius Politicus*, no. 251 (29 March–5 April 1655), p. 5244; *The Faithful Scout*, no. 221 (30 March–6 April 1655), p. 1765; *Certain Passages of Every dayes Intelligence*, no. 229 (30 March–6 April 1655), p. 23; *The Weekly Post*, no. 221 (3–10 April 1655), p. 1767; *The Weekly Intelligencer*, no. 120 (3–10 April 1655), p. 23; Firth (ed.), *Clarke Papers*, vol. 3, p. 32; *Mercurius Politicus*, no. 252 (5–12 April 1655), last page; *The Faithful Scout*, no. 222 (6–13 April 1655), p. 1776; *Certain Passages of Every dayes Intelligence*, no. 222 (6–13 April 1655), p. 23.
63 *The Weekly Post*, no. 124 (24 April–1 May 1655), pp. 1785, 1792.
64 *Mercurius Fumigosus*, no. 52 (23–30 May 1655), p. 412.
65 *Certain Passages of Every dayes Intelligence*, no. 5 (22–30 June 1655), p. 28.
66 Birch (ed.), *Thurloe State Papers*, vol. 3, p. 512; *A Perfect Account*, no. 230 (30 May–6 June 1655), p. 1838; T.C. Wales and C.P. Hartley (eds.), *The Visitation of London begun in 1687* (London, 2004), part 1, pp. 490–91.
67 Birch (ed.), *Thurloe State Papers*, vol. 3, pp. 512, 629; *A Perfect Account*, no. 198 (18–25 October 1655), p. 1584.
68 *The Faithful Scout*, no number (6–13 July 1655), p. 1876.
69 TNA: PRO, SP 18/99, fol. 235; *CSPD 1655*, pp. 263–64.
70 *Certain Passages of Every dayes Intelligence*, no number (24–31 August 1655), pp. 55–56.
71 Lilburne, *Resurrection*, p. 4.
72 *Mercurius Fumigosus*, no. 68 (5–12 September 1655), p. 532; Worc. Coll., MS Clarke 27, fol. 132r, printed in Firth (ed.), *Clarke Papers*, vol. 3, p. 53.
73 *The Perfect Diurnall*, no. 277 (26 March–2 April 1655), pp. 4258–59; *CSPD 1655*, pp. 556, 558.
74 Luke Howard, *A Warning from the Lord unto the Rulers of Dover* (1661), p. 1; Kent H & L Centre, N/FQz/2, pp. 23–24; William Batcheller, *A New History of Dover* (Dover, 1828), pp. 37–38, 72, 261; see also William Darell, *The History of Dover Castle* (1786), pp. 27–28.
75 Worc. Coll., MS Clarke 27, fol. 137r, printed in Firth (ed.), *Clarke Papers*, vol. 3, p. 60.
76 The cinque ports were, however, exempt 'from writs issuing from courts in Westminster Hall in suits between private parties'; see Halliday, *Habeas Corpus*, pp. 82–83, 366 n. 87, 368 n. 103; *Habeas Corpus Act* (27 May 1679), www.bsswebsite.me.uk/History/BillofRights/habeascorpus.html.
77 Lilburne, *Resurrection*, pp. 7–8 (although the reference to Harding as '*Mayor*' is evidently a misprint); Birch (ed.), *Thurloe State Papers*, vol. 3, pp. 194–95; *CSPD 1652–53*, p. 350; *CSPD 1656–57*, p. 62.
78 Kent H & L Centre, N/FQz/2, p. 13, printed in Penney (ed.), *First Publishers of Truth*, p. 144.
79 FHL, MS Swarthmore III 151; Luke Howard, *Love and truth in plainness manifested* (1704), p. 7–8, 14, 32, 107–8; William Caton, *A Journal of the Life of that Faithful Servant* (1689), pp. 15–16.

80 Kiffin had been employed as Lilburne's servant and wrote the preface to the second edition of Lilburne's *The Christian Mans Triall* (1641).
81 Lilburne, *Resurrection*, pp. 2, 3, 4, 5, 7.
82 Lilburne, *Resurrection*, pp. 2, 3, 5, 7, 8. Thomason dated his copy of Nayler's *Something further in answer* 29 September 1655; his copy of Dewsbury's *Discovery of the great enmity of the Serpent* 20 July 1655; and his copy of Dewsbury's *The Discovery of Mans Returne* 14 February 1654. Another work that Lilburne may have read is Humphrey Smith's *The Cruelty of the Magistrates of Evesham* (1655). This was dated by the author 15 October 1655 and may have been one of the 'printed speeches' of several Quaker prisoners in Northampton and Evesham gaols referred to in a marginal note.
83 Lilburne, *Resurrection*, pp. 5, 8; FHL, Tract vol. 309/3, MS annotation following J[ohn] J[ackson], *Strength in Weakness* (1655), printed in G.F. Nuttall, '"Overcoming the world": the early Quaker programme', in Geoffrey Nuttall, *Early Quaker Studies and The Divine Presence* (Weston Rhyn, 2003), p. 39. Jackson's title may have been suggested by Lilburne's *Strength out of Weaknesse* (1649).
84 Although John and Elizabeth's son John was baptised at St Martin, Ludgate on 17 October 1650, I have found no evidence that Elizabeth had her youngest child baptised. Moreover, Elizabeth had attended a meeting of John Spilsbury's congregation at Ratcliffe, Stepney on 21 September 1641; see TNA: PRO, KB 9/823, no. 113; Keith Lindley, *Popular Politics and Religion in Civil War London* (Aldershot, 1997), pp. 80–82.
85 Lilburne, *Resurrection*, pp. 1–2, 4, 5–6, 8.
86 Lilburne, *Resurrection*, pp. 7–8.
87 *Publick Intelligencer*, no. 11 (10–17 December 1655), p. 276; Worc. Coll., MS Clarke 27, fol. 150r, printed in Firth (ed.), *Clarke Papers*, vol. 3, p. 62.
88 Lilburne, *Resurrection*, pp. 9–14; Worc. Coll., MS Clarke 28, fol. 30v.
89 Lilburne, *Resurrection*, pp. 16–17; TNA: PRO, Prob 11/280 fol. 226r–v; William Berry, *County Genealogies. Pedigrees of the families of the county of Sussex* (1830), p. 37; John Gurney, 'Maynard, Sir John (1592–1658)', *ODNB*.
90 TNA: PRO, Prob 11/227 fols. 56v–57v; TNA: PRO, Prob 11/358 fols. 45v–47r; William Robinson, *The history and antiquities of the parish of Stoke Newington in the county of Middlesex* (1820), p. 194. It should be noted that the register records the birthday rather than baptism of the child, presumably in accordance with Commonwealth legislation of August 1653 that required the registration of births, marriages, and burials. Moreover, given that John and Elizabeth Lilburne had named two of their children Tower and Providence, Benoni ('son of my sorrow') may have merely signified their doleful condition.
91 Lilburne, *Resurrection*, p. 16.
92 Lilburne, *Resurrection*, pp. 18–22; see also Jeremiah Ives, *Innocency above impudency* (1656), p. 31.
93 Francis Duke, *The Fulness and Freeness of Gods Grace in Jesus Christ … The Third Part* (1656), pp. 94–114; *CSPD 1656–57*, p. 222; Francis Duke, *An Answer To some of the Principal Quakers* (1660), pp. 67–85; see also George Whitehead, *The True Light expelling the Foggy Mist of the Pit* (1660), p. 9; Samson Bond, *A publick tryal of the Quakers in Barmudas* (Boston, 1682), p. 96; Francis Estlake, *A Bermudas preacher proved a persecutor* (1683), p. 22.
94 Thomas Winterton, *The chasing the young Quaking Harlot Out of the City* (1656), title page, pp. 17–19.
95 Lilburne, *Resurrection*, p. 21; Richard Hubberthorne, *The Horn of the He-goat broken* (1656), pp. 10–11.
96 Kent H & L Centre, N/FQz/2, pp. 2, 13, printed in Penney (ed.), *First Publishers of Truth*, pp. 131–33, 143–45; Joseph Besse, *A Collection of the Sufferings of the people called Quakers* (2 vols., 1753), vol. 1, p. 288; Braithwaite, *Beginnings of Quakerism*, pp. 366–67. A Quaker meeting house was subsequently established 'at the lower part of St. James's-street, opposite the stone masons' yard'; see Batcheller, *New History of Dover*, p. 260.
97 FHL, MS vol. 367, no. 2, John Lilburne to Margaret Fell (Woolwich, 27 May 1657) [Thirnbeck MSS], printed in *Journal of the Friends Historical Society*, 9 (1912), p. 56;

Kent H & L Centre, N/FQz/2, pp. 15–16; Penney (ed.), *First Publishers of Truth*, pp. 30, 33, 163; Besse, *Sufferings of Quakers*, vol. 1, p. 289.
98 FHL, MS vol. 367, no. 2, printed in *J.F.H.S.*, 9 (1912), pp. 54, 55; Henry Clark, *A Rod Discover'd* (1659), p. 46.
99 FHL, MS Swarthmore IV 14, printed in A.R. Barclay (ed.), *Letters, &c., of early Friends* (1841), p. 55; Braithwaite, *Beginnings of Quakerism*, p. 186.
100 FHL, MS Swarthmore III 96v; Braithwaite, *Beginnings of Quakerism*, pp. 416–17.
101 FHL, MS vol. 367, no. 2, printed in *J.F.H.S.*, 9 (1912), pp. 53–59.
102 A.E. Wallis, 'The establishment of a monthly meeting in Durham (1654) and a note on Anthony Pearson (*d*. 1666)', *J.F.H.S.*, 48 (1957), pp. 119–22; A.E. Wallis, 'Anthony Pearson (1626–1666): an early Friend in Bishoprick', *J.F.H.S.*, 51 (1965–67), pp. 77–95; Richard L. Greaves, 'Pearson, Anthony (*bap.* 1627, *d*. 1666)', *ODNB*; Christopher Durston, 'Hesilrige, Sir Arthur, second baronet (1601–1661)', *ODNB*.
103 FHL, MS vol. 367, no. 2, printed in *J.F.H.S.*, 9 (1912), pp. 53–59; Gibb, *Lilburne the Leveller*, pp. 342–43; Gregg, *Free-Born John*, pp. 304–11, 313–14, 340, 345.
104 Anon., *Selfe afflicter*, p. 12.
105 TNA: PRO, SP 18/157A, fol. 129a.
106 *Registers of Stationers*, vol. 2, pp. 145, 151.
107 Anon., *Lilburns Ghost* (1659); Maureen Bell, 'Chapman, Livewell (*fl.*1643–1665)', *ODNB*.
108 H.N., *An Observation and Comparison Between the Idolatrous Israelites, and Judges of England* (1659), pp. 2, 4, 9.
109 Francis Howgill, *The Popish Inquisition* (1659), p. 42; George Bishop, *New England judged* (1661), p. 70; Sewel, *History of Quakers*, p. 193.
110 Wales and Hartley (eds.), *Visitation of London*, part 1, pp. 490–91; 1 Chronicles 4:18.
111 TNA: PRO, SP 18/157A, fol. 129a; *CSPD 1657–58*, p. 148.
112 TNA: PRO, Prob 6/34 fol. 51r.
113 TNA: PRO, SP 18/200 fol. 107; *CSPD 1658–59*, pp. 260–61.
114 William Huntington, *A True Narrative Concerning Sir Arthur Haslerigs Possessing of Lieutenant-Colonel John Lilburnes estate in the County of Durham* (1653); TNA: PRO, C 7/467/106; TNA: PRO, C 7/176/5; see also Gregg, *Free-Born John*, pp. 306–8, 313–14.
115 John Rutt (ed.), *Diary of Thomas Burton* (4 vols., 1828), vol. 3, pp. 68, 503–9; *CJ*, vii, 608, 682, 751, 760, 776, 879; *The Publick Intelligencer*, no. 166 (28 February–7 March 1659), p. 263; *CSPD 1658–59*, p. 371; *CSPD 1659–60*, pp. 346, 593, 594; *CJ*, viii, 31; Gibb, *Lilburne the Leveller*, pp. 346–47; Gregg, *Free-Born John*, pp. 347–48.
116 Lilburne, *Resurrection*; FHL, Tract vol. 309/3, MS annotation; FHL, MS vol. 367, no. 2; James Hedworth, *The oppressed man's out-cry* (1651), p. 10; Gervase Benson, *The Cry of the Oppressed* (1656), p. 27.
117 Brailsford, *Levellers and English Revolution*, pp. 637–40; Hill, *World Turned Upside Down*, pp. 240–41; Hill, *Experience of Defeat*, p. 131.
118 Barry Reay, *The Quakers and the English Revolution* (Hounslow, 1985), pp. 19–20.
119 James Naylier, *The Foxes Craft Discouered* (1649), p. 7; John Lilburne, *The Legal Fundamental Liberties Of the People of England* (1649), p. 31; see also J. Peacey, 'The parliamentary context of political radicalism in the English Revolution', in Laurent Curelly and Nigel Smith (eds.), *Radical voices, radical ways. Articulating and disseminating radicalism in seventeenth- and eighteenth-century Britain* (Manchester, 2016), pp. 151, 161–62.
120 J.L. Nickalls, 'The Problem of Edward Byllynge. II. His writings and their evidence of his influence on the first constitution of West Jersey', in Howard Brinton (ed.), *Children of Light. In Honor of Rufus M. Jones* (New York, 1938), pp. 111–31.
121 A.S.P. Woodhouse (ed.), *Puritanism and Liberty. Being the army debates (1647–49) from the Clarke Manuscripts* (1938; 3rd edn., 1992), pp. 81, 107; Richard Falconer, *A true and perfect narrative of the several proceedings in the case concerning the Lord Craven* (1653), p. 1; Ralph Farmer, *Sathan Inthron'd in his Chair of Pestilence* (1656), pp. 15, 37–38; cf. Nuttall, '"Overcoming the world"', pp. 36–37 n. 41; G.E. Aylmer, *The State's Servants. The Civil Service of the English Republic 1649–1660* (1973), pp. 272–74; Maryann S. Feola, 'Bishop,

George (*d.* 1668)', *ODNB*; K. Peters, 'The Quakers and the Politics of the Army in the Crisis of 1659', *Past & Present*, 231 (2016), pp. 111–16.
122 Richard L. Greaves, 'Fox, George, the younger (*d.* 1661)', *ODNB*.
123 George Fox, *A declaration against all profession and professors* (1653), p. 4; George Fox, *A Word from the Lord* (1654), p. 13; cf. FHL, Tapper MSS, Box C 4/2, fol. 29; Ralph Farmer, *The great mysteries of godlinesse and ungodlinesse* (1659), p. 59.
124 FHL, MS Swarthmore I 36; Francis Harris, *Some Queries Proposed* (1655), p. 23; Rutt (ed.), *Burton's diary*, vol. 1, p. 50; Claudius Gilbert, *The Libertine School'd* (1657), p. 19.
125 Charles Severn (ed.), *Diary of the Rev. John Ward* (1839), p. 141; cf. Thomas Comber, *Christianity No Enthusiasm* (1678), p. 5.
126 Francis Higginson, *A brief relation of the Irreligion of the Northern Quakers* (1653), p. 10.
127 Thomas Collier, *A Looking-Glass for the Quakers* (1656), p. 12.
128 Rutt (ed.), *Burton's diary*, vol. 1, p. 169.
129 Birch (ed.), *Thurloe State Papers*, vol. 6, pp. 167–68.
130 James Nayler, George Fox and John Lawson, *Saul's Errand to Damascus* (1653), p. 30.
131 John Lilburne, *A manifestation from Lieutenant Col. John Lilburne ... and others, commonly (though unjustly) styled Levellers* (1649).
132 Anon., *Selfe afflicter*, p. 13; S. Carrington, *The history of the life and death of His Most Serene Highness, Oliver, late Lord Protector* (1659), pp. 22–23; James Heath, *A brief chronicle of the late Intestine War* (1663), pp. 3–4.
133 S.C. Lomas (ed.), *The Letters and Speeches of Oliver Cromwell with elucidations by Thomas Carlyle* (3 vols., 1904), vol. 2, pp. 342–43.

8

REBORN JOHN?

The eighteenth-century afterlife of John Lilburne[1]

Edward Vallance

> This man proved a great trouble-world in all the variety of Governments afterward, being chief of a faction called *Levellers*: he was a great proposal-maker and modeller of State, which by his means was always restless in the Usurpation. He died a Quaker; and such as his life was, such was his death.
>
> James Heath, *Chronicle of the Late Intestine War (1661), 1676*

In so describing the Leveller activist and pamphleteer John Lilburne (1615?–57) in his 1661 history of the civil wars, James Heath, best known as the hostile biographer of Oliver Cromwell, was outlining a figure he assumed would already be well-known to his readership. Indeed, he referred to him as 'that famously known person John Lilburne'.[2] Today, Lilburne remains the most celebrated of all seventeenth-century English radicals, commemorated in popular biography, television drama (Channel 4's *The Devil's Whore*), and even rock opera.[3]

Many scholars argue that the relatively high profile of the Levellers today, in both popular and academic works, is a recent phenomenon. Historians such as Royce MacGillivray, Alistair MacLachlan, and, most notably, Blair Worden, have claimed that the Levellers received virtually no attention from historians until the late nineteenth century and only really gained prominence in the twentieth century, through the work of liberal, socialist, and Marxist authors.[4] The one exception to this historical neglect, as Worden notes, was John Lilburne, who continued to be deemed worthy of the attention of biographers and historians through the eighteenth and nineteenth centuries. Even so, he was treated as a fairly minor player and did not figure prominently in many histories of the civil wars. Moreover, Lilburne's relative visibility in contrast to his associates Richard Overton, John Wildman, and William Walwyn had very little to do with his connections to what was identified as the Leveller movement. Instead, Lilburne was given eighteenth-century labels like 'enthusiast' or 'patriot'. The Levellers, when mentioned at all, were crudely caricatured as 'social levellers' (those advocating the redistribution of property and/or the obliteration of marks of status), and scant attention was paid to the ideas manifested in documents such as the many versions of the Levellers' written manifesto, the *Agreement of the People*. Rather than being remembered as a political radical, it has been argued, Lilburne was memorialised for his many courtroom battles, which struck a chord with eighteenth-century legal controversies, especially over freedom of the press.[5] On this reading, it was Lilburne the litigant who was remembered, not Lilburne the Leveller.

This is a persuasive presentation of the historical influence of the radicalism of the civil war, and one which reflects a broader scholarly unease with the conception of a 'radical tradition'. The notion of a tradition of radical thought was powerfully evoked in the classic works of British Marxist historians such as Christopher Hill and Edward Thompson and retains some importance in the popular historical imagination.[6] Academics have become increasingly critical, however, both of the use of the term 'radical' to describe pre-modern politics and of the idea of a continuum of radical ideas and movements. Scholars have pointed out that the term 'radical' – not even in common political use until the early nineteenth century – had a very different meaning in the seventeenth century, indicating not ideas that would dramatically transform the status quo but instead a return to fundamentals or to the root. Using the term 'radical' in its modern sense, then, risks distorting the political outlook of historic individuals who did not necessarily view themselves as advocating anything new or novel. The notion of a radical tradition is now seen as equally problematic, as it implies both a similarity in radical thought over the ages and a degree of influence from one radical group to the next that is often not supported by empirical evidence.[7] At best, the idea of a radical tradition is seen as a poor way of thinking about intellectual influence. At worst, the concept is viewed as a historical fabrication, little more than an exercise in wish-fulfilment on the part of modern left-wing academics and journalists.[8]

In consequence, academic arguments for the enduring influence of civil war radicalism are now thin on the ground (and tend to come mainly from North American scholars such as Robert Zaller and F.K. Donnelly).[9] The evidence presented by eighteenth-century representations of John Lilburne, however, suggests that historians should be more cautious about dismissing the influence of the memory and ideas of the English Revolution upon later politicians and campaigners. Lilburne's case also indicates that the invocation of seventeenth-century figures in eighteenth-century political battles was not simply part of a process of historical reinvention. As will be seen, early eighteenth-century historical treatments of the civil wars show considerable effort to represent Lilburne's life and ideas accurately. Indeed, Lilburne's memory had an enduring power precisely because of the element of continuity both in the ideals at stake and in how they were contested. And it was just because these ideals remained 'radical' (however problematic that word) that there was no need for historians unsympathetic to Lilburne and the Levellers to distort their aims: they could just as easily be condemned by rehearsing their actual political principles, which remained anathema.

Paradoxically, as Lilburne's public profile grew over the second half of the eighteenth century – to the extent that eighteenth-century Patriot Whig writers adopted 'Lilburne' as a *nom de plume* – so awareness of the broader aspects of his life and career appeared to diminish, including his connection with the Levellers.[10] But decreasing emphasis on Lilburne as Leveller did not equate to the severing of Lilburne's public memory from radical politics. Rather, in the later eighteenth century Lilburne became ever more closely identified with contemporary radicals, from John Wilkes, to John Horne (later Horne Tooke), to Charles James Fox. The parallel ensured that he remained a contentious, ambiguous figure: a radical hero for some, a demagogic anti-hero to others. The affinity these figures and their supporters felt for Lilburne again reflected similarities of style (the emphasis on charismatic personality, the use of the courtroom as a political theatre) and of ideals (individual liberty, freedom of the press, and the importance of the jury system). But, as this chapter will demonstrate, Lilburne's memory did not simply legitimate arguments in support of these concepts and institutions. More than this, his legal struggles exerted a tangible influence on British law, helping to change legislation relating to libel, the power of juries, and even the legal status of slaves on British soil.

A seventeenth-century life

Lilburne, as Rachel Foxley and Jason Peacey (among others) have shown, was one of the most written-about individuals of the 1640s and the subject of sophisticated propaganda campaigns.[11] Indeed, Lilburne's fame was such that Mike Braddick has christened him the 'celebrity radical'.[12] A celebrity today, according to Simon Morgan, is a 'known individual who has become a marketable commodity'.[13] Lilburne was certainly 'monetised': his name alone sold books (even when he did not write or even appear in them) and his face graced a number of prints and medallions, prefiguring the similar commodification of eighteenth-century political figures such as Wilkes.[14] The extent to which both Lilburne and his critics personalised his political struggle is also suggestive of modern celebrity, though the occasional focus of biographers on the minutiae of his life perhaps less so.[15]

Lilburne's contemporary fame means that the details of his life can be traced with relative ease. Born probably in Sunderland around 1615, Lilburne was the second son of a minor Durham gentleman, Richard Lilburne. The family had had some connections with the royal court, but Lilburne's career as an opponent of Charles I was set by his apprenticeship in 1630 to a London clothier, Thomas Hewson. It was Hewson, a Puritan, who introduced Lilburne into the circle of 'Godly' opponents of the personal rule of Charles I and the church policies of his archbishop, William Laud. Lilburne became an acolyte of Dr John Bastwick, a leading critic of Laud's episcopate, and Bastwick in turn helped mould the young Lilburne both intellectually and socially. Bastwick, along with William Prynne and Henry Burton, fell foul of the Laudian authorities in 1637, the three suffering brutal corporal punishments (ear-cropping and branding) for their anti-episcopal writings. Lilburne soon followed. Arrested for circulating unlicensed literature (further tracts by Bastwick), Lilburne compounded his problems by refusing to take the so-called 'etcetera oath', which required the swearer to answer truthfully all questions posed. A charge of contempt of court was added and Lilburne was found guilty. He was sentenced to be whipped from the Fleet Prison to New Palace Yard, Westminster, placed in the pillory and then imprisoned. In Lilburne's own account, the brutal punishment was taken as a sign of divine favour: 'my wedding day, in which I was married to the Lord Jesus Christ: for now I know hee loves me, in that hee hath bestowed so rich apparel upon mee, and counted mee worthy to suffer for his sake'.[16]

Lilburne's trial and punishment in 1637–38 set a pattern for most of the rest of his life, in which dramatic courtroom battles were followed by lengthy periods of imprisonment that nonetheless did not stop him from continuing his arguments in print. By 1638 Lilburne had already joined the ranks of Burton, Bastwick, and Prynne as a celebrated puritan 'martyr'. The calling of the Long Parliament in 1640 brought an end to his first spell in prison. He was freed as a result of the pleading of the newly elected Member of Parliament for Cambridge, Oliver Cromwell, who was, like Lilburne, a 'godly' man of gentry stock but modest means. It was the beginning of a relationship that would profoundly influence Lilburne's life, as Cromwell turned in the course of the 1640s from his saviour and supporter to his nemesis.

Lilburne might have retired from public affairs at this point: in or before September 1641 he married Elizabeth Dewell, daughter of a London merchant, and a woman, by his own report, 'deare in my affections severall years before from me she knew anything of it'.[17] His uncle, George Lilburne, provided him with capital to set up in business as a brewer, and there was the prospect of further money from Parliament as compensation for his punishment by Star Chamber. A stable family life seemingly beckoned, but the pull of the political arena proved irresistible. The England into which Lilburne emerged free had changed dramatically. Now it was the crown's opponents who held the upper hand: hated royal ministers such as the Earl of Strafford were tried and executed; the organs of press censorship which had suppressed critical opinions were abolished; and Laud's church policies, deemed 'popish' by the 'godly', were being reversed. When the king resorted to arms to resist this assault on his authority, Lilburne was quick to volunteer for the parliament's cause. Captured by the royalists at Brentford in November 1642, he would have been tried for treason but the Commons threatened to treat royalist prisoners in kind if charges were brought, and Lilburne was released. (To add to the drama, it was Lilburne's heavily pregnant wife Elizabeth who assured his salvation by riding from London to Oxford to deliver the House's message.) With further support and encouragement from Cromwell, Lilburne continued his successful career in the parliamentarian army, but he left in the spring of 1645, unwilling to take the new loyalty oath, the Solemn League and Covenant: a test, Lilburne said, 'fram'd in Scotland, and most basely, illegally and unjustly obtruded upon England'.[18] Before this point, however, Lilburne had already fallen out with more conservative 'Presbyterian' figures in the army, including his general, the parliamentarian Earl of

Manchester. Not only was Lilburne antagonising powerful figures like Manchester, he was also associating with more radical individuals such as Richard Overton, a printer of unlicensed tracts and a staunch advocate of religious toleration. These associations added to Lilburne's own readiness to attack conservative opponents, including his one-time ally John Bastwick, prompted a phase in his life in which he was rarely out of either court or prison.

In July 1645 Lilburne was gaoled because of charges by Bastwick that he had slandered the Speaker of the Commons. These charges did not result in a trial and Lilburne was eventually released that October, but his ongoing quarrels with powerful Presbyterians, especially the Earl of Manchester, meant that he was not out of trouble for long. In June 1646 he was called to the House of Lords to answer accusations that he had libelled Manchester in one of his pamphlets. Lilburne argued that Lords had no right to try a commoner, a stance which put him in prison once again. As in 1637–38, incarceration proved no impediment to Lilburne's productivity as a writer, and only a month later he was tried by the Lords for scandal and illegal printing, found guilty, heavily fined, and imprisoned in the Tower. He would not be freed until 2 August 1648.

This period transformed Lilburne's political philosophy. Until then, he had retained some support among leading Independents in Parliament, especially Cromwell. In the Tower, however, his ideas increasingly diverged from those of his old associates. Now he saw Parliament exercising the same 'unjust power' as Charles I's Star Chamber, even against those who had been the two Houses's 'cordiall friends'.[19] As Lilburne was breaking away from Cromwell ('my pretended friend'), he was making new alliances with men such as Overton, William Walwyn, and John Wildman.[20] These individuals were later christened 'Levellers' by their opponents (a pejorative term previously applied to anti-enclosure rioters and meant to associate them with social revolt).[21] However, Leveller ideas, as represented in their manifesto, the *Agreement of the People*, were quite distinct from those of earlier agrarian rebels: they sought a new 'representative' to replace Parliament, elected on a much broader franchise, a simplified legal code under which all would have equal protection, and a set of 'reserved' rights, such as freedom of conscience and/or worship, that neither the legislature nor the executive could abrogate. It was a settlement on this basis that Lilburne and the other Levellers urged on his eventual release in 1648. But though Cromwell's son-in-law Henry Ireton presented a version of the *Agreement of the People* to the Commons late that year, Lilburne viewed the 'Officers' Agreement' (as it has become known) as little more than a diversionary tactic, designed to distract radical attention from army leadership's 'main work', the trial and execution of the king in January 1649.

Lilburne had opposed Charles's trial (he argued that it was in the Levellers' interest to 'keep up one Tyrant to balance another'), a stance which, combined with his associations with royalist prisoners in the Tower, prompted insinuations about his political loyalties.[22] By the spring of 1649 he was back in the Tower, accused of writing a number of tracts against the new republican government. On 24 October he was put on trial for treason at the Guildhall. It was here that he pulled off his most memorable escape from death. According to the letter of the new treason law passed in July of that year, which had made it a capital offence to write works describing the republic as tyrannical, Lilburne was undoubtedly guilty as charged. Yet he succeeded over two days in convincing his jury that they, not the magistrates, were judges of the law, the only 'pronouncers of their Sentence, Will and Minde'.[23] (This radical 'pro-jury' position represented a significant departure from the traditional view of the jury as only judges of fact, a view which, until late 1648, Lilburne himself had largely endorsed.)[24] He was acquitted to rapturous applause and medallions were struck to commemorate his release.

For a short time, Lilburne retreated from politics. The Leveller movement itself had largely been crushed that year, as Leveller-inspired mutinies in the army were suppressed and its power base in the separatist churches of London was weakened by the republic's offer of religious toleration to these groups. But Lilburne's period at liberty did not last long. A property dispute between his uncle, George Lilburne, and the influential Rump MP Sir Arthur Hesilrige led John Lilburne to make a number of printed attacks on Hesilrige that the parliament deemed not only libellous but also treasonable. Lilburne was this time denied a chance to speak at his own trial – the Rump had learnt the lesson from its humiliation in 1649 – and was found guilty, fined £7,000, and banished for life.

The final phase of Lilburne's life began with his unauthorised return from exile in the Netherlands in 1653. Under the terms of the judgment in 1651 this was treasonable, but Lilburne hoped that the change in government in England (the republic had been replaced by Cromwell's Protectorate) might invalidate the law on which he originally been tried. The hope proved vain, and he was put on trial for treason at the Old Bailey in July of that year. Once again, he convinced a jury to acquit him (or rather, in the carefully chosen words of the jurymen, to find him 'not guilty of any crime worthy of death'), but there was to be no repeat of the celebrations of 1649.[25] Viewed as a serious threat to the regime, Lilburne was kept in prison for most of the remainder of his life, first in the Tower, then in Castle Orgueil on Jersey, and finally, as his health failed him, in Dover Castle. It was while on parole from this last prison that Lilburne made his conversion to Quakerism and renounced political activity. Following this declaration, and because of his declining health, Lilburne was given increasing freedom to visit his wife and children, and he died on 29 August 1657 while at liberty in Eltham, Kent.[26]

'The great darling of the sectaries'

The drama and turmoil of Lilburne's life would alone have attracted the attention of contemporary writers. However, the fact that he was a major political player, capable of attracting significant popular support, meant he drew the fire of hostile pamphleteers and propagandists. Before moving on to discuss Lilburne's reputation in the eighteenth century, we need to look at how he was portrayed in the 1640s and '50s, for these delineations of his character, especially those by his opponents, established key features that heavily influenced subsequent accounts.

Strikingly absent from hostile portrayals of Lilburne was any strong assertion of a connection between him and the Leveller movement. When he first emerged as a noteworthy figure, it was as, to use the 'heresiographer' Thomas Edwards's phrase, 'the great darling of the sectaries'.[27] Edwards recorded that radical preachers prayed regularly for his release from prison. Later, he claimed that a 'great sectary' prayed for the downfall of earthly monarchies and that Lilburne might be lifted up in their place. The implications of this story were rammed home with repeated allusions to Lilburne as a new Thomas Muntzer or John of Leiden, both of whom were seen as representing the worst excesses of the popular reformation in Germany.[28] Here, Lilburne was presented as the messianic leader of religious fanatics, not the director of a political movement. It was an image which persisted even after the label 'Leveller' became common. Another of Lilburne's hostile biographers, the Presbyterian Cuthbert Sydenham, claimed that it was de facto toleration which had fuelled the growth of the Leveller movement: 'all that turn Levellers, first leave the Principles of Scripture-Religion, that they may be without check of conscience for any civil disorder'.[29] A mock 'last will and testament' produced in 1654 as Lilburne languished in prison in Jersey (notably before his public conversion to Quakerism) continued to harp on this theme. It depicted the erstwhile sectary leaving his lips to the 'Saints of the Feminine' and the will itself was presented as being dictated to 'sister Abigail Lemmon and since published by Ruth Dox'.[30]

Hostile presentations of Lilburne often portrayed him (and his followers) as being of the 'meaner sort': in Edwards's words, he was that 'unworthy, mean man'.[31] This could be linked to 'social levelling' and thereby to the kinds of misrepresentations of Levellerism noted by Worden; but it was also a way of knocking Lilburne's own pretensions, notably his insistence on the ancient pedigree of the Lilburne family and his acquisition of gentlemanly manners and dress.[32] The tactic also delegitimised appeals to the lower house, as Edwards railed:

> Let Lilburne, Overton, Larner [the radical printer], and the rest of that rable who talk so much of the House of Commons being their chosen ones, and that a man ought to obey none but whom he chuses with such like, name any Knight or Burgesse whom they chose, or were capable to chuse; for I beleeve they were of so mean estate that they had not so much free-land *per annum* required by the Statute for them who have voices Election of Knights of the shire.[33]

Sydenham, who described the Levellers as 'mechanic' (meaning plebeian, vulgar, and coarse), similarly depicted Lilburne as a man of 'such an inconsiderable Interest, one who could hardly ever challenge more Land in England then might Geometrically serve to make his grave'.[34] Others mocked his involvement in the unglamorous trades of brewing and soap-boiling.[35]

One of the most enduring tropes in anti-Lilburne propaganda was the image of him as the source of all contention. Quarrelsome behaviour in general came to be described as 'to play Lilburne'.[36] Death itself, it was jokingly suggested, would not bring an end to Lilburne's mania for controversy. His mock will ordered that his body be embalmed and his coffin encased in a double-sheath of lead 'lest it cause either mutiny in Creatures, or Earthquakes'.[37] The theme was returned to in the famous epitaph produced following Lilburne's death:

> Is John departed, and is Lilburn gone!
> Farewel to both, to Lilburn and to John…
> But lay John here, lay Lilburn here about,
> For if they ever meet they will fal out.[38]

These three elements in contemporary portraits of Lilburne, that he was a 'sectary', that he had a seemingly insatiable appetite for controversy, and that he was of lowly status all proved enduring. But even as Edwards moved from attacking religious radicalism to targeting the army and political Independents, in part three of *Gangraena* he seems to have felt no need to present Lilburne as a 'social leveller'. Some critics of the Levellers did argue that demands for equality of rights would soon lead to demands for equality of estates, and Edwards might also be seen to be implying this when he compared Lilburne with sixteenth-century German Anabaptists, who argued for the community of goods.[39] However, when Edwards shifted from attacking Lilburne as a religious radical to targeting him as a significant political actor, he did so on the grounds that Lilburne and his associates sought 'the overthrow of the three Estates and the Lawes of the Kingdome, and in the stead of the Fundamentall Government Lawes and Constitution of this Kingdome to set up an Utopian Anarchie of the promiscuous multitude'.[40] The line of attack here remained largely political and ideological, not social, and – the word 'Anarchie' apart – was arguably only a partisan reading of what the Levellers did indeed pursue.

Significantly, much more was made of Lilburne's connections with royalists than of his collusion with radical elements in the army, or links with political fellow travellers such as Richard Overton. In part, this was a parliamentarian response to the royalist press, where his harsh treatment during his imprisonments was used increasingly as evidence of the tyrannical rule of the Army 'Junto'.[41] The parliamentarian press responded in turn by depicting Lilburne as a royalist plotter, colluding in the Tower with the Welsh judge David Jenkins.[42] In 1649, the rumours even became an occasion for humour, when *Mercurius Elencticus* reported that Lilburne's gaolers had been ordered to keep him under close watch as his cell window in the Tower faced that of the royalist Countess of Carlisle, Lucy Hay. (It was feared that, 'though the distance be very great', the two might enter into communication via sign-language, which might be 'very prejudiciall to the present Government'.)[43] For the parliamentarian press, and later the Commonwealth's propagandists, Lilburne's royalist intrigues seemed an effective means to undermine his credibility, especially with the army. For the royalists, the same claims demonstrated how the parliamentarian cause was divided, but also how far the Junto's 'tyranny' had pushed one former supporter.

The connections established between Lilburne and the royalist cause proved of lasting significance for his subsequent reputation. These unlikely alliances became part of the dispute over the accuracy and objectivity of the greatest post-Restoration narrative of the civil wars, Edward Hyde, Earl of Clarendon's *History of the Rebellion*, published posthumously in 1702.

Post-Restoration Lilburne

Lilburne's high profile in the political press of the 1640s and '50s as well as his relationship with Oliver Cromwell ensured him a place in many of the chronicles and histories of the civil wars published after the Restoration of monarchy in 1660. In some respects these accounts fit Worden's description of them as partisan, overtly hostile to the Levellers (misrepresented as social levellers), and factually inaccurate. Heath's discussion of the Levellers, for example, was accompanied by a marginal note: 'they lay all things common'. Yet, as with Edwards earlier, he also attacked the Levellers and Lilburne by acknowledging their political radicalism, describing Lilburne as a supporter of 'democracy' (with all the evils implicit in that form of government for most seventeenth-century, and especially royalist, commentators). Heath even followed Lilburne in referring to the Officers' *Agreement of the People* as merely a Machiavellian ploy by Cromwell to placate and distract radical opposition to his seizure of power.[44]

Similarly, Anthony Wood – who was deeply critical of Heath's history for its inaccuracy – nonetheless largely followed Heath's characterisation of Lilburne in his *Athenae Oxonienses* (first published 1691–92), describing him as the chief of the Levellers and a 'trouble-world', and picking out the witticism, generally attributed to the republican MP Henry Marten, that if 'the world was emptied of all but John Lilbourne, Lilbourne would quarrel with John, and John with Lilbourne'.[45] The reputation for contentiousness established in the 1640s and '50s was emphasised by other royalist historians: Sir William Sanderson depicted Lilburne as an 'undaunted troublesome spirit',[46] and John Nalson called him a 'perpetual trouble to himself and disease to the ruling Authority'.[47] Nalson's history also returned to the theme of Lilburne's lowly status: 'from this obscure rise crawling up the stairs of a pretended Sanctimony to be a great favourite of the People and asserter of their Liberty'.[48]

Significantly, though, the most important post-Restoration history of the civil wars took a different tack. The Earl of Clarendon's *History of the Rebellion* delivered a more complex, and at points conflicting, reading of Lilburne and the Levellers. Some elements of his history chimed with the familiar denunciations of other royalist historians: Clarendon described Lilburne, along with Overton, as a 'fanatic', and argued that, in general, the Levellers 'held great malice' against the king.[49] However, a more extensive discussion of Lilburne came in book 14, where Clarendon delivered short biographies of both Lilburne and John Wildman in the context of discussing royalist conspiracies against the Protectorate. Clarendon's treatment of Lilburne extends over several pages, running from his emergence as a martyr for the Puritan cause in the late 1630s through to his career in the parliamentary army and on to his engagement with radical politics in the mid- to late 1640s.[50] Elements of the established picture of Lilburne remained in Clarendon's description of him as a 'poor bookbinder'. But Clarendon's purpose in rehearsing Lilburne's biography was rather different from that of most Restoration royalist historians: for him, the case of both Wildman and Lilburne represented evidence (admittedly strained) 'of the temper of the nation, and how far the spirits of that time were from paying a submission to that power, when nobody had the courage to lift up their hands against it'.[51]

Clarendon's discussion of Lilburne and Wildman, unlike that of most other royalist historians, was based in part on personal knowledge. As Peacey has noted, during the 1650s Clarendon, then a leading figure in the exiled court, had seriously considered an alliance between Levellers and royalists as potentially fruitful, and certainly a better prospect than forging a partnership with Presbyterians to restore Charles II. His reasoning even displayed some sympathy for Leveller ideas, stating that, in seeking to establish a new representative in place of Parliament, they struck at the 'roote and foundacion' of the country's past and present misery. He also felt that the Levellers were less guilty than the Presbyterians of starting the war and had expressed less personal animosity to Charles I while he was alive.[52] Of course, Clarendon was also swayed by more cynical considerations in suggesting an alliance with the Levellers: they were 'lesser men' and could be more easily manipulated than the Presbyterians. Generally, Clarendon appears to have viewed the Levellers as well-meaning but naive: individuals, therefore, who could easily be bought off with some 'spetious concessions'.[53] So, though Clarendon's royalist allegiance was transparently on display, he did not present Lilburne as consistently hostile to monarchy – a portrait which fitted with his earlier assessment of the Levellers in the 1650s.

As noted by Philip Hicks, Daniel Woolf, and Mark Knights, partisan politics came to dominate historical writing in the first half of the eighteenth century. This was not just a question of the authors' perspectives but was due also to the production and marketing of expensive works of history which were largely dependent on subscriptions gathered from political activists.[54] In the eyes of many contemporaries, history – as a literary form the highest of the polite arts – suffered as a result. A belated target for such complaints was Clarendon's *History*, in part because the lofty neo-Classical standards that he had sought to attain were seemingly not met in the finished work, which had been subjected to the excisions of editors and marred by a blatantly pro-Tory preface.[55]

Clarendon's unusual treatment of Lilburne provided a potentially fruitful point of weakness for his eighteenth-century critics to explore. Volume five of the *Biographia Britannica* (1760), edited by William Oldys, contained a lengthy biography of Lilburne. According to its author, Philip Nicolls, it was also to serve as a partial 'commentary on the History of the Rebellion'.[56] In scrutinising the accuracy and objectivity of Clarendon's *History*, Nicolls provided the fullest biography yet of Lilburne, based on close reading of Lilburne's own works as well as other available printed civil war sources. Here we can see evidence of Oldys's editorial influence. MacGillivray has noted that post-Restoration historians of the civil war often viewed pamphlets and newssheets as too unreliable to be used as evidence. Wood attacked Sanderson's histories on just these grounds, as 'not much valued, because they are mostly taken from printed authors and lying pamphlets'.[57] Oldys, on the other hand (as one might expect of the editor of the *Harleian Miscellany* of rare pamphlets), took a very different view:

> Pamphlets, and such short Tracts, risest [i.e. increase or proliferate] in great Revolutions; which tho' looked upon, by some, but as *Paper Lanterns*, set a flying to be gaped at by the Multitude (in illuminating whom, they have not always escaped the Flames themselves) yet are they beheld, by politic, or penetrating Eyes, as the *Thermometers* of *State*, fore-shewing the Temperature and Changes of Government.[58]

The value of print was, according to Oldys, particularly clear in the case of English history:

> surely, no Nation, has ever given more conspicuous Instances, to what immeasurable Lengths, Animosity, and Indignation will advance, upon the least Imposition, or even Umbrage of Tyrannical or Arbitrary Power; as might be exemplified, among many others, in the restless *John Lilburn*, and the endless *William Prynne*, who had both been bleeding Witnesses thereof. There are near a Hundred Pamphlets, written by, and concerning the *first* of these Authors.[59]

Nicolls's use of Lilburne's writings, today still the main source for biographical information on him, highlighted key factual errors in Clarendon's account: that Lilburne was not a 'poor bookbinder' but came from a gentry family and had not died in prison but was on parole at the end of his life. He also took issue with the presentation of Lilburne as a royalist conspirator – there was always, Nicolls said, a 'mental reservation' present in any statements Lilburne made in favour of monarchy.[60] Moreover, even though Nicolls's editorial interventions indicated he was not entirely sympathetic to his subject (he referred to Lilburne's 'supreme vanity'), he did engage thoughtfully with the Levellers' political programme in the *Agreement of the People*, describing it, albeit with faint praise, as a 'not being ill-digested' plan for settlement.[61]

Nicolls explicitly linked Lilburne with the Leveller movement, describing him as its 'coryphaeus' (meaning leader of the group).[62] Tellingly, neither he nor Oldys seem to have felt the need to add any explanation of who the Levellers were: besides Cromwell's biography, there were no further references to the Levellers in Oldys's *Biographia* and no other Leveller writer was deemed worthy of an entry. Nicolls clearly expected, then, that an educated readership would know who the Levellers were and what they stood for. This was a reflection of the fact that many early eighteenth-century histories of the civil wars did indeed discuss the Levellers and identify Lilburne as their leader. Moreover, both hostile and sympathetic histories had given fairly accurate descriptions of Leveller ideology.

This was because for pro-royalist historians of the eighteenth century, just as for Presbyterian and cavalier commentators in the seventeenth century, it was possible to condemn Lilburne and the Levellers simply by rehearsing their principles. The Huguenot historian Isaac de Larrey's account of the reign of Charles I, published in 1716, was clearly written from a pro-Stuart perspective. De Larrey evidently viewed the Levellers and 'their head, one Lilburn' with disdain, but his description of their ideas was scarcely a calumny upon them. He described their affirmation of popular sovereignty, their proposals for the reform of Parliament and the electoral system, and their belief in equality before the law, and even discussed the Levellers' manifesto, *The Agreement of the People*, though he felt it was more likely to breed 'Confusion than Order'.[63] Similarly, the flagrantly royalist additions to Sir Richard Baker's *Chronicle of the Kings of England* in its last eighteenth-century edition claimed that the Levellers espoused not the 'levelling' of social status or the abolition of private property but 'the equal distribution of justice in government to all degrees of people'.[64] So, too, the Tory Jacobite Thomas Carte's *General History of England*:

> There was a great part of the army, which still adhered to the old *independent* principles; and thinking themselves to have the same natural rights as their superior officers, took it ill to be left without any share in a government, which was deemed democratical: these men were called *Levellers. John Lilburne* ... was one of their chieftains.[65]

So although some early eighteenth-century Tory and Jacobite histories did characterise the Levellers as social levellers, the Whig polemicist John Oldmixon was already tackling something of a caricature of Tory/royalist presentations of them when he stated that 'for what is said of their being against all Degrees of Honour or Riches, and levelling the Count with the Cobler is false'.[66]

Some common characteristics emerge from both Tory and Whig histories of the 1640s in their treatments of Lilburne. He was frequently connected with the Levellers and identified as their chief or head. Though the Levellers were occasionally presented in crude terms as advocating social levelling, most historical accounts depicted them more accurately as supporting political and legal reform. (For many of these historians, however, that was at least as bad as advocating the redistribution of property or the abolition of social distinctions.)[67] Yet, while partisan prejudices were clearly on display in most early eighteenth-century histories of the civil wars, Lilburne and the Levellers sat rather awkwardly in this Whig/Tory historiographical battlefield. Clarendon's picture of Lilburne and the Levellers, as has been noted, was ambivalent – they were culpable in the regicide but had also joined the royalist cause in the 1650s – but so, too, was Oldmixon's. While Oldmixon was keen to demonstrate, by way of knocking Clarendon, that the Levellers were not ardent royalists, neither were they seventeenth-century Whigs but rather regicidal republicans. It was no coincidence, then, that only in the writing of a self-confessed republican, Catherine Macaulay, would the Levellers be embraced as worthy political ancestors.[68] As a result, the presentation of the Levellers was less distorted by eighteenth-century party politics than other elements of the history of the civil wars. Indeed, the urge of some writers such as Oldmixon and Nicolls to critique Clarendon's account meant that a considerable premium was set on factual accuracy and thorough research.

Lilburne the litigant

If the presentations of Lilburne and the Levellers by Whig and Tory historians were often impressively accurate, they were scarcely sympathetic. Lilburne was treated as a figure of some historical significance, but certainly not as a heroic one. It was not until the second half of the eighteenth century, in Joseph Towers's *British Biography* (1766–72), that a straightforwardly positive presentation of Lilburne emerged. Towers's biography of Lilburne was clearly built upon that constructed earlier for the *Biographia Britannica*. Although Towers's used some different sources, there were obvious similarities with Nicolls's biography in terms of phrasing and quotations from Lilburne's works.[69] Like Nicolls, Towers also used his life of Lilburne to criticise the accuracy of Clarendon's *History*.[70] However, Towers's portrait diverged from its predecessor in two significant ways. First, Towers removed the reference to the 'Levellers', and second, in place of Nicolls's heavily annotated text, he produced a smoothly flowing and glowing account of Lilburne's life, describing his subject as an 'undaunted spirit, in his private life irreproachable, and attracted to the cause of liberty to a degree even of enthusiasm'.[71]

So, at the same time as Lilburne's own character was being rehabilitated, his connection to the Leveller movement was being obscured. One explanation for this shift might be a change in the type of source material exploited by biographers. Those early eighteenth-century historical works had, by and large, been lengthy and very expensive tomes readily available only to wealthy subscribers. They had been based on compendia of civil war sources (John Rushworth's *Historical Collections* – part four published in 1701; Bulstrode Whitelocke's *Memorials*, 1682; and Edmund Ludlow's *Memoirs*, 1698–99), which were equally costly. But from the evidence of eighteenth-century booksellers' catalogues, the most commonly available work relating to Lilburne was Clement Walker's account of his 1649 treason trial, *The Triall of Lieut. Collonell John Lilburne*, which was issued in two editions, the first printed by Henry Hills in the year of the trial, the second by his son, Henry Hills Junior, in 1710.[72]

Given the timing of the publication of the second edition, it is tempting to see a connection between Lilburne's case and another celebrated 'state trial', that of the High Church clergyman Henry Sacheverell. However, though Hills Junior's edition was advertised with an anti-Sacheverell pamphlet, this doesn't appear to have been the main motivation behind the reissue.[73] Instead, Hills lived up to his reputation

FIGURE 8.1 Frontispiece to Theodorus Verax (Clement Walker), *The Triall of Lieut. Collonell John Lilburne* (1649), British Museum AN514450001

Source: The Trustees of the British Museum.

as, in John Dunton's words, an 'Arch-pirate' by remarketing his father's old stock as a cut-price alternative to buying existing copies of the first edition: 'price 1s … former edition was sold at 2s. 6d.', as the advert ran.[74] The pamphlet remained available and relatively cheap in booksellers' catalogues; only very good copies retaining the original print of Lilburne at the bar (Figure 8.1) commanded higher prices.[75] Besides the two pamphlet editions of the 1649 trial, it was also reproduced in the periodical press and featured in a number of collections of state trials that were also serialised.[76]

Hills Junior's advertisement, attached to the end of the 1710 edition, suggested that there was a greater market for Lilburne's works:

> There being several Pamphlets, written by Lieutenant Colonel *John Lilburn* (besides this Tryal,) Therefore all Gentlemen that have any of his Works by 'em, if they please to communicate them to the Printer, he having several by him already, they shall be justly and faithfully Printed and Published, and the Favour most thankfully acknowledg'd by H. H.[77]

The widespread availability of this tract might also suggest, however, that supply very much outstripped demand. The evidence from booksellers' advertising is mixed. On the one hand, Lilburne's name, as in the seventeenth century, was clearly seen as a useful marketing ploy, even in the case of pamphlets not authored by him or which were only tangentially related to his career.[78] On the other, whole volumes of Lilburne's tracts regularly featured in catalogues priced at only a few shillings, hardly indicating an insatiable public thirst for his writings.[79] In addition, besides the 1710 edition of Lilburne's trial, there were few other eighteenth-century reprints of his works. Excluding trial proceedings, Lilburne's *An Impeachment of High Treason against Oliver Cromwell* (1649) was reprinted in the *Harleian Miscellany*; and *The Picture of the Councel of State* (1649) was included in the first edition of a planned series of reissues, *Valuable and Scarce Tracts* (1769), though this never went beyond the first edition.[80]

The greater availability of accounts of Lilburne's trials, especially that of 1649, does not alone explain why, in the later eighteenth century, interest in Lilburne the Leveller decreased and focus upon Lilburne's legal battles intensified. In fact, later eighteenth-century courtroom struggles over the freedom of the press encouraged comparisons with Lilburne's seemingly equivalent disputes in the seventeenth century. By the beginning of the 1760s, Lilburne's name was being invoked in the press along with that of John Peter Zenger. (Zenger was the German-American printer whose 1735 case established that actions for seditious libel could be challenged on the basis of the truth of the claims, even if the substance of what was published was slanderous.)[81]

As Worden notes, Lilburne's name came to be firmly connected to the freedom of the press cause in the wake of the notorious *North Briton* case of 1763, when John Wilkes was accused of libelling George III in issue 45. (Wilkes had attacked the king's speech which had praised the peace terms secured with France at the Treaty of Paris.)[82] The comparison was so keenly felt that in June 1763 Wilkes was even presented with a copy of Lilburne's 1649 trial and the medallion commemorating it.[83] It is worth adding that Lilburne was already being invoked ironically by the supporters of Lord Bute's government before this celebrated trial. *The Briton*, the loyalist precursor of Wilkes's journal, cited the cases of Lilburne, Bastwick, Burton, and Prynne to suggest ironically that the only remedy to the evils of the times must be to print treason. In the same journal, an associate of the pro-Wilkes Mayor of London, William Beckford, was described as a 'modern Lilburne in war and patriotism'.[84] By far the most frequent comparison made, however, was between the treatment of Wilkes and that of Lilburne during the trial of 1637.[85] The allusion was made frequently in the Wilkesite press, and one loyalist author complained that, reading the writings of Wilkes's supporters, one would think Lord Bute was also accountable for the treatment of Lilburne over a century earlier.[86]

Consequently, as much as supporters of freedom of the press identified Lilburne as a worthy predecessor, the affinity suggested between him and Wilkes was also used to attack the Wilkesite cause. One anti-Wilkes satire, *An Epistle from Col. John Lilburn, in the shades, to John Wilkes Esq.*, probably published in 1765, imagined Lilburne corresponding to Wilkes from the 'infernal shades'. These attacks returned to familiar themes in hostile biographies of Lilburne: that he was of low birth (Clarendon's description of him as a 'poor bookbinder' was recycled); that he was congenitally argumentative; and that he used his struggles primarily to advance himself, the press allowing Lilburne to acquire a reputation 'in a sphere more extensive than I seemed intended for, by my birth, or station in life'.[87] The satire imagined Lilburne and his radical associates toasting Wilkes in the underworld:

> For you must know, we lead very merry lives here in the infernal shades: our wine is as good as that which you drink in the upper world; and you are become so much my favourite, that whenever I go to a tavern to drink a bottle with a friend, the first toast I give is to W[il]kes and Liberty.[88]

Lilburne's public commemoration in the eighteenth century therefore revealed a character whose attributes remained highly contested. To compare a contemporary figure with him was to make a political statement. 'Lilburne' continued to be used as a byword for contentiousness and rabble-rousing. As the conflict between Britain and its 13 American colonies heated up in the 1770s, one correspondent, signing himself 'Yankee', complained of the presentation of American legislators as 'so many Col. Lilburne's'.[89] Advocates of political reform, such as Charles Lennox, 3rd Duke of Richmond, were also, like Wilkes, presented in the loyalist press as the political descendants of 'John Lilburn of notorious memory'.[90] Yet, at the same time, 'the famous John Lilburne' continued to be invoked by defenders of freedom of the press and his struggles in the 1630s and '40s compared with those of contemporary figures. The behaviour of John Horne (later Horne Tooke) at his libel prosecution in 1777 (for drawing up an advertisement to raise a public subscription for the American colonists injured at the battles of Lexington and Concord) was compared to that of the 'celebrated Col. John Lilburne who was tried at Guildhall for a treasonable libel, in the year 1694 [*sic*]; a man whose daring spirit gave Cromwell and his Council the greatest apprehensions'.[91]

This was not simply a case of eighteenth-century reformers searching for convenient historical predecessors. The invocation of Lilburne reflected the continuing importance of the law to late eighteenth-century radicalism.[92] Moreover, the arguments voiced by Lilburne at his 1649 trial had a real impact on the law and, by extension, the role of juries. Allusions to Lilburne's legal struggles persisted into the era of more self-conscious radicalism in the 1790s. In a speech given in Parliament on 20 May 1791, Charles James Fox compared the contemporary libel case involving John Luxford, printer of the *Morning Herald*, with that of Lilburne in 1649, with the qualification that, while he agreed with Lilburne that juries were sometimes required to be judges of law as well as fact, he did not endorse Lilburne's vitriolic attack on the judiciary.[93] The connections drawn by Fox between Lilburne and Luxford were significant since the speech laid the ground for the 1792 Libel Act, also known as Fox's Act. This legislation, only repealed in 2010, clarified the role of juries in trials for libel, confirming that they might give a 'general verdict on the whole matter put in issue'.[94]

Lilburne was invoked across a broader range of issues than simply press freedom. This was evident in the later work of Joseph Towers. Aside from his biographical work, Towers was also a major eighteenth-century advocate of the role of juries as judges of law.[95] The process of revising Philip Nicolls's original biography clearly influenced Towers: while his 1764 pamphlet on the rights of juries (published the year after Wilkes's *North Briton* libel case) carried no mention of Lilburne, his 1784 book on the same subject listed Lilburne as an important authority in support of the 'pro-jury' view.[96] The work of James Epstein indicates that Lilburne's arguments informed later eighteenth- and nineteenth-century radical arguments concerning the power of the jury.[97] Lilburne has also been seen as an important influence on the conception of jury rights in the American colonies in the eighteenth century, although there is little direct evidence of his trial of 1649 being invoked as a precedent.[98]

Given the enduring importance of the 1649 trial to these discussions, identifying Lilburne as a defender of the rights of juries was, of course, only a relatively small development from seeing him as an advocate of press freedom. A more dramatic legal allusion to Lilburne was made in 1772 in the case of James Somerset. Somerset was the slave of a Scottish merchant and senior colonial customs official, Charles Stewart. Somerset left his master's service while Stewart was on a visit to London but was recaptured two months later and kept in captivity. The case, often seen as a landmark in the history of the abolition of the slave trade, hinged on whether a writ of habeas corpus which had been made to free Somerset could apply to a slave.[99] One of the lawyers supporting the writ, Francis Hargrave, employed an obscure sixteenth-century precedent, 'Cartwright's Case', to demonstrate that 'England was too pure an air for a slave to breathe in'.[100]

But the only reference to Cartwright's case came in the arguments of Lilburne's lawyers, the future regicides John Cook and John Bradshaw, as they sought compensation for their client from Parliament in 1645/46.[101] The case supposedly revolved around the treatment of a Russian slave owned by the eponymous Cartwright, an English merchant. Cartwright was indicted for having severely beaten his slave in public, actions that the merchant felt were lawful given the slave's status as his chattel. The court, however (at least as Lilburne and his lawyers reported it), rejected this defence on the grounds that slavery was incompatible with English common law, upheld the charge of battery, and freed the Russian. Hargrave noted that although the case had been cited by the 'famous John Lilburne' there was scant supporting evidence to corroborate this account of the trial. Nonetheless, Somerset's lawyer argued, the account was credible as it had been endorsed by the Lords when they deemed Lilburne's sentence unjust and illegal.[102] Lord Chief Justice Mansfield's verdict in the case may have been rather limited in law, essentially affirming that a writ of habeas corpus might apply even to a slave. However, the decision was widely read as rendering slavery incompatible with English law.[103] Lilburne's rhetoric of the 'freeborn Englishman' had been extended dramatically. Lilburne was now being celebrated not just as a litigant but as a liberator.

Lilburne, then, continued to be seen as a 'martyr to liberty' in the broadest sense, not merely as a defender of the liberty of the press, or even of the rights of juries.[104] Moreover, he was a figure who was most often invoked positively by eighteenth-century reformers and radicals.[105] By the late eighteenth century, 'Leveller' appeared to have lost any specific historical meaning and, in its use by John Reeves' loyalist associates, had come to be taken as applying to any who would attack private property.[106] But though connections between Lilburne and the Leveller movement were less frequently drawn in the later eighteenth century, they had not been obscured altogether. Loyalist histories and biographies of the late 1790s certainly continued to make the link. Stephen Jones's *A New Biographical Dictionary* (1796) referred to Lilburne as 'the ring-leader of the Levellers', while Noble's *Lives of the English Regicides* (1798) discussed 'the well-known John Lilburne of factious memory' alongside the *Agreement of the People* – 'a plan of jurisprudence just one remove from what would be sufficient for a nation in the first years of its emerging from absolute barbarism'.[107] Lilburne's works also continued to be read and admired by early nineteenth-century radicals. The publisher-printers William Hone and Richard Carlile, the former in private, the latter in public, both invoked Lilburne as an advocate of 'true liberty' who understood the revolutionary potential of the printing press.[108]

The above suggests that Lilburne continued to divide opinion: loyalists could still cite him as a dangerous mob demagogue while a variety of reformers, from comparative moderates such as Charles James Fox to self-identified republican 'atheists' such as Carlile, could treat him as an illustrious predecessor. That the connection between Lilburne and the Levellers was still being made in the 1790s, although infrequently, suggests that Reeves's loyalist campaign against 'Levellers and Republicans' did not completely dissuade radicals from identifying with him. The more cautious, such as Hone, might prefer to keep allusions to Lilburne submerged within their texts; the more daring and outspoken, such as Carlile, were prepared to make their admiration public.

Conclusion

Lilburne's reputation unquestionably dipped in the early nineteenth century, just as the reputation of Oliver Cromwell began to rise. For the historian Thomas Carlyle, for example, Lilburne was merely 'noisy John', the irritating gnat perpetually bothering the 'great man' Cromwell.[109] Even some of Lilburne's nineteenth-century descendants came to endorse this view. In the mid-nineteenth century, Charles Lilburn, a Sunderland Justice of the Peace, began constructing his own biography based largely on his private collection of more than 50 of Lilburne's pamphlets.[110] The resultant portrait of his ancestor was, however, scarcely glowing, a result of the influence of William Godwin's *History of the Commonwealth* (1824), a work which had compared Lilburne's 'self-interested' behaviour with the 'patriotic' actions of Cromwell.[111]

The Victorian cult of Cromwell only goes some way to explaining why Lilburne's reputation diminished in the nineteenth century. For one thing, the negative character traits identified by hostile biographers of Lilburne had altered little from the seventeenth to the early nineteenth century: he was still presented as an ambitious, habitual controversialist, driven by religious zeal. Indeed, much of this picture remained in place in twentieth-century representations of Lilburne.[112] A more convincing explanation can be found in the increasingly politicised uses of Lilburne's life in the later eighteenth century. As has been shown, early eighteenth-century historians often delivered reasonably accurate, if largely unsympathetic, depictions of Lilburne and the Levellers. From the 1760s onwards, however, a more heroic image of Lilburne developed, built in part on his own writings and emphasising his own courtroom struggles rather than the wider history of the Leveller movement. This Lilburne was invoked in later eighteenth-century controversies over freedom of the press, the power of juries, and even the rights of slaves. One reason why Lilburne's star dimmed, it might be suggested then, was because these battles had largely been won (in part through the persistent influence of his arguments and example).[113]

Unquestionably these later depictions of Lilburne (including visual ones: see Figure 8.2) diminished or even completely obscured his connections with the broader context of mid seventeenth-century radicalism. But the focus on Lilburne as an individual did not significantly distort his self-presentation in the seventeenth century, which had concentrated heavily on his personal struggles.[114] Neither is it the case, as argued by F.K. Donnelly, that Lilburne's ideals were a poor fit with eighteenth-century radicalism.[115] The causes in which Lilburne's name was invoked were all ones that connected with his own political philosophy: the rights of juries and their role as a bulwark against royal and parliamentary tyranny; the importance of a free press – 'a liberty of greatest concernment to the Commonwealth' – and even the incompatibility of slavery with the rights of freeborn Englishmen.[116] Of course, the exact parameters of these disputes had changed over the course of more than a century: the late eighteenth-century debate over slavery had very different targets than that engaged in by Lilburne and the Levellers.[117] Similarly, Lilburne's more radical stance on the jury was moderated in Fox's Act to regulating the judiciary's role rather than usurping it.[118]

However, there is a danger that in emphasising the separateness of historical epochs, historians have undervalued the degree of intellectual sympathy and continuity between the radicalism of the seventeenth century and that of the

FIGURE 8.2 Image of Lilburne from 'WALKS ROUND LONDON', in *Boys of England: A Young Gentleman's Journal of Sport, Travel, Fun and Instruction*, no. 79 (Friday 22 May 1868), p. 4. The 1649 image (Figure 8.1) clearly offered the template for this nineteenth-century illustration, but Lilburne is now divorced from the original legal setting and he is now reading the Bible rather than Sir Edward Coke's *Institutes*

Source: The British Library Board, BL Shelfmark P. P. 5993. s.

eighteenth.[119] As has already been shown, the editor of the *Biographia Britannica* assumed, probably correctly, that an educated readership would already know who Lilburne and the Levellers were. Indeed, Donnelly has recently suggested that over-familiarity rather than a lack of awareness, may explain why at least one eighteenth-century revolutionary, Thomas Jefferson, didn't refer to the arguments of his famous ancestor John Lilburne.[120] As John Rees has also noted, Marx and Engels identified the Levellers as forerunners of the proletariat long before the emergence of Marxist and socialist historical scholarship on the movement.[121] They surely would not have alighted upon the Levellers if they had truly sunk into obscurity. We do not need to invest in a grand narrative of an English 'radical tradition' to acknowledge that the English revolution of the seventeenth century had both intellectual and practical consequences for the eighteenth century. A life which ended in political retreat in Eltham in 1657 was resurrected in the 1700s to take up the 'temporal sword' once more.

Notes

1 I would like to thank Mike Braddick, Victoria Gardner, Jason Peacey, and the anonymous reviewers of *History Workshop Journal* for their comments on this article. This chapter is a revised version of my article 'Reborn John? The Eighteenth-century Afterlife of John Lilburne', *HWJ*, 74:1 (2012), 74, pp. 1–26. I am grateful to Oxford University Press and the editors of the journal for allowing me to reproduce the article here.
2 James Heath, *A Chronicle of the Late Intestine War in the Three Kingdoms of England, Scotland and Ireland … to which is added A Continuation to this present year 1675* (London, 1676), p. 2.
3 Pauline Gregg, *Free-Born John: the Biography of John Lilburne*, 3rd edn. (London: Phoenix Press, 2000); Martine Brant and Peter Flannery, *The Devil's Whore*, four episodes (Channel 4, 2008); Rev Hammer, *Free-Born John: The Story of John Lilburne, the Leader of the Levellers*, CD (Cooking Vinyl, 1997).
4 Royce MacGillivray, *Restoration Historians and the English Civil War* (The Hague: Marinus-Nijhoff, 1974), p. 234; Alistair MacLachlan, *The Rise and Fall of Revolutionary England* (Basingstoke: Macmillan, 1996), esp. ch. 5; Blair Worden, 'The Levellers and the Left', in *Roundhead Reputations* (London: Penguin, 2002), ch. 12; Blair Worden, 'The Levellers in History and Memory, c. 1660–1960', in Michael Mendle (ed.), *The Putney Debates of 1647* (Cambridge: CUP, 2001), pp. 256–82.
5 Worden, 'The Levellers and the Left', pp. 316, 330.
6 The radical tradition was sketched more subtly and cautiously than critics of Hill and Thompson often allow. For the clearest examples, see Thompson, *Witness Against the Beast: William Blake and the Moral Law* (Cambridge: CUP, 1994); Hill, 'From Lollards to Levellers', in Maurice Cornforth (ed.), *Rebels and their Causes: Essays in Honour of A.L. Morton* (London: Lawrence and Wishart, 1978), ch. 3. For a recent popular invocation of the idea, see Billy Bragg, *The Progressive Patriot: A Search for Belonging* (London: Bantam Press, 2007).
7 On this see the excellent introduction by Glenn Burgess to Burgess and Matthew Festenstein (eds.), *English Radicalism, 1550–1850* (Cambridge: CUP, 2007); Philip Baker, 'Radicalism in Civil War and Interregnum England', *History Compass* 8 (2010), pp. 152–65.
8 For the more extreme position, see, aside from the work of MacLachlan, Jonathan Clark, *Revolution and Rebellion: State and Society in England in the Seventeenth Century* (Cambridge: CUP, 1986), esp. ch. 6.
9 Robert Zaller, 'The Continuity of British Radicalism in the Seventeenth and Eighteenth Centuries', *Eighteenth-Century Life*, 6 (1981), pp. 17–38; Frederick K. Donnelly, 'Levellerism in Eighteenth and Early Nineteenth-Century Britain', *Albion*, 20:2 (1988), pp. 261–69; and, in more polemical vein, Marcus Rediker and Peter Linebaugh, *The Many-Headed Hydra: Sailors, Slaves, Commoners and the Hidden History of the Revolutionary Atlantic* (London: Verso, 2000), esp. ch. 4.
10 For the use of 'Lilburne', 'Lilburn' or 'Lilbourne' as a pen name, see *Gazetteer and New Daily Advertiser* (7 March 1770), no. 12,797; *Gentleman's Magazine* 40 (1770), p. 120; *Middlesex Journal or Chronicle of Liberty* (23–26 Feb. 1771), no. 297; *Morning Chronicle and London Advertiser* (24 Oct. 1781), no. 3,881. (Unless otherwise indicated, newspapers and periodicals are unpaginated.)

11 Rachel Foxley, 'Citizenship and the English Nation in Leveller Thought, 1642–1653', PhD dissertation (University of Cambridge, 2001); see also Rachel Foxley, *The Levellers: Radical Political Thought in the English Revolution* (Manchester: MUP, 2013); Jason Peacey, 'Hunting the Leveller: the Sophistication of Parliamentarian Propaganda, 1647–53', *Historical Research* 78: 199 (2005), pp. 15–42; Jason Peacey, 'John Lilburne and the Long Parliament', *Historical Journal* 43 (2000), pp. 625–45.
12 Mike Braddick, 'The Celebrity Radical', *BBC History Magazine* 8: 10 (October 2007), pp. 34–36.
13 Simon Morgan, 'Celebrity: Academic "Pseudo-event" or a Useful Concept for Historians?', *Cultural and Social History*, 8: 1 (2011), pp. 95–114, at p. 98.
14 Foxley, 'Citizenship', pp. 156, 208–9; David Adams, 'The Secret Printing and Publishing Career of Richard Overton the Leveller, 1644–46', *The Library* 11: 1 (2010), pp. 3–88, at p. 73; Morgan, 'Celebrity', p. 104.
15 See Thomas Edwards, *The first and second part of Gangraena* (1646), pt. 2, pp. 23–24, 84–85; Ann Hughes, *Gangraena and the Struggle for the English Revolution* (Oxford: OUP, 2004), p. 117. (Unless otherwise stated, pre-1800 works are published in London.)
16 John Lilburne, *The Christian Mans Triall* (1641), p. 21.
17 John Lilburne, *L. Colonel John Lilburne Revived* (1653), p. 1, quoted in Andrew Sharp, 'John Lilburne', *ODNB*. These wistful, romantic memories were undercut, as Ann Hughes notes, by Lilburne's complaint on the same page about the 'sneaking terms' that Elizabeth was prepared to make with Cromwell in order to secure his release. See Ann Hughes, 'Elizabeth Lilburne', *ODNB*; and Ann Hughes, *Gender and the English Revolution* (Abingdon: Routledge, 2012), pp. 57–58, 100–1.
18 John Lilburne, *Rash Oaths Unwarrantable* (1647), p. 10.
19 Lilburne, *Rash Oaths*, p. 30.
20 John Lilburne, *The Legall Fundamentall Liberties of the People of England Revived* (1649), p. 26.
21 Edwin F. Gay, 'The Midland Revolt and the Inquisitions of Depopulation of 1607', *Transactions of the Royal Historical Society*, 18 (1904), pp. 195–244, at p. 214.
22 Lilburne, *Legall Fundamentall Liberties*, p. 29.
23 Theodorus Verax [Clement Walker], *The triall of Lieut. Collonell John Lilburne* (1649), p. 121.
24 Thomas A. Green, *Verdict According to Conscience: Perspectives on the English Criminal Trial Jury 1200–1800* (London: University of Chicago Press, 1985), p. 169.
25 Green notes that the response of the jury in 1653 demonstrated that they had been convinced again by Lilburne's arguments, in this case that juries could protect the citizen against unjust laws; *Verdict According to Conscience*, pp. 192–97.
26 This brief overview of Lilburne's life is indebted to Sharp, 'John Lilburne', *ODNB*; and Gregg, *Free-Born John*.
27 Thomas Edwards, *The third part of Gangraena* (1646), p. 153.
28 Edwards, *Gangraena*, pt. 3, p. 151. As Hughes notes, Lilburne was a favourite target of Edwards, so much so that he claimed he had planned to write a biography: Hughes, *Gangraena and the English Revolution*, pp. 64–65.
29 Cuthbert Sydenham, *An Anatomy of Lieut. Col. John Lilburn's Spirit and Pamphlets* (1649), A3v.
30 Anon., *The Last Will and Testament of Lieutenant Col. John Lilburn* (1654), p. 4. 'Lemon' and 'Dox' evoke 'leman' (illicit mistress) and 'doxy' (prostitute).
31 Edwards, *Gangraena*, pt. 3, p. 195.
32 See Lilburne's comment in *A Worke of the Beast* (1638): 'I am the Sonne of a Gentleman, and my Friends are of rancke and quality in the Countries where they live', quoted in Gregg, *Free-Born John*, p. 21.
33 Edwards, *Gangraena*, pt. 3: 'A new and further discovery of the errours and proceedings of the sectaries 7' [unpaginated, should be p. 25], astutely picking up on shifts in Lilburne's attitude to Parliament. See Peacey, 'Lilburne and the Long Parliament', pp. 640–42.

34 Sydenham, *Anatomy*, A2v.
35 *Last Will and Testament*, p. 5; *Mercurius Politicus* (6–13 June 1650), no. 1, p. 16.
36 *Mercurius Pragmaticus* (25 April–2 May 1648), no. 5 [unpaginated, p. 2].
37 *Last Will and Testament*, p. 3.
38 *The Selfe Afflicter Lively Described in the whole course of the life of Mr. John Lilburn* (1657), p. 14.
39 See Jonathan Scott, 'What were Commonwealth Principles?', *Historical Journal*, 47 (2004), pp. 591–613, at p. 604–5.
40 Edwards, *Gangraena*, pt. 3, p. 217.
41 *Mercurius Pragmaticus* (5–12 Oct. 1647), no. 4 [p. 3]; (18–25 Jan. 1648), no. 19 [p. 7]. On this campaign, see Peacey, 'Hunting of the Leveller'.
42 Sydenham, *Anatomy*, B2v; *Mercurius Anti-Pragmaticus* (20–27 Jan. 1648), no. 7, p. 7.
43 *Mercurius Elencticus* (10–17 Sept. 1649), no. 21, p. 162.
44 Heath, *Chronicle*, pp. 131, 187.
45 Anthony Wood, *Athenae Oxonienses*, vol. 2 (1692), pp. 101–2.
46 Sir William Sanderson, *A Compleat History of the Life and Raigne of King Charles from His Cradle to his Grave* (1658), p. 867.
47 John Nalson, *An Impartial Collection of the Great Affairs of State from the Beginning of the Scotch Rebellion in the Year MDCXXXIX to the Murther of King Charles*, vol. 1 (1682), p. 514.
48 Nalson, *Impartial Collection*, vol. 1, p. 512.
49 Worden, 'Levellers and the Left', p. 327.
50 Edward Hyde, *The History of the Rebellion and Civil Wars in England Begun in the Year 1641*, ed. W. D. Macray, 6 vols (Oxford, 1888), vol. 5, pp. 305–8.
51 Hyde, *History of the Rebellion*, vol. 5, p. 308.
52 Edward Nicholas, *The Nicholas Papers: Correspondence of Sir Edward Nicholas, vol. 1 1641–1652* (Camden Society, 1886), pp. 141–42; Peacey, 'Hunting the Leveller', p. 29n.
53 Nicholas, *Nicholas Papers, vol. 1*, p. 143.
54 Philip Hicks, *Neoclassical History and English Culture from Clarendon to Hume* (Basingstoke: Macmillan, 1996); Daniel Woolf, *Reading History in Early Modern England* (Cambridge: CUP, 2000), ch. 5; and Mark Knights, 'The Tory Interpretation of History in the Rage of Parties', in Paulina Kewes (ed.), *The Uses of History in Early Modern England* (San Marino, CA: Huntingdon Library, 2006), pp. 347–66.
55 Hicks, *Neoclassical History*, pp. 69–73.
56 *Biographia Britannica*, ed. William Oldys, 6 vols, 1747–66, p. 2961; for that publication, see Donald W. Nichol, 'Biographia Britannica', in Steven Serafin (ed.), *Eighteenth-Century British Literary Biographers*, vol. 142 of Dictionary of Literary Biography (Detroit: Gale Research, 1994), pp. 287–93; Donnelly, 'Levellerism', p. 264.
57 MacGillivray, *Restoration Historians*, p. 12.
58 [William Oldys], 'A Dissertation on Pamphlets, and the Undertaking of Phoenix Britannicus, To Revive the most Excellent among Them', in J. Morgan, Gent., *Phoenix Britannicus: Being a Miscellaneous Collection of Scarce and Curious Tracts, Historical, Political, Biographical, Satirical, Critical, Characteristical, &c. Prose and Verse*, vol. 1 (containing nos. 1–6) (London, 1732), pp. 553–64 at p. 555; for *Phoenix Britannicus*, a short-lived (one-volume) series reissuing rare sixteenth- and seventeenth-century pamphlets, see Harry Sirr, *J. Morgan and His Phoenix Britannicus, with notes about his other works* (Margate: H. Keble, 1906). For further evidence of Oldys's interest in the civil wars, see his commonplace books, British Library, Add MS 12522, f. 42v and Add MS 12523 f. 9.
59 [Oldys], 'A Dissertation on Pamphlets', p. 556.
60 *Biographia Britannica*, vol. 5, p. 2959.
61 *Biographia Britannica*, vol. 5, p. 2956.
62 *Biographia Britannica*, vol. 5, p. 2937.
63 Isaac de Larrey, *The History of the Reign of King Charles I*, 2 vols. (1716), vol. 2, p. 289–90.
64 Richard Baker, *Chronicle of the Kings of England* (1733 edn.), p. 526.
65 Thomas Carte, *A General History of England*, 4 vols. (1747–55), vol. 4, pt. 2, p. 615.

66 John Oldmixon, *The History of England during the Reigns of the Royal House of Stuart* (1730), p. 338; for an example of Levellers portrayed as 'social levellers', see Robert Menteith, *The History of the Troubles of Great Britain*, trans. James Ogilvy (1735), p. 325.
67 For Lilburne as an enduring example of sectarian 'enthusiasm', see the High Church periodical *Scourge* (Tuesday 21 May 1717), no. 16 [unpaginated]; for Lilburne as a troublemaker, see the comparison made between Daniel Defoe and Lilburne as controversialists in the *Weekly Journal or British Gazetteer* (22 Nov. 1718), p. 1208.
68 Catharine Macaulay, *The History of England From the Accession of James I to that of the Brunswick Line Vol IV* (London, 1769), p. 388; Macaulay owned many Leveller tracts, [Catharine Macaulay] *A Catalogue of [Mrs Macaulay's] Tracts* (1790).
69 Joseph Towers, 'The Life of John Lilburne', in *British Biography*, ed. Towers, 7 vols, 1766–72, vol. 6, pp. 44–69. For similarities of phrasing, see Towers, 'Life of Lilburne', p. 44; and *Biographia Britannica*, p. 2937; for similar choice of quotation, see Towers, 'Life of Lilburne', p. 49; and *Biographia Britannica*, p. 2941. Although Alexander Gordon's *DNB* article on Towers suggested that the 'biography contained much original work, the fruit of his research in the British Museum', Towers's notebook, which details books borrowed and bought, contains no mention of him having looked at Lilburne's works independently, Bodleian Library, Oxford, MS. Eng. Misc. e. 334. The main differences in terms of the sources used appear to be Towers's use of Bulstrode Whitelocke's *Memorials* (1682) and the 1710 edition of Lilburne's 1649 trial. See Towers, 'Life of Lilburne', pp. 60, 61–63 and 67.
70 Towers, 'Life of Lilburne', p. 66.
71 Towers, 'Life of Lilburne', p. 69.
72 From a sample of 50 booksellers and library catalogues accessed via Eighteenth Century Collections Online that contained mention of Lilburne's works, 29 listed the 1649 trial. The next most commonly occurring work was *A Picture of the Councel of State* (1649), with just two listings. For Hills's pamphlet, see also Donnelly, 'Levellerism', p. 263.
73 See *Evening Post* (26 August 1710), no. 162. The anti-Sacheverell pamphlet was *A New Map of the Laborious and Painful Travels of our blessed High-Church Apostle* (1710).
74 Dunton quoted in Ian Gadd, 'Henry Hills jnr', *ODNB*; *Daily Courant* (3 Aug 1710), no. 2,739.
75 See Thomas Payne, *A New Catalogue for 1797* (1797), p. 132, which advertised a 'very neat' copy of the trial with portrait for 9s, compared to a typical price of between one and three shillings.
76 *Weekly Journal or British Gazetteer* (16 Sept. 1721), p. 2028; *A Compleat Collection of State-Tryals, and Proceedings upon Impeachments for High Treason and other Crimes and Misdemeanours*, 4 vols (1719), pp. 580–640; reprinted in eight vols in *A Collection of State Trials, and Proceedings, upon High Treason, and other Crimes and Misdemeanours, from the reign of King Edward VI to the present*, (1730–35). For serialisations, see adverts in *Read's Weekly Journal or British Gazetteer* (31 Aug. 1734), no. 493; (5 Oct. 1734), no. 497; (2 Nov. 1734), no. 501.
77 *Tryal* (1710 edn.), p. 132.
78 See the continuing success of Overton's tactic of linking *A Remonstrance of Many Thousand Citizens* (1646) to Lilburne's imprisonment: John Hildyard, *A Catalogue of Several Libraries and Parcels of Books* (York, 1751), p. 126; John Hinxman, *A Catalogue of above 15000 Volumes* (York?, 1759), p. 79.
79 John Manson, *Manson's Catalogue for 1791* (1791), offered a volume of eight tracts by or about Lilburne for only five shillings, p. 23.
80 *Public Advertiser* (9 March 1769), no. 10,720; William Oldys, *A Compleat and exact Catalogue of all the Pamphlets contained in the VIII volumes of the Harleian Miscellany* (1746), p. 38. For the reprint of other Leveller tracts, see Donnelly, 'Levellerism', p. 264.
81 *Public Ledger or the Daily Register of Commerce and Intelligence* (20 Feb. 1760), no. 34.
82 Worden, 'Levellers in History and Memory', p.269; Braddick, 'Celebrity Radical', p. 35.

83 Donnelly, 'Levellerism', p. 263. This copy of Lilburne's trial pamphlet is now owned by Andrew Whitehead. I thank him for this information.
84 *The Briton* (11 Sept. 1762), no. XVI, p. 95; (10 Nov. 1762), XXV, p. 149.
85 *Lloyd's Evening Post* (3–6 June 1763), no. 920, p. 530; *Public Advertiser* (6 June 1763), no. 8,916; *London Evening Post* (26–28 Feb. 1765), no. 5,824.
86 *Public Advertiser* (15 Oct. 1765), no. 9,658; reprinted in *Gazetteer and New Daily Advertiser* (16 Oct. 1765), no. 11,418.
87 *An Epistle from Col. John Lilburn, in the Shades to John Wilkes Esq. Late A Colonel in the Buckinghamshire Militia* (n.d. 1765?), p. 2. Noted by Donnelly, 'Levellerism', p. 263.
88 *An Epistle*, p. 11.
89 *St James's Chronicle or the British Evening Post* (26–9 Oct. 1776), no. 2,441.
90 *Gazetteer and New Daily Advertiser* (6 Sept. 1779), no. 15,777.
91 *General Evening Post*, 3–5 July 1777, no. 6,789.
92 See John Brewer, 'The Wilkites and the Law, 1763–1774', in Brewer and John Styles (ed.), *An Ungovernable People: the English and Their Law in the Seventeenth and Eighteenth Centuries* (London, 1980), pp. 128–71.
93 *Speeches of the Rt Hon. Charles James Fox in the House of Commons*, ed. Goldwin Smith, 6 vols (London), vol. 6, pp. 254–55; see pp. 244–70 for the whole speech on the bill. The speech was widely reported in the press: *St. James' Chronicle or the British Evening Post* (19–21 May 1791), no. 4,696; *Diary or Woodfall's Register* (21 May 1791), no. 674; and *Morning Post and Daily Advertiser* (21 May 1791), no. 5,638.
94 For the text of the act as it currently remains in force, see www.legislation.gov.uk/apgb/Geo3/32/60/body.
95 Green, *Verdict According to Conscience*, pp. 340–41; Donnelly, 'Levellerism', p. 267.
96 Joseph Towers, *An Enquiry into the Question, Whether Juries are, or are Not, Judges of Law as well as of Fact* (1764); Towers, *Observations on the Rights and Duties of Juries* (1784), pp. 27–28. Towers, 'Life of Lilburne', pp. 61–67 contains an extensive discussion of the argument that jurors were judges of law as well as fact, with reflections on eighteenth-century libel cases.
97 J.A. Epstein, *Radical Expression: Political Language, Ritual and Symbol in England, 1790–1850* (Oxford: OUP, 1994), pp. 34–35; J.A. Epstein, *In Practice: Studies in the Language and Culture of Popular Politics in Modern Britain* (Stanford: Stanford University Press, 2003), pp. 80–81.
98 For the assumption of influence, see Hugo Lafeyette Black, *A Constitutional Faith* (New York: Knopf, 1969), pp. 4–5; for an attempt to trace the actual basis for the pro-jury position, see Stanton D. Kraus, 'An Inquiry into the Right of Criminal Law Juries to Determine the Law in Colonial America', *Journal of Criminal Law and Criminology* 89 (1998), pp. 11–214.
99 George Van Cleve, 'Somerset's Case and its Antecedents in Imperial Perspective', *Law and History Review*, 24 (2006), pp. 601–47; Ruth Paley, 'Imperial Politics and English Law: the Many Contexts of Somerset', in the same volume, pp. 659–65; Steven M. Wise, *Though the Heavens May Fall: the Landmark Trial that Led to the End of Human Slavery* (London: Pimlico, 2006).
100 Francis Hargrave, *An Argument in the Case of James Sommersett A Negro, Lately Determined by the Court of King's Bench* (London, 1772), p. 50. A famous quotation, but one not spoken at the trial: see Hargrave, *Argument*, p. 9.
101 *A true relation of ... Lilburnes sufferings* (1646), pp. 5–6, 11; *L.J.*, viii, pp. 164–65.
102 Hargrave, *Argument*, p. 51. Hargrave was dependent on Rushworth for this information and followed Rushworth in misdating the judgment to 1640: Rushworth, *Historical Collections* (London, 1680), pp. 468–69.
103 On the contrast between the content of Mansfield's judgment and the public perception of the verdict, see Ruth Paley, 'James Somerset', *ODNB*.
104 *General Evening Post* (8–10 July 1777), no. 6,791.
105 See *Morning Chronicle* (13 Oct. 1794), no. 7,802.
106 Worden, 'Levellers in History and Memory', p. 270; Donnelly, 'Levellerism', pp. 265–66.

107 Stephen Jones, *A New Biographical Dictionary* (1796), p. 280; Mark Noble, *The Lives of the English Regicides*, 2 vols (1798), vol. 1, p. 378, vol. 2, p. 117.
108 See Jason McElligott, 'William Hone, Print Culture, and the Nature of Radicalism', in Ariel Hessayon and David Finnegan (ed.), *Varieties of Seventeenth and Eighteenth-Century English Radicalism in Context* (Franham: Ashgate, 2011), pp. 241–60; Mark Clement, 'True Religion: Christianity and the Rhetoric of Early Nineteenth-Century English Popular Radicalism', *Journal of Religious History* 20: 1 (1996), pp. 1–20, at p. 19. Epstein, *Radical Expression*, p. 35.
109 Thomas Carlyle, *Oliver Cromwell's Letters and Speeches with elucidations*, 2 vols. (London, 1845), vol. 1, p. 297.
110 See University Library Durham, Add MS. 763, 'The Lilburne M.S.'. The Lilburne tracts were bound into three volumes: see Durham University Library Special Collections, SB 1614–16. I am grateful to Alex Barber for bringing the Lilburne MS to my attention.
111 See William Godwin, *History of the Commonwealth of England from its Commencement, to the Restoration of Charles the Second*, edited with an introduction by John Morrow (Bristol: Thoemmes, 2002), vol. 1, p. xxix.
112 See, for example, Fenner Brockway, *Britain's First Socialists* (London: Quartet, 1980), p. 25.
113 I owe this point to Victoria Gardner.
114 For which, see Braddick, 'Celebrity Radical', throughout.
115 Donnelly, 'Levellerism', p. 269. For a contrasting argument that emphasises radical re-engagement with English revolution in the later eighteenth century, see Zaller, 'Continuity', p. 35.
116 John Lilburne, *England's New Chains Discovered*, 1649, B2v.
117 D. Alan Orr's contention that Lilburne was developing an important new conception of 'negative liberty' in his trial pamphlets might suggest that there remained intellectual affinities here: Orr, 'Law, Liberty and the English Civil War: John Lilburne's Prison Experience, the Levellers and Freedom', in Michael J. Braddick and David L. Smith (eds.), *The Experience of Revolution* (Cambridge: CUP, 2011), ch. 8. See also John Donoghue, *'Fire Under the Ashes': An Atlantic History of the English Revolution* (Chicago: University of Chicago Press, 2013).
118 Green, *Verdict According to Conscience*, p. 381.
119 For an argument for just such continuity, see T. Morton and N. Smith, *Radicalism in British Literary Culture, 1650–1850* (Cambridge: CUP, 2002), pp. 1–2.
120 F.K. Donnelly, 'Thomas Jefferson, John Lilburne and the English Levellers', *Albion Magazine Online*, Autumn 2010 [http://zyworld.com/albionmagazineonline/jefferson_lilburne.htm, accessed 9 March 2015]. I thank Professor Donnelly for sending me a copy of his article, which unfortunately, as of 1 July 2017, is no longer available online.
121 John Rees, 'Leveller Organisation and the English Revolution' (unpublished, Goldsmiths, University of London, PhD, 2014), pp. 28–29 [http://research.gold.ac.uk/10465/1/HIS_thesis_Rees_Thesis_2014.pdf, accessed 9 March 2015].

BIBLIOGRAPHY

Works by John Lilburne

Lilburne, J, *A Copy of a Letter Written to Collonel Henry Marten* (London, 1647).
Lilburne, J, *A Defensive Declaration* (London, 1653).
Lilburne, J, *A Letter ... to Mr John Price* (London, 1651).
Lilburne, J, *A Light for the Ignorant* (London, 1641), published anonymously in Amsterdam, 1638.
Lilburne, J, *A preparative to an hue and cry* (London, 1649).
Lilburne, J, *A Whip for the present House of Lords* (London, 1648).
Lilburne, J, *An anatomy of the Lords tyranny* (London, 1646).
Lilburne, J, *An impeachment of high treason* (London, 1649).
Lilburne, J, *An outcry of the youngmen and apprentices* (London, 1649).
Lilburne, J, *As You Were* (Amsterdam, 1652).
Lilburne, J, *As You Were* (London, 1652).
Lilburne, J, *Christian Mans Triall* (London, 1641).
Lilburne, J, *Colonel Lilburne Revived* (London, March 1653, np).
Lilburne, J, *Englands New Chaines Discovered* (London, 1649).
Lilburne, J, *Foundations of Freedom, or an Agreement of the People* (London, 1648).
Lilburne, J, *His Letter to his dearly beloved wife, Mrs Elizabeth Lilburne, March 1652* (1653, np).
Lilburne, J, *Innocency and truth justified* (London, 1646).
Lilburne, J, *L. Col. John Lilburne his apologeticall narration* (London, 1652).
Lilburne, J, *L. Colonel Lilburne his Letter to his Dearely Beloved Wife* (Amsterdam, 1652).
Lilburne, J, *L. Colonel Lilburne Revived* (Amsterdam, 1653).
Lilburne, J, *London's Liberties in Chains discovered ... published by Lieutenant Colonell John Lilburn, prisoner in the Tower of London* (London, 1646).
Lilburne, J, *Malice Detected* (London, 1653).
Lilburne, J, *Rash Oaths Unwarrantable* (London, 1647).
Lilburne, J, *Regall Tyranny Discovered* (London, 1647).
Lilburne, J, *Severall Informations and Examinations* (London, 1653).
Lilburne, J, *Strength out of Weakness* (London, 1649).
Lilburne, J, *The additionall plea of Lieut. Col. John Lilburne* (London, 1647).
Lilburne, J, *The copy of a letter ... to a freind* (London, 1645).

Lilburne, J, *The free-mans freedom vindicated* (London, 1646).
Lilburne, J, *The grand plea of Lieut. Col. John Lilburne* (London, 1647).
Lilburne, J, *The Innocent Man's Second Proffer* (London, 1649).
Lilburne, J, *The Just Defence of John Lilburne*, in Morton, A L, (ed.), *Freedom in Arms* (London: Lawrence and Wishart, 1975).
Lilburne, J, *The juglers discovered* (London, 1647).
Lilburne, J, *The Lawes Funerall* (London, 1648).
Lilburne, J, *The Legall Fundamentall Liberties* (London, 1649, 1st edn.).
Lilburne, J, *The peoples prerogative* (London, 1648).
Lilburne, J, *The prisoners plea for a habeas corpus* (London, 1648).
Lilburne, J, *The reasons of Lieu Col. Lilbournes sending his letter to Mr Prin* (London, 1645).
Lilburne, J, *The resolved mans resolution* (London, 1647).
Lilburne, J, *The resurrection of John Lilburne, now a prisoner in Dover-Castle* (London, 2nd edn., 1656).
Lilburne, J, *The Upright Mans Vindication or An Epistle writ by John Lilburne Gent. Prisoner in Newgate, August 1 1653* (London, 1653).
Lilburne, J, et al., *A Plea for Common-Right and Freedom* (London, 1648).
Lilburne, J, Walwyn, W, Prince, T, and Overton, R, *An Agreement of the Free People of England, Tendered as a Peace-Offering to this distressed Nation* (London, 1649).

Primary sources

A Conference with the Souldiers (London, 1653).
A Declaration of Some Proceedings of Lt Colonel John Lilburne (London, 1648).
A Declaration of the Armie (London, 1652).
A Declaration of the High and Mighty Lords (London, 1652).
A Declaration of the Proceedings of Major General Massey (London, 1652).
A Declaration: or, Representation from His Excellencie Sir Thomas Fairfax and the Army under his command (London, 14 June 1647).
A Petition from His Excellency Thomas Lord Fairfax and the General Council of officers of the Army, to the Honourable the Commons of England in Parliament Assembled (London, 1649).
An Agreement of the People for a firme and present Peace, upon grounds of common-right and freedome (London, 1647).
An Epistle from Col. John Lilburn, in the Shades to John Wilkes Esq. Late A Colonel in the Buckinghamshire Militia (n.d. 1765?).
An Exact Collection of all the Remonstrances, Declarations, Votes, Orders, Ordinances, Proclamations, Petitions, Messages, Answers, and other remarkable passages between the Kings Most Excellent Majesty, and his High Court of Parliament beginning with his Majesties return from Scotland, being in December 1641, and continued until March the 21, 1643.
Anon., *A Declaration To the Free-born People of England* (London, 1654).
Anon., *The History of King-Killers* (1720), vol. 2.
Anon., *The Last Will and Testament of Lieutenant Col. John Lilburn* (London, 1654).
Bloudy Newes from Holland (London, 1652).
Englands birth-right justified (London, 1645).
The Humble Petition of divers well-affected women (London, 1649).
The Selfe Afflicter Lively Described in the whole course of the life of Mr. John Lilburn (London, 1657).
The Speech spoken by Prince Robert (London, 1642).
The Triall of Mr John Lilburn (London, 1653).
To the Parliament of the Commonwealth of England. The humble petition of divers afflicted Women, in behalf of M John Lilburn Prisoner in Newgate (London, June 25 1653).

To the Supreme Authority of England. The Commons Assembled in Parliament, The Humble Petition of divers well-affected women (London, May 1649).

Unto every individual Member of Parliament: The humble representation of divers afflicted Women-Petitioners to the Parliament, on the behalf of Mr John Lilburn (London, July 29 1653).

Bastwick, J, *A Just Defence of John Bastwick* (London, 1645).
Bethel, S, *The world's mistake in Oliver Cromwell* (London, 1668).
Birch, T (ed.), *A Collection of the State Papers of John Thurloe*, 7 vols. (1742), vol. 3.
Chidley, S, *The Dissembling Scot* (London, 1652).
Cockeram, H, *The English Dictionarie* (London, 1626; 2nd edn.).
Coke, E, *The first part of the Institutes* (1639).
Cowell, J, *The Interpreter* (London, 1637 edn.).
Edwards, T, *Gangraena*, Pt. III (London, 1646).
Freize, J, *The Levellers vindication* (London, 1649).
Larner, W, *A true relation of all the remarkable Passages and Illegall Proceedings ... Against William Larner* (London, 1646).
Larner, W, *A Vindication of Every Free-mans Libertie* (London, 1646).
Lilburne, E, *To the Chosen and betrusted Knights, Citizens, and Burgesses, assembled in the High and Supream Court of Parliament* (1646).
Locke, J, *A Letter concerning Toleration* (London, 1689).
Marten, H, *Rash Censures Uncharitable*, BL Add. MS 71532.
Milton, J, *Areopagitica; A Speech of Mr. John Milton, for the Liberty of Unlicens'd Printing, to the Parliament of England* (London, 1644).
Overton, R, *The Araignement of Mr Persecution* (London, 1645).
Overton, R, *An Appeale from the degenerate representative body* (London, 1647).
Overton, R, *Commoners Complaint* (London, 1647).
Overton, R, *Remonstrance of Many Thousand Citizens* (London, 1646).
Owen, J, *A Sermon Preached to the Honourable House of Commons* (London, 1649).
Oxford, W, *A Prospective for King and Subjects* (Leyden, 1652).
Oxford, W, *The Unexpected Life* (Leyden?, 1652).
Oxford, W, *Vincit qui Patitur* (London, 1653).
Peter, H, *Good Work for a Good Magistrate* (London, 1651).
Prynne, W, *A new discovery of free-state tyranny* (London, 1655).
Prynne, W, *Mount-Orgueil* (London, 1641).
Rastell, J, *Les Termes de la Ley* (1629 edn.).
Rushworth, J, *Historical Collections of private passages of state* (London, 8 vols., 1721).
Scott, T, *The Belgicke Pismire* (London, 1622).
Sanderson, W, *A Compleat History of the Life and Raigne of King Charles from His Cradle to his Grave* (London, 1658).
Stalham, J, *The reviler rebuked* (1657).
Sydenham, C, *An Anatomy of Lieut. Col. John Lilburn's Spirit and Pamphlets* (1649).
Twisse, W, et al., *Certaine considerations to dis-swade men from further gathering of churches in this present juncture of time* (London, 1643).
Varax, T (Clement Walker), *The Triall of Lieu. Colonell John Lilburne* (London, 1649).
Walwyn, W, *The Poore Wise-mans Admonition* (London, 1647).
Williams, R, *The Bloudy Tenent, of Persecution, for Cause of Conscience, discussed, in a Conference betweene Truth and Peace* (London, 1644).
Winstanley, W, *England's Worthies* (1660).
Winterton, T, *The chasing the young Quaking Harlot Out of the City* (1656).
Wood, A, *Athenae Oxonienses* (2 vols., 1691–92).

Secondary sources

Adams, D, 'The secret printing and publishing career of Richard Overton the Leveller, 1644–46', *The Library*, 11: 1 (2010).
Allen, J W, *A History of Political Thought in the Sixteenth Century* (London, 1928).
Aylmer, G E, *The Levellers in the English Revolution* (London, 1975).
Baker, P, 'Radicalism in Civil War and Interregnum England', *History Compass*, 8 (2010).
Baker, R, *Chronicle of the Kings of England* (1733 edn.).
Bernstein, E, *Cromwell and Communism: Socialism and Democracy in the Great English Revolution* (1895), trans. H.J. Stenning (1930; reprinted, Nottingham, 1980).
Birchall, I, 'The wrong kind of secularism', *Jacobin*, www.jacobinmag.com/2015/11/charlie-hebdo-france-secular-paris-attacks-lacite/, online only.
Black, A, *Guilds and Civil Society in European Political Thought from the Twelfth Century to the Present* (London: Methuen, 1984).
Black, A, *Political Thought in Europe, 1250–1450* (Cambridge: Cambridge University Press, 1992).
Braddick, M, 'The celebrity radical', *BBC History Magazine*, 8: 10 (October 2007).
Bragg, B, *The Progressive Patriot: a Search for Belonging* (London, 2007).
Brailsford, H N, *The Levellers and the English Revolution* (Nottingham, 1983).
Braithwaite, W, *The Beginnings of Quakerism to 1660* (1912; 2nd edn., revised Cambridge, 1955; reprinted York, 1981).
Brewer, J, 'The Wilkites and the law, 1763–1774', in J. Brewer and J. Styles (eds.), *An Ungovernable People: the English and Their Law in the Seventeenth and Eighteenth Centuries* (London, 1980).
Brockway, F, *Britain's First Socialists* (London, 1980).
Burgess, G, 'Protestant polemic: the Leveller pamphlets', *Parergon*, n.s.11 (1993).
Burgess, G, *Absolute Monarchy and the Stuart Constitution* (New Haven and London, 1996).
Burgess, G, *The Politics of the Ancient Constitution: An Introduction to English Political Thought, 1603–1642* (Basingstoke, 1992).
Carlin, C, 'Liberty and fraternities in the English revolution', *International Review of Social History*, 39 (1994).
Carlin, N, 'Toleration for Catholics in the Puritan revolution', in Ole Peter Grell and Bob Scribner (eds.), *Tolerance and Intolerance in the European Reformation* (Cambridge: Cambridge University Press, 1996).
Carlin, N, 'Leveller organisation in London', *Historical Journal*, 27 (1984).
Carlyle, T (ed.) *Letters and Speeches of Oliver Cromwell* (London, 1888 edn.).
Carte, T, *A General History of England*, 4 vols. (1747–55).
Clark, J C D, *Revolution and Rebellion: State and Society in England in the Seventeenth Century* (Cambridge, 1986).
Clement, M, 'True religion: Christianity and the rhetoric of early nineteenth-century English popular radicalism', *Journal of Religious History*, 20: 1 (1996).
Coffey, J, *Persecution and Toleration in Protestant England 1558–1689* (Harlow: Longman, 2000).
Condren, C, 'Liberty of office and its defence in seventeenth-century political argument', *History of Political Thought*, 18 (1997).
Condren, C, 'Radicals, conservatives and moderates in early modern political thought: a case of Sandwich Islands syndrome?', *History of Political Thought*, 10 (1989).
Cromartie, A, 'The constitutionalist revolution: the transformation of political culture in early Stuart England', *Past and Present*, 163 (1999).
Davis, J C, 'Reassessing radicalism in a traditional society', in G. Burgess and M. Festenstein (eds.), *English Radicalism, 1550–1850* (Cambridge, 2007).
Davis, J C, 'Radicalism in a traditional society: the evaluation of radical thought in the English commonwealth 1649–1660', *History of Political Thought*, 3 (1982).

Davis, J C, 'Religion and the struggle for freedom in the English Revolution', *Historical Journal*, 35 (1992).
de Larrey, I, *The History of the Reign of King Charles I*, 2 vols. (1716).
Donnelly, F K, 'Levellerism in eighteenth and early nineteenth-century Britain', *Albion*, 20: 2, 1988.
Donnelly, F K, 'Thomas Jefferson, John Lilburne and the English Levellers', *Albion Magazine Online*, Autumn 2010, http://zyworld.com/albionmagazineonline/jefferson_lilburne.htm.
Donoghue, J, *'Fire Under the Ashes': An Atlantic History of the English Revolution* (Chicago, 2013).
Duke, A, Lewis, G, and Pettegree, A (eds.), *Calvinism in Europe 1540–1610* (Manchester: Manchester University Press, pb edn. 1997).
Ellis, H (ed.), *The Obituary of Richard Smyth* (London: Camden Society, 1849).
Epstein, J A, *In Practice: Studies in the Language and Culture of Popular Politics in Modern Britain* (Stanford, 2003).
Epstein, J A, *Radical Expression: Political Language, Ritual and Symbol in England, 1790–1850* (Oxford, 1994).
Farr, D, *Henry Ireton and the English Revolution* (Woodbridge: Boydell, 2006).
Firth, C H (ed.), *The Clarke Papers, Selections from the Papers of William Clarke, Secretary to the Council of the Army* (London: Camden Society, 1894).
Foxley, R, 'Freedom of conscience and the agreements of the people', in P. Baker and E. Vernon (eds.), *The Agreements of the People, the Levellers and the Constitutional Crisis of the English Revolution* (Basingstoke: Palgrave Macmillan, 2012).
Foxley, R, *The Levellers: Radical Political Thought in the English Revolution* (Manchester: Manchester University Press, 2013).
Frank, J, *The Levellers: A History of the Writings of Three Seventeenth-Century Social Democrats (Lilburne, Overton and Walwyn)* (Cambridge, MA, 1955).
Gardiner, S R (ed.), *The Constitutional Documents of the Puritan Revolution* (Oxford, 1906 edn.).
Gay, E F, 'The Midland Revolt and the Inquisitions of Depopulation of 1607', *Transactions of the Royal Historical Society*, 18 (1904).
Gentles, I, 'Rich, Nathaniel (d. 1700x02)', *Oxford Dictionary of National Biography*.
Gibb, M A, *John Lilburne The Leveller* (London: Lindsay Drummond, 1947).
Gleissner, R, 'The Levellers and natural law', *Journal of British Studies*, 20 (1980–81).
Glover, S, 'The Putney Debates: popular vs. elitist republicanism', *Past and Present*, 164 (1999).
Godwin, W, *History of the Commonwealth of England from its Commencement, to the Restoration of Charles the Second*, edited with an introduction by John Morrow (Bristol, 2003).
Greaves, R L, 'Owen, John (1616–1683)', *Oxford Dictionary of National Biography*.
Green, T A, *Verdict According to Conscience: Perspectives on the English Criminal Trial Jury 1200–1800* (London, 1985).
Gregg, P, *Free-Born John: The Biography of John Lilburne* (London, 1961).
Guérin, D, *Class Struggle in the First French Republic*, trans. Ian Patterson (London: Pluto, 1977).
Halliday, P, *Habeas Corpus. From England to Empire* (Cambridge, MA, 2010).
Hampsher-Monk, I, 'The political theory of the Levellers: Putney, property and Professor Macpherson', *Political Studies*, 24 (1976).
Heath, J, *A Chronicle of the Late Intestine War in the Three Kingdoms of England, Scotland and Ireland … to which is added A Continuation to this present year 1675* (London, 1676).
Heinemann, M, 'Popular drama and Leveller style', in M. Cornforth (ed.), *Rebels and Their Causes: Essays in Honour of A. L. Morton* (London: Lawrence and Wishart, 1978).
Henderson, F, 'Drafting the Officers' Agreement of the People, 1648–9', in P. Baker and E. Vernon (eds.), *The Agreements of the People, the Levellers and the Constitutional Crisis of the English Revolution* (Basingstoke: Palgrave Macmillan, 2012).
Henderson, F (ed.), *The Clarke Papers Volume 5: Further Selections from the Papers of William Clarke*, Camden Society, 5th series, 27 (Cambridge, 2006).

Hessayon, A, *'Gold Tried in the Fire': The Prophet TheaurauJohn Tany and the English Revolution* (Ashgate, 2007).
Hicks, P, *Neoclassical History and English Culture from Clarendon to Hume* (Basingstoke, 1996).
Higgins, P, 'The reactions of women with special reference to women petitioners', in Brian Manning (ed.), *Politics, Religion and the English Civil War* (London: Edward Arnold, 1973).
Hildyard, J, *A Catalogue of Several Libraries and Parcels of Books* (York, 1751).
Hill, C, '"Till the conversion of the Jews"', in *Religion and Politics in 17th Century England* (Brighton: Harvester, 1986).
Hill, C, *The Experience of Defeat* (London: Verso, 2016 edn.).
Hill, C, 'From Lollards to Levellers', in Maurice Cornforth (ed.), *Rebels and their Causes: Essays in Honour of A. L. Morton* (London, 1978).
Hill, C, *The Experience of Defeat: Milton and Some Contemporaries* (1984).
Hill, C, *The World Turned Upside Down. Radical Ideas during the English Revolution* (1972; Harmondsworth, 1984 edn.).
Hinxman, J, *A Catalogue of above 15000 Volumes* (York?, 1759).
Hopfl, H (ed.), *Luther and Calvin on Secular Authority* (Cambridge: Cambridge University Press, 1991).
Houston, A, '"A way of settlement": the Levellers, monopolies and the public interest', *History of Political Thought*, 14 (1993).
Howell, R, and Brewster, D E, 'Reconsidering the Levellers: the evidence of the *Moderate*', *Past and Present*, 46 (1970).
Hughes, A, 'Elizabeth Lilburne', *Oxford Dictionary of National Biography*.
Hughes, A, 'Gender and politics in Leveller literature', in Susan D. Amussen and Mark A. Kishlansky, (eds.), *Political Culture and Cultural Politics in Early Modern England* (Manchester: Manchester University Press, 1995).
Hughes, A, *Gangraena and the Struggle for the English Revolution* (Oxford, 2004).
Hughes, A, *Gender and the English Revolution* (London: Routledge, 2011).
Hyde, E, *The History of the Rebellion and Civil Wars in England Begun in the Year 1641*, ed. W. D. Macray, 6 vols, (Oxford, 1888).
Johnson, R C, et al. (eds.), *Commons Debates 1628* (6 vols., New Haven, 1977–83).
Jones, S, *A New Biographical Dictionary* (1796).
Judson, M A, *The Crisis of the Constitution: An Essay in Constitutional and Political Thought in England 1603–1645* (New Brunswick and London, 1988 edn., originally 1949).
Katz, D S, *Philo-Semitism and the Readmission of the Jews to England 1603–1655* (Oxford: Clarendon, 1982).
Kenyon, J P, *The Stuart Constitution: Documents and commentary* (Cambridge, 1966).
Knights, M, 'The Tory interpretation of history in the rage of parties', in P. Kewes (ed.), *The Uses of History in Early Modern England* (San Marino CA, 2006).
Lake, P, 'Constitutional consensus and Puritan opposition in the 1620s: Thomas Scott and the Spanish Match', *Historical Journal*, 25 (1982).
Larry Ingle, H, *First Among Friends: George Fox & the Creation of Quakerism* (New York, 1994).
Levy, M, 'Freedom, property and the Levellers', *Western Political Quarterly*, 36 (1983).
Lindley, K, *Popular Politics and Religion in Civil War London* (Aldershot: Scolar, 1997).
Lysons, D, *The Environs of London*, 4 vols. (1796–1800).
Macaulay, C, *The History of England From the Accession of James I to that of the Brunswick Line*, Vol. IV, 9 (London, 1769).
MacGillivray, R, *Restoration Historians and the English Civil War* (The Hague, 1974).
MacLachlan, A, *The Rise and Fall of Revolutionary England* (Basingstoke, 1996).
Macpherson, C B, *The Political Theory of Possessive Individualism* (Oxford, 1962).

Manning, B, *1649, The Crisis of the English Revolution* (London: Bookmarks, 1992).
Manson, J, *Manson's Catalogue for 1791* (1791).
McElligott, J, and Smith, D (eds.), *Royalists and Royalism during the English Civil Wars* (Cambridge, 2007).
McElligott, J, and Smith, D (eds.), *Royalists and Royalism during the Interregnum* (Manchester, 2010).
McElligott, J, 'William Hone, print culture, and the nature of radicalism', in A. Hessayon and D. Finnegan (eds.), *Varieties of Seventeenth and Eighteenth-Century English Radicalism in Context* (Basingstoke, 2011).
McGregor, J F, Capp, B, Smith, N, and Gibbons, B J, 'Fear, myth and furore: reappraising the "Ranters"', *Past and Present*, 140 (1993).
McIntee, A M, '"The [Un]civill-sisterhood of Oranges and Lemons": female petitioners and demonstrators, 1642–53', *Prose Studies*, 14 (1991).
McMichael, J R, and Taft, B (eds.), *The Writings of William Walwyn* (Athens, GA and London: University of Georgia Press, 1989).
Mendle, M, 'Putney's pronouns: identity and indemnity in the great debate', in Mendle (ed.), *The Putney Debates of 1647* (Cambridge, 2001).
Menteith, R, *The History of the Troubles of Great Britain*, trans. James Ogilvy (1735).
Morgan, S, 'Celebrity: academic "pseudo-event" or a useful concept for historians?', *Cultural and Social History*, 8: 1 (2011).
Morton, T, and Smith, N, *Radicalism in British Literary Culture, 1650–1850* (Cambridge, 2002).
Mowry, M, '"Commoners wives who stand for their freedom and liberty": Leveller women and the hermeneutics of collectivities', *Huntington Library Quarterly*, 77 (2014).
Nalson, J, *An Impartial Collection of the Great Affairs of State from the Beginning of the Scotch Rebellion in the Year MDCXXXIX to the Murther of King Charles*, vol. 1 (1682).
Nicholas, E, *The Nicholas Papers: Correspondence of Sir Edward Nicholas, vol. 1 1641–1652*, (London: Camden Society, 1886).
Noble, M, *The Lives of the English Regicides*, 2 vols. (1798).
Ogle, O, Bliss, W H, Macray, W D, and Routledge, F J (eds.), *Calendar of the Clarendon State Papers Preserved in the Bodleian Library*, 5 vols. (Oxford, 1869–1970).
Oldmixon, J, *The History of England during the Reigns of the Royal House of Stuart* (1730).
Orr, D, 'Law, liberty and the English Civil War: John Lilburne's prison experience, the Levellers and freedom', in M. Braddick and D. Smith (eds.), *The Experience of Revolution* (Cambridge, 2011).
Pagden, A (ed.), *The Languages of Political Theory in Early-modern Europe* (Cambridge: Cambridge University Press, 1987).
Parkin-Speer, D, 'John Lilburne: a revolutionary interprets statutes and common law due process', *Law and History Review*, 1 (1983).
Peacey, J, 'Hunting the Leveller: the sophistication of parliamentarian propaganda, 1647–53', *Historical Research*, 78: 199 (2005).
Peacey, J, 'John Lilburne and the Long Parliament', *Historical Journal*, 43 (2000).
Pease, T, *The Leveller Movement: A Study in the History and Political Theory of the English Great Civil War* (Washington, DC, 1916; reprinted, Gloucester, MA, 1965).
Penney, N (ed.), '*The First Publishers of Truth*'. *Being early records (now first printed) of the introduction of Quakerism into the counties of England and Wales* (1907).
Peters, K, *Print Culture and the Early Quakers* (Cambridge: Cambridge University Press, 2005).
Pocock, J G A, *The Ancient Constitution and the Feudal Law: A Study of English Historical Thought in the Seventeenth Century* (Cambridge, 1987 edn.).
Pocock, J G A, *The Machiavellian Moment* (Princeton, 1975).

Polizzotto, C, 'Liberty of conscience and the Whitehall Debates of 1648–9', *Journal of Ecclesiastical History*, 26 (1975).
Polizzotto, C, 'What really happened at Whitehall? A new source', *Historical Journal*, 57 (2014).
Rappaport, S, *Worlds Within Worlds: Structures of Life in Sixteenth-Century London* (Cambridge, 1989).
Rediker, M, and Linebaugh, P, *The Many-Headed Hydra: Sailors, Slaves, Commoners and the Hidden History of the Revolutionary Atlantic* (London, 2000).
Rees, J, 'Leveller organisation and the English Revolution' (Goldsmiths: University of London, PhD, 2004).
Rees, J, *The Leveller Revolution* (London: Verso, 2016).
Robertson G, *The Tyrannicide Brief: The Story of the Man who Sent Charles I to the Scaffold* (Random House, 2006).
Robertson, G, *The Levellers: The Putney Debates* (Verso, 2007).
Robinson, H, *Liberty of Conscience, or the Sole Means to Obtaine Peace and Truth* (London, 1643).
Russell, C, *The Causes of the English Civil War* (Oxford, 1990).
Sacks, D, 'Parliament, liberty and the commonweal', in J. H. Hexter (ed.), *Parliament and Liberty* (Stanford, 1992).
Sanderson, J, *'But the People's Creatures': The Philosophical Basis of the English Civil War* (Manchester, 1989).
Scott, J, 'What were Commonwealth Principles?', *Historical Journal*, 47 (2004).
Scott, J, *Commonwealth Principles* (Cambridge, 2004).
Seaberg, R B, 'The Norman Conquest and the common law', *Historical Journal*, 24 (1981).
Sharp, A, 'John Lilburne and the Long Parliament's *Book of Declarations*', *History of Political Thought*, 9 (1988).
Sharp, A, 'John Lilburne's discourse of law', *Political Science*, 40 (1988).
Sharp, A (ed.), *The English Levellers* (Cambridge, 1998).
Sharp, A, *Political Ideas of the English Civil Wars 1641–1649* (London, 1983).
Skinner, Q, 'History and ideology in the English Revolution', *Historical Journal*, 8 (1965).
Skinner, Q, *The Foundations of Modern Political Thought*, 2 vols. (Cambridge, 1977–78).
Smith, D, *Constitutional Royalism and the Search for Settlement, c.1640–1649* (Cambridge, 1994).
Smith, J, *A Descriptive Catalogue of Friends' Books*, 2 vols. (1867).
Sommerville, J P, 'History and theory: the Norman conquest in early Stuart political thought', *Political Studies*, 34 (1986).
Taft, B, 'Walwyn, William (*bap.* 1600, d. 1681)', *Oxford Dictionary of National Biography*.
Taft, B, 'The council of officers' Agreement of the people, 1648/9,' *Historical Journal*, 28 (1985).
Thomas, K, 'The Levellers and the franchise', in G. E. Aylmer (ed.), *The Interregnum: The Quest for Settlement* (London, 1972).
Thompson, E P, *Witness Against the Beast: William Blake and the Moral Law* (Cambridge, 1994).
Tolmie, M, 'Thomas Lambe, soapboiler, and Thomas Lambe, merchant, general Baptists', *Baptist Quarterly*, 27: 1 (January 1977).
Tolmie, M, *The Triumph of the Saints, The Separatist Churches of London 1616–1649* (Cambridge: Cambridge University Press, 1977).
Towers, J, 'The life of John Lilburne', in Towers (ed.), *British Biography*, 7 vols. (1766–72).
Towers, J, *An Enquiry into the Question, Whether Juries are, or are Not, Judges of Law as well as of Fact* (1764).
Towers, J, *Observations on the Rights and Duties of Juries* (1784).
Tubbs, J W, *The Common Law Mind* (Baltimore and London, 2000).
Tuke, H, *Biographical Notices of Members of the Society of Friends*, 2 vols. (York, 1815).
Wales, T C, and Hartley, C P (eds.), *The Visitation of London Begun in 1687* (London, 2004).

Wende, P, '"Liberty" und "property" in der politischen Theorie der Levellers', *Zeitschrift für historische Forschung*, 1 (1974).
Weston, C, 'England: ancient constitution and common law', in J.H. Burns and Mark Goldie (eds.), *The Cambridge History of Political Thought, 1450–1700* (Cambridge, 1991).
White, S, *Sir Edward Coke and the Grievances of the Commonwealth* (Manchester, 1979).
Whiting, J, *A Catalogue of Friends Books; Written by Many of the People, Called Quakers, From the Beginning or First Appearance of the Said People* (London, 1708).
William Sewel, W, *The History of the Rise, Increase, and Progress of the Christian People Called Quakers* (1722, 3rd edn., Philadelphia, 1728).
Wolfe, D M, *Leveller Manifestoes of the Puritan Revolution* (New York, 1944).
Woodhouse, A S P (ed.), *Puritanism and Liberty* (London, 1992).
Woolf, D, *Reading History in Early Modern England* (Cambridge, 2000).
Wootton, D, 'Leveller democracy and the Puritan Revolution,' in J.H. Burns and M. Goldie (eds.), *The Cambridge History of Political Thought, 1450–1700* (Cambridge, 1991).
Worden, B, 'The Levellers and the left', in *Roundhead Reputations* (London, 2002).
Wright, S, *The Early English Baptists 1603–1649* (Woodbridge: Boydell, 2006).
Zaller, R, 'The continuity of British radicalism in the seventeenth and eighteenth centuries', *Eighteenth-Century Life*, 6 (1981).

INDEX

Additional Plea, The (Lilburne, J.) 21
Agreement of the Free People of England (Levellers) 43
Agreement of the People (Levellers' manifesto) 4, 22, 23, 25, 121, 125, 127, 128, 134; and Army Remonstrance (1648), impact of 39–40; modern view of 118; purpose and aims of 63; religious toleration, conflict over 39–40; the state and religion, view of and challenges to 37, 38, 40–3
Apologeticall Narration (Lilburne, J.) 20, 83; bilingual editions of 85–6
apprenticeships: apprentices' 'riot' 71; Lilburne, J. 1, 119; nature of (in London) 1
Araignement of Mr Persecution, The (Overton, Richard) 34–5, 36
Areopagitica (Milton, J.) 35
Army Council (Whitehall, 1648) 32; religion, debate on 34
Army Remonstrance (1648) 38–40; the state and religion, challenges to 41–2
army revolt (1647) 72
Assembly of Divines (Westminster) 34
Athenae Oxonienses (Wood, A.) 125

Baker, Sir Richard 128
Barkstead, John 98
Bastwick, John 2, 75, 119, 121
Beckford, William 131–2
Bernstein, Eduard 98
Béza, Theodore 40
Billing, Edward 109
Biographia Britannica (1760) 126

Birkenhead, Isaac 81
birth-right: definition, and use of 12–13; and legal tradition 13
Bishop, George 109
Blasphemy Act (1650) 44
Bloudy Tenent of Persecution for Cause of Conscience (Williams, R.) 33, 34, 36
Book of Declarations 71
Book of Martyrs (Foxe, J.) 2
Braddick, Mike 119
Bradshawe, John 65
Brailsford, Henry 98
Bramhall, Bishop John 80
British Biography (Towers, J.) 129
Buckingham, Duke of 79–80; Lilburne, John, involvement with 80
Bull and Mouth Inn (Aldersgate) 95
Burgess, Glenn 19
Burton, Henry 2, 119

Calvert, Giles 104
Calvin, John 40; civil authority and correct religious belief 40–1
Carlile, Richard 134
Carlin, Norah 3
Carlyle, Thomas 95, 134–5
Carte, Thomas 128
'Cartwright's Case' 133
Case of the Armie, The (Lilburne, J.) 23, 24
Certain Passages (Lilburne, J.) 102
Chapman, Livewell 107
Charles I: execution of 43; street protests against 2; trial of, and Leveller view 63–4
Cheesman, Christopher 109

Chidley, Katherine 68, 71, 73
Chidley, Samuel 75
Christian Man's Trial (Lilburne, J.) 2, 70; Kiffin, William, foreword by 72
Chronicle of the Kings of England (Baker, R.) 128
Chronicle of the Late Intestine War (Heath, J.) 117
citizens and citizenship: and birth-right 12; subjects, comparison with 8
Civil War 3, 120; Edgehill, battle at 62; outcomes of 4; Scots, role in 3
Clarendon, Earl of 79, 80, 125; *History of the Rebellion* 125; Levellers, and a possible alliance with 126; Lilburne, John, view of 125–6
Clarendon Code (1660) 44
Clark, Henry 106
Cockeram, Henry 10–11
Coke, Edward 2, 12; common law and parliamentary statute, views of 19; denizen, use of word 10; legal writings of 14–15; Magna Carta, reinvention of 61; monopoly, use and interpretation of 15
Commentaries (Plowden, E.) 15
Committee of Examinations 12
common law 26n6; Coke, Edward, writings on and interpretation of 14; and law of nature 16–17, 20; and parliamentary statute 19; principles and maxims of 14–15; and royal prerogative 15
Commoners Complaint or a Dreadful Warning from Newgate to the Commons of England, The (Overton, R.) 53
Compassionate Samaritane (Walwyn, W.) 36
Condren, Conal 13–14
Cooke, John 62; Charles I, trial and prosecution of 63–4; *King Charles: His Case* 67; Lilburne, John, legal support of 62
Cornelius, Lambert 103
Cowell, John 11, 13; denizen, use of word 11
Crome, Elizabeth 101
Cromwell, Oliver 3; Gibbon, Robert, letter from 101; Judaism, toleration of 35; Levellers, attitude towards and opposition from, 4, 64; Lilburne, Elizabeth, letter from 96–7; Lilburne, John, relationship with 62, 120, 121; Owen, John, view of 44

de Larrey, Isaac 128
Declaration to the Free-born People of England, A (1654) 99
Defencive Declaration (Lilburne, J.) 83; Dutch edition of 86; Scott, Thomas, and criticism of 84
denizen: definition, and Lilburne's use of 10–11, 12; interpretation of 10–11; status and rights of 11–12
Dewell, Henry 101
Dewsbury, William 104
Dictionary (Cockeram, H.) 10–11
Diggers 71
Discovery of Mans Returne To his First Estate (Dewsbury, W.) 104
Discovery of the great enmity of the Serpent against the seed of the Woman, The (Dewsbury, W.) 104
Dover Castle 82, 103, 104, 105, 122
Duke, Francis 106

Edwards, Thomas 37, 69, 72, 123; *Gangraena* 124; Lilburne, John, view of 123, 125
Englands Birthright Justified (Lilburne, J.) 20, 24
Englands New Chaines Discovered (Lilburne, J.) 4, 20, 25; presentation of to the House of Commons 54; purpose and aims of 64
English Commonwealth 43
Englishness: concept of 21; and English liberties 21–2; treason and forfeiting of rights 22
entitlements (and English law) 13
Epistle from Col. John Lilburne, in the shades, to John Wilkes Esq., An 132
Epstein, James 133
Evelyn, John 96
Exact and true narration of the life and death of that famous & most unsatisfied and unbound person, An (Stafford, J.) 107

Fairfax, Thomas, Lord 38; Levellers, attitude towards 64
Faithful Scout, The (newsbook) 99, 100, 102
Fell, Margaret 107
female activism 50; petitioning by women 50
Fleetwood, Charles 97
Fox, Charles James 133, 134
Fox, George 97, 106, 109
Frank, Joseph 98
'free-born Englishman' (meaning and use of phrase) 7–8
Free-Born John (Gregg, P.), 98
'free-man', and freeman (different meanings of) 8–9

Freemans Freedom, The (Lilburne, John) 20
Freize, James 72
Funeral exercise or sermon, spoken at ye solemnization of ye obsequies of that precious Saint and dearly beloved brother, A (Harper, R.) 107

Gangraena (Edwards, T.) 124
General History of England (Carte, T.) 128
Gibb, M. A. 69
Gibbon, Robert 101; Cromwell, Oliver, letter to 101; Lilburne, John, captor of (Jersey) 101–2
Good Work for a Good Magistrate (Peter, H.) 88
Gregg, Pauline 69, 98

habeas corpus, writ of: Channel Islands, application of? 98–9, 100; *Declaration to the Free-born People of England, A* (1654), and reference to 99; investigation in to use/abuse of 100; Lilburne, John, writ applied for 98–9, 100
Harding, William 103, 105
Hargrave, Francis 133–4
Harper, Richard 107
Harrington, James 91
Harris, John 74–5
Harrison, George 106
Harwood, John 107
Hesilrige, Sir Arthur 56, 63, 67, 79; property dispute with John Lilburne 107, 108, 122
Heane, James 98, 99; death of 101; Lilburne, John, captor of (Jersey) 100
Heath, James 117, 125
Heselrig, Sir Arthur *see* Hesilrige, Sir Arthur
Hessayon, Ariel 4
Hewson, Thomas 1, 119
Higgins, John 106
Hill, Christopher 69, 98, 109, 118
Hills, Henry (and Jr.) 129–31
History of King-Killers, The (1720) 96
History of the Commonwealth (Godwin, W.) 135
History of the Rebellion (Clarendon, Earl of) 125, 126
Hone, William 134
Honywood, Benoni 105
Honywood, Elizabeth 105
Hopton, Lord 81
Horne, John 132
Howard, Luke 103–4, 106
Hubberthorne, Richard 106
Hyde, Edward *see* Clarendon, Earl of

Innocency and Truth (Lilburne, John) 17
Innocent Man's Second Proffer, The (Lilburne, J.) 70
Institutes (Coke, Edward) 2, 15
Institutes of the Christian Religion, The (Calvin, J.) 40
Interpreter (Cowell, John) 11
Ireton, Henry: Army Remonstrance (1648) 38–9; Levellers, attitude towards 41–2; 'Officers' Agreement' 121; Putney Debates 23, 24, 25; the state and religion, view of 41–2

Jackson, John 104
Jenkins, David 124
Jersey: Lilburne, John, confinement at 4, 98; Mont Orgueil Castle 98, 100, 101
Jones, Stephen 134
Judaism: Cromwell, Oliver, toleration of 35; and persecution of Jews 35
juries, and rights of 122, 132–3
Juryman's Judgement, A (Lilburne, J.) 68
Just Defence of John Lilburne, The (Lilburne, J.) 70
Just Man in Bonds or Lieutenant Colonel John Lilburne close Prisoner in Newgate (1646) 50

Keble, Judge 65–7
Kiffin, William 72, 103
King Charles: His Case (Cooke, J.) 67

Lamb Contending with the Lion, The (Cheesman, C.) 109
Lambe, Thomas 72
'Large Petition' (September 1648) 38, 39; Leveller wives, support for 54–5
Larner, Ellen 50; petitioning by, in support of her husband 53
Larner, William 2, 51, 73; imprisonment of 53
Last Will & Testament (of John Lilburne) 99–100
Laud, Archbishop William 2, 119, 120
Law and Liberties of the People of England (Lilburne, J.) 101
Les Termes de la Ley (Rastell, John) 10; privileges, and definition of 13
Letany (Bastwick, J.) 2
Letter Concerning Toleration (Locke, J.) 44
Letter to his Dearly Beloved Wife (Lilburne, J.) 83, 84
Levellers: *Agreement of the Free People of England* 43; *Agreement of the People* (manifesto) 4, 22, 23, 25, 121, 125,

127, 128, 134; army, impact on 72; Assembly of Divines (Westminster) 34; collective leadership of 73; and common law, view of 7; and consent theory 24–5; Cromwell, Oliver, opposition to 4; English Commonwealth, establishment of and impact on 43; female activism 50; gender relations 50; households of, and their representations of 51, 52, 53; inclusivity and exclusivity 22–3; 'Large Petition' (September 1648) 38, 39, 54; modern view of 117–18; naming of and origin 1, 121; political theories, and classification of 6–7; post-Restoration, view of 125–9; and Quaker conversions 109; and religious motivation and toleration 32–3, 37; Rump Parliament, challenges of 64; the state and religion, view of 33, 37; voting and petitioning, significance of to 24–5; wives of, and their roles 49–50, 51–2, 53–6; women, treatment and view of 51–2; writings and publications of 74–5

liberty: sources of in English common law 16–17; and status 14; use and interpretation of the word 14

Liberty of Conscience (Robinson, H.) 35

'liberty' of the law, and citizenship rights 12

Light for the Ignorant, A (Lilburne, John) 33

Lilburn, Charles 135

Lilburne, Elizabeth: abuse and treatment of 52; Cromwell, Oliver, letter to 96–7; estate and property, disputes after John's death 108; and Leveller pamphlets, depictions of 52; *Londons Liberty in Chains*, petition in 50–1, 53; marriage and relationship with her husband 49, 56–8; Oxford, her defence of John at 3, 62, 120; petition to Protector, John's release from Jersey 102; Quakerism, and John's conversion to 104; support of her husband 49, 50–1, 104, 105, 120

Lilburne, John *136*; 17th/18th century view of 119, 123, 129; 19th/20th century view of 117–18, 135–7; Amsterdam, and exile in and influence on 82, 87–9; ancient liberties and current/future laws, views of 18–19; apprenticeship of 1, 119; arrest and imprisonment of 2, 4, 98, 100–2, 120; background of 1, 120; banishment and exile 4, 56, 67, 68, 78–9, 122; Baptists, disagreements with 105–6; biographies of 126–30; *Book of Declarations*, use of 71; bravery and courage of 73–4; Buckingham, Duke of, involvement with 80; Charles I, trial and view of 63–64; Civil War, role in 3; Coke, Edward, influence on 14, 15–16; Committee of Examinations, speech to 12; consent theory, view of 24–5; Cromwell, Oliver, relationship with 62, 120, 121; death and rumours of 95, 99–100, 122; denizen, use of word 10–11, 12; Dover Castle, interment 82, 103, 104, 105, 122; Edgehill, battle at and role in 62; Elizabeth, support from 49, 50–1, 62, 104, 105, 120; and Englishness, sense of 21–2; European influence of 86; final years of 107–9; 'free-born', use of 2, 7–8, 61; 'free-man', use of term 8–9; funeral of 95–6; gathered churches, alliance with 72; God's will, submission to 37; habeas corpus, application on behalf of 98–9, 100; Hesilrige, Sir Arthur, dispute with 63, 67, 122; inclusivity and use of language 22–3; Isle of Wight, transfer to 102; Jersey, interment 4, 98, 100–2; *Last Will & Testament* (of) 99–100, 123; law of nature and common law, interpretation of 17, 20; legal system and British law, impact on 64–8, 119, 132–3; and legalistic vocabulary 13–14; *Letany*, smuggling of 2; liberties, legal understanding and interpretation 16–17; London, writings on 9; Low Countries, exile in and impact on 78, 83; Magna Carta, impact on 61; marriage and relationship with his wife 49, 56–8, 120; nature and personality of 69; Norman laws, view of 20; oppositional stance of 70–1; Oxford, Captain Wendy, disputes with 83, 85; parliamentary statute and common law, views of 19; post-Restoration, view of 125–9; print ban (Netherlands) 87–8; prisoners, support for 72; privileges, use of word 13; 'pro-jury' position of 122, 132–3; propaganda against 123–4; Quakerism, and conversion to 96–8, 103–4, 105–6; and religious motivation and toleration 32–3; royalists, and claims of collusion with 78, 79–81, 85, 121, 124–5; spying, claims of 80–1; the state and religion, view of 33, 41–3; 'subject', and rejection of the term 8; Titus, Captain John, disputes with 83–4; trials for treason 4, 62, 64–7, 121–2; use of name of (18th century) 119; women, treatment and view of 56–7; writings and publications of 70, 74–5

Lilburne, Richard 102; petition to Protector, John's release from Jersey 102
Lilburns Ghost, With a Whip in One Hand, to Scourge Tyrants Out of Authority (Chapman, Livewell) 107
Lives of the English Regicides (Noble, 1798) 134
Locke, John 44
Lockyer, Robert, funeral of 52
'London agents' 1
Londons Liberty in Chains (Lilburne, John) 9; disenfranchise, use of word in 11; Lilburne, Elizabeth, petition of 50–1, 53
Low Countries: Amsterdam, Lilburne's exile in 82, 83; and Anglo-Dutch political culture 90–1; Dutch editions of Lilburne pamphlets 86–7, 91; English texts and printed works available in 84; pamphlets printed from 83–4; royalist exiles, presence in 79–81; spying against Lilburne, claims of 80–1; and tensions with England 86–7

Macaulay, Catherine 129
Magna Carta: and assertion of ancient rights 20; Chapter 29, free-man, and rights of 8, 15; and English law 16; Lilburne, John, impact of on 61
Malice Detected (Lilburne, J.) 81–2
Manchester, Earl of 120–1
Marten, Henry 39, 69, 73, 125; Lilburne, John, view of 69–70
Masterson, George 38
Maynard, John 105
Mendle, Michael 24
Mercurius Elencticus 124
Mercurius Politicus 80, 84, 87; Lilburne, John, reporting on 87–8
Milton, John 3, 35
monopoly, definition, and use of 15
Mowry, Melissa 51, 56

Nalson, John 125
National Secular Society 44–5
Nayler, James 44, 104, 110
New Biographical Dictionary, A (Jones, S.) 134
New Model Army 72; Army Remonstrance (1648) 38–9; religious toleration and the state, view of 37
Nicholas, Edward 79, 80
Nicolls, Philip 126, 127–8, 129, 133
North Briton case (1763) 131
Nye, Philip 42

Oldmixon, John 128–9
Oldys, William 126–7; Lilburne, John, biography of 126–7

Overton, Mary 49–50; abuse and treatment of 52–3; depicted in her husband's pamphlets 52, 53; petitioning by 50–1
Overton, Richard 3, 22, 34–5, 36, 62, 121; Netherlands and the Dutch society model, advocate for 90; pamphlets of, and depictions of his wife 52, 53; petitioning by wife of 50–1; *Remonstrance of Many Thousand Citizens*, message of 70–1; the state and religion, view of 41; writings and publications of 74–5
Owen, John 43–4
Oxford, Captain Wendy 80–1; Lilburne, John, disputes with and reports on 83, 85; pamphlets produced by 83

Parnell, James 106
Peacey, Jason 4
Pearson, Anthony 107
Pease, Theodore 97
Peter, Hugh 88; Netherlands and the Dutch society model, advocate for 89–90
Petition of Right 15
Plowden, Edmund 15
Pocock, J. G. A. 25–6
Praise-God Barebone 68
Prideaux, Edward 65–6
privilege: and liberties 14; use and interpretation of the word 13–14
Providence (Rhode Island, USA) 33
Prynne, William 2, 21, 98, 119
Publick Intelligence 105
'Puritan martyrs' 2
Putney Debates 1, 23–4, 26, 63; the state and religion, view of and challenges to 37, 38
Pym, John 3

Quakers: Bull and Mouth Inn (Aldersgate), meeting house 95; funeral ceremonies 96; hostile views of 109–10; and Leveller conversions 109; Lilburne, John, conversion of 96–8, 103–4, 105–6

radical, use of the term 118
Rainsborough, Thomas 72; Putney Debates 23
Rastell, John 10
Reay, Barry 109
religion: Assembly of Divines (Westminster) 34; Blasphemy Act (1650) 44; Clarendon Code (1660) 44; gender and spiritual equality 51; as motivation 32; and persecution of Jews 35; and political

debate 32, 40; secularism, development of 44–5; and 'spiritual rape' 34; and the state 32–3, 36, 37–8, 40–4; Toleration Act (1689) 44; toleration of 32, 34–6; true religion, and struggle for 34
Remonstrance of Many Thousand Citizens (Overton, R.) 70, 90
Resurrection of John Lilburne, now a prisoner in Dover Castle, The (Lilburne, J.) 97, 103, 105
Rich, Nathaniel 42, 95
Riley, Hugh 84
Robertson, Geoffrey 2–3
Robinson, Henry 35, 36
Rump Parliament 25, 68; challenge to 64
Rushworth, John 96

Sacheverell, Henry 129
Sanderson, William 125, 127
Scotland, Civil War, role in 3
Scott, Thomas 80–1; *Defencive Declaration* (Lilburne, J.) 84; Netherlands and the Dutch model, advocate for 89; spying against Lilburne, claims of 80–1, 84
'Second son' 2; use of phrase 1
Secularism: development of 44–5; France, impact of 45; USA, religious toleration and the state 45
Servet (Servetus), Miguel 40
Severall Informations and Examinations 81; *Malice Detected* (Lilburne, J.), response to 81–2
Sewel, William 97
Sexby, Edward 62, 103; Putney Debates 24
Sidney, Algernon 91
Simmons, Thomas 95
slavery 133–4
Smith, Sir Thomas 9
Somerset, James 133–4
Something further in answer to John Jacksons book called Strength in weaknesse (Nayler, J.) 104
Spilsbury, John 72
Spratt, Mr 66
Sprigge, Joshua 42
Stafford, John 107
Staplehill, John 81
Stewart, Charles 133–4
Streater, John 99
Strength in Weakness (Jackson, J.) 104
Stubbs, John 106
Sydenham, Cuthbert 123; Lilburne, John, view of 123

Thompson, Edward 118
Titus, Captain John 81; Lilburne, John, disputes with 83–4
Toleration Act (1689) 44
Tolleration Justified, and Persecution Condemned (Walwyn, W.) 36
Towers, Joseph 129, 133
Triall of Liet. Collonell John Lilburne (Walker, C.) 129–31, *130*
true and perfect Dutch-Diurnall, The (newsbook) 99
Truths Triumph (Wildman, John) 21
Tuke, Henry 97

Upright Mans Vindication, The (Lilburne, J.) 86

Valance, Edward 4
Vaughan, Richard 52

Walker, Clement 129
Walwyn, William 3, 36, 37, 51, 62, 73; *Book of Declarations*, use of 71; conscience of individuals, defence of 37; imprisonment of 99; Leveller writings of 74–5; and religious toleration 36
Wansey, Henry 72
Ward, John 109
Watcher, The (Parnell, James) 106
Watson, Richard 79
Wende, Peter 15; and 'liberty' of the law 12
Wildman, John 21, 42, 62, 73, 126
Wilkes, John 131–2
Williams, Roger 33, 34, 36, 40; the state and religion, view of 33, 34
Wilson, Thomas 106
Windmill Tavern (Lothbury, London) 34, 36
Winstanley, Gerrard 71
Winterton, Thomas 97, 106
women: abuse and treatment of 55; inferiority of 51; Leveller wives, roles of 49–50, 51, 53–4; petitioning and interventions by 53, 54–6; and political rights 56; religion and spiritual equality 51
Wood, Anthony 125, 127
Word of Reproof, and Advice to my Late Fellow-Souldier and Officers (Billing, E.) 109
Worden, Blair 117, 125

Zenger, John Peter 131

Taylor & Francis eBooks

Helping you to choose the right eBooks for your Library

Add Routledge titles to your library's digital collection today. Taylor and Francis ebooks contains over 50,000 titles in the Humanities, Social Sciences, Behavioural Sciences, Built Environment and Law.

Choose from a range of subject packages or create your own!

Benefits for you
- Free MARC records
- COUNTER-compliant usage statistics
- Flexible purchase and pricing options
- All titles DRM-free.

Benefits for your user
- Off-site, anytime access via Athens or referring URL
- Print or copy pages or chapters
- Full content search
- Bookmark, highlight and annotate text
- Access to thousands of pages of quality research at the click of a button.

REQUEST YOUR FREE INSTITUTIONAL TRIAL TODAY

Free Trials Available
We offer free trials to qualifying academic, corporate and government customers.

eCollections – Choose from over 30 subject eCollections, including:

Archaeology	Language Learning
Architecture	Law
Asian Studies	Literature
Business & Management	Media & Communication
Classical Studies	Middle East Studies
Construction	Music
Creative & Media Arts	Philosophy
Criminology & Criminal Justice	Planning
Economics	Politics
Education	Psychology & Mental Health
Energy	Religion
Engineering	Security
English Language & Linguistics	Social Work
Environment & Sustainability	Sociology
Geography	Sport
Health Studies	Theatre & Performance
History	Tourism, Hospitality & Events

For more information, pricing enquiries or to order a free trial, please contact your local sales team:
www.tandfebooks.com/page/sales

Routledge
Taylor & Francis Group

The home of
Routledge books

www.tandfebooks.com

Made in United States
North Haven, CT
23 August 2022

23151326R00093